Praise for *God Attachment*

"The deepest part of us was designed to be connected to God's person and presence. However, we often feel detached from Him in many ways. *God Attachment* will show you how to become more profoundly attached to the Lord and experience all the benefits of that endeavor."
—Dr. John Townsend, psychologist, leadership consultant, and author of the bestselling book *Boundaries*

"Anyone who has struggled with their relationship with God and others will find this book refreshing. . . . The most relevant book ever written dealing with the subject of our attachment to God."
—Josh McDowell, author of *Evidence That Demands a Verdict*

"The clear, concise way that our individual 'attachment styles' are explained by Tim and Josh will lead each reader to break free from preconceived relationship patterns and bring them into a fresh, exciting experience with God."
—Mike Huckabee, previous governor of Arkansas and host of the Fox News Channel talk show *Huckabee*

"The theological integrity, coupled with the psychological perspective, that Drs. Clinton and Straub employ in *God Attachment* will leave you thirsting for your own relationship with God to go deeper and to grow stronger."
—Tim LaHaye, author of the bestselling *Left Behind* series

"The Bible emphasizes the fact that human beings are created in 'the image of God.' That makes us different and unique in all of God's creation. Clinton and Straub build the case from both Scripture and scientific research that humans are 'hard-wired' for a relationship with God. While He obviously seeks us, we also are designed to seek Him. 'You will seek me and find me when you seek me with all of your heart' (Jeremiah 29:13). Don't miss this dynamic and insightful study!"
—Ed Hindson, D.Phil., Distinguished Professor of Religion, Liberty University

"*God Attachment* is the kind of book I would give to someone who is lost, who is without confidence, who is without strength, and who is seeking answers. God IS the answer, and this wonderful book will help lead you to Him."

—Delilah, international radio personality

"Have you ever played hide-and-seek with three-year-olds? Try as they may, you'll see them run out from their hiding place because they want to be 'found' so much! Adults play hide-and-seek in their relationship with God as well. Using a powerful blend of clinical and practical insights, Drs. Clinton and Straub show us both why we tend to hide from God—and how life brings so much joy and purpose when we finally run out and 'find' Him! Attach yourself to this book as a great way to understand, launch, and build your faith!"

—John Trent, Ph.D., president, StrongFamilies.com
and the Institute for the Blessing at Barclay College

GOD
Attachment

WHY YOU BELIEVE,
ACT, AND FEEL
THE WAY YOU DO
ABOUT GOD

Dr. TIM CLINTON
AND
Dr. JOSHUA STRAUB

HOWARD BOOKS
A DIVISION OF SIMON & SCHUSTER, INC.
New York Nashville London Toronto Sydney

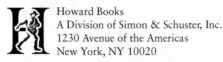 Howard Books
A Division of Simon & Schuster, Inc.
1230 Avenue of the Americas
New York, NY 10020

First Howard Books hardcover edition August 2010

HOWARD BOOKS and colophon are trademarks of Simon & Schuster, Inc.

Figure on page 69 is reprinted from "Avoidance of Intimacy: An Attachment Perspective," by Kim Bartholomew, *Journal of Social and Personal Relationships*. Reprinted by permission. All rights reserved.

Survey on pages 79-81 is from *Why You Do the Things You Do: The Secret to Healthy Relationships,* by Tim Clinton and Gary Sibcy (Nashville: Thomas Nelson, Inc., 2006). Reprinted by permission. All rights reserved.

For information about special discounts for bulk purchases, please contact Simon & Schuster Special Sales at 1-866-506-1949 or business@simonandschuster.com.

The Simon & Schuster Speakers Bureau can bring authors to your live event. For more information or to book an event, contact the Simon & Schuster Speakers Bureau at 1-866-248-3049 or visit our website at www.simonspeakers.com.

Designed by Davina Mock-Maniscalco

Manufactured in the United States of America

10 9 8 7 6 5 4 3 2 1

Library of Congress Cataloging-in-Publication Data

Clinton, Timothy E., 1960–
  God attachment : why you believe, act, and feel the way you do about God /
Tim Clinton and Joshua Straub.
     p. cm.
1. Spirituality. 2. Interpersonal relations—Religious aspects—Christianity.
3. Intimacy (Psychology)—Religious aspects—Christianity. I. Straub, Joshua. II. Title.
  BV4501.3.C55 2010
  248.4—dc22

                                                                    2010014223

ISBN 978-1-5011-0813-6
ISBN 978-1-4391-8683-1 (ebook)

To all those who hunger and thirst
after God and righteousness . . .
and to those who have yet to start the journey.

Acknowledgments

I N LIFE, WE ARE to give honor to whom honor is due—and there are many. To Jonathan Merkh, publisher of Howard Books at Simon & Schuster, and Ted Squires, our agent and friend, thank you for believing in this project and taking a bold step forward in making it happen.

To Tom Winters, literary agent, and his wonderful executive assistant, Ms. Debbie Boyd, you guys are the best, always encouraging and standing ready to help in any way. To Ron Hawkins and Gary Sibcy for your friendship and the many, many long hours of thought and discussion on who God is and what he means to us, attachment theory and practice, and what it means to journey with someone to freedom in this life. The work of God in your life echoes forth from each page.

To Cindy Lambert, our editor, you are a gracious conceptual thinker and word surgeon. Thanks for spending *real* time and effort in this work. To our research, writing, and editing team, Pat Springle and Laura Faidley, we offer a huge thank you.

To Team AACC—the entire leadership team and staff of the American Association of Christian Counselors—we are grateful for your support and encouragement throughout this journey. The world is a better place because of your commitment to encouraging and equipping counselors all over the world with the message of hope we have in Christ.

To the administration, faculty, and students at Liberty University—and in particular, Scott Hawkins, David Jenkins, Kevin Corsini, Fred Milacci, and all those who serve in the Center for Counseling and Family Studies.

To my (Josh) parents, David Straub and Sharon Hess, for your unconditional love and always believing in me. And to my beautiful wife, Christi. Thank you for your patience and support through the long hours devoted to this book. I love you!

Last but not least, to my (Tim) wife, Julie, my daughter, Megan, and my son, Zach. You color every day of my life with joy. I can't imagine life without you.

Contents

PART I
WHY GOD FASCINATES

1

Does God Matter?

God is dead. God remains dead.
And we have killed him.
—Friedrich Nietzsche[1]

ALBERT EINSTEIN ONCE SAID that "there are two ways to live: you can live as if nothing is a miracle; you can live as if everything is a miracle." Either God is there or he isn't. It takes a lot of faith to believe he isn't.

There is no better place to see this unfold than in the counseling office. As a licensed professional counselor, marriage and family therapist, and life coach, I (Tim) see people at their best and worst. Unfortunately for most of us, we don't make that call for help until the "wheels have come off" and our lives are in total chaos. As a result, we usually walk in and out of counseling sessions, buy the latest self-help book, or go to church hoping and praying for God to perform some huge miracle in our lives. Yet some of us haven't prayed to God in years except to say grace over McDonald's cheeseburgers. And now we want God to show up and give us some special sign that he hears and still answers our prayers. A burning bush. Some cloud configuration in the sky, a sign along the road with the word GOD in it . . . we want anything to prove that he is listening, all-powerful and there for us in the abuse we wrongly endured, or with the spouse who is leaving, the fear of job loss and paying the bills, the death sentence of a vicious cancer, living with the pain of a child's death, the onset of deep depression, the loneliness of being single, and the list goes on.

Josh and I have been there—both personally and professionally. You may be thinking of a time in your life even now, a situation when you wondered if God really cared about you and the circumstances you were in. Are you living with that question right now? What have you faced that has caused you to question whether God really exists?

Each one of us has faced, or will soon face, the reality that life isn't turning out at all as we had imagined it would; and often when that happens, it leads to a "crisis of belief"—a time when our world gets rocked, doubt explodes within us, and we wonder if God really cares. Suddenly we are jolted to wonder if a relationship with him even matters. It's a question that lies at the core of human existence—a tension that cuts so deep into our souls that people of every race, culture, ethnic background, educational level, socioeconomic status, and age have wrestled with it since the beginning of written history. Some resolve the "crisis of belief," but still others repress or suppress it until the wheels come off again or they're up against a *giant*.

In ancient Hebrew history, believing in *Yahweh*, the God of Israel, was a given. Belief was taught to every citizen and even written on tablets of stone. David, a common shepherd boy at the time who would later become king, believed emphatically. God was real, and David was willing to do anything to stand for him. David, the young man that he was, may have seemed a bit naive and a little overconfident. Sent by his father to visit his brothers in battle, David was stunned by what he saw. As the armies of the Philistines lined up to battle Israel, one huge Philistine named Goliath mocked and terrified the entire Israelite army. Even David's older brothers were afraid. How could one man scare an entire army?

David contested, "Who is this uncircumcised Philistine that he should defy the armies of the living God?"[2] Wholeheartedly believing his army served his *living* God, David made a decision to fight Goliath, a decision that would have him summoned to the king of Israel—King Saul. David's uncompromising belief in God led into a conversation with the king that went something like this:

DAVID: King, don't lose heart! There is hope when your army is God's army. Sit back and relax. I'll go fight him.

SAUL: Are you kidding me? Fight that monster? You're just a boy. Goliath is a man's man. You stand no chance.

DAVID [SPEAKING EMPHATICALLY]: I have been keeping my father's sheep for years and God was with me. When a bear or a lion would come and try to take away a sheep, I would go after it, strike it down, and kill it. This uncircumcised Philistine will be no different. Since he defied the armies of the living God, I'll kill him, too. God has my back. He delivered me from the bear and the lion and sure enough he will also deliver me from this Philistine.

SAUL: Well, then. Go ahead. And may God be with you.[3]

With three smooth stones and a sling, David set out to face Goliath. One-on-one. A nine-foot, "I am going to kill you" monster. When Goliath saw him coming, he mocked David.

"Am I a dog, that you come at me with sticks?" The Philistine then cursed David by his gods. "Come here," he said, "and I'll give your flesh to the birds of the air and the beasts of the field!"[4]

David responded, "You come against me with sword and spear and javelin, but I come against you in the name of the LORD Almighty, the God of the armies of Israel, whom you have defied. This day the LORD will hand you over to me, and I'll strike you down and cut off your head. Today I will give the carcasses of the Philistine army to the birds of the air and the beasts of the earth, and the whole world will know that there is a God in Israel."[5]

What? Are you kidding? Don't we all wish we had that kind of confidence in God to come through for us? If you're not familiar with this story, know that David goes on to defeat Goliath, just as he said he would. But stop for a moment and put yourself in David's shoes. Do you so confidently believe that God is alive and able to help you face your Goliath? What are your Goliaths? Perhaps your finances, your rebellious teen, maybe cancer or marital problems.

Who doesn't want God on their side? We certainly all do.

But, as we call on God to help us, do we really believe it makes a difference? Will we, like David, stake our lives on it?

Some go to a different extreme.

• • •

Some are God crazy . . .

Consider the 1993 government siege of the Branch Davidian compound in Waco, Texas, where David Koresh and seventy-five followers, including twenty-one children, were killed. Or the 1978 mass suicide of 918 followers at the Peoples Temple, a pseudo-religious organization founded by Jim Jones. The mass suicide is known as the single greatest loss of civilian life in America by a nonnatural disaster until 9/11. Every death in the name of religion.

On October 6, 2009, a Marathon County, Wisconsin, circuit judge sentenced Dale and Leilani Neuman to serve ten years' probation and thirty days a year for the next six years in jail.

The charge?

Second-degree reckless homicide for the death of their eleven-year-old daughter, Madeline. Instead of seeking medical attention for the young girl's undiagnosed diabetes, they reportedly gathered people around her on the floor of the living room in their rural home and prayed over her, waiting for God to perform a miracle. Though she couldn't talk, walk, or eat, they ignored the everyday God-given wisdom and the resources of God to help her. It wasn't until after she stopped breathing that anybody called 911.[6]

For some, God is offensive and doesn't matter at all . . .

Bill Maher, political comedian and writer, and producer of the documentary *Religulous*, a film that investigates and subsequently uses sarcasm to ridicule religion around the world, said, "I think flying planes into a building was a faith-based initiative. I think religion is a neurological disorder." Also, "We are a nation that is unenlightened because of religion. I do believe that. I think religion stops people from thinking. I think it justified crazies."[7]

At the opening ceremonies of the 2009 Little League season in Falls Church, Virginia, a Methodist preacher walked onto the field to deliver an invocation, followed by the young players' reciting the Little League pledge, "I trust in God, I love my country. . . ." Opening ceremonies as usual. But for assistant coach Bob Ritter, whose son was a first-year player on the team, the religious language found in the pledge was offensive. "It interferes with the ability to teach your child," said Ritter, and does not represent "Falls Church's religiously diverse community." Ritter, a civil rights attorney for the American Humanist Association, started a petition to have the religious language removed from the Little League pledge.[8] We wonder if he let his son pray for safety with the team before the game.

To those ready to engage in combat, God seems to be all that matters . . .

Major General (Retired) Robert Dees, U.S. Army, has served in a wide variety of command and staff positions, culminating in his last two assignments as Commander, Second Infantry Division, U.S. Forces Korea; and as Deputy Commanding General, V (U.S./GE) Corps in Europe, concurrently serving as Commander, U.S.–Israeli Combined Task Force for Missile Defense. When speaking to a group of men recently he began his talk by showing video footage of what it was like to be in night combat in the Middle East. Then he added, "When soldiers in Iraq hold hands and pray before going on a dangerous patrol, they are not concerned with being 'politically correct'— they want to be 'God correct'! They want to know that God is their Rock, Fortress, Deliverer . . . their Strong Tower to Whom they can run."[9] My (Tim) dad used to tell me similar stories about being on the *USS Pennsylvania* during WWII, and how as a teenager he felt and prayed to God for help when the sirens would go off as the Japanese fighters attacked.

Reaching for God . . .

From the hospital room, to the dad who tucks his daughter in bed at night, to the mom who prays for her son to get a hit in the ball game, to the family who holds hands and prays over Thanksgiving dinner, the soldier in combat, the woman with the mass on her ovary, to the president who prays for God to bless his country, the reaching out for someone or something transcendent is clear. From the Little League field to the legislative war room, individuals and countries throughout history have wanted—and many have claimed to have— God on their side.

But does it matter? Does God really care about you and me? Can we trust him for everyday life? Can he or will he be there when we need him? Or even more, why would he? Most of us would like to think it matters, especially when life is not the way it is supposed to be.

Consider those who seek God. Just ask . . .

- The fifty-nine-year-old man diagnosed with multiple my-eloma cancer at Duke University.
- The dad who holds his little girl, now fighting for her life because of an accident involving a drunk driver.
- The mom and dad whose daughter went missing at a local rock concert, and there is still no word.
- The parents who tuck their daughter into bed at night with a high fever and asthma flaring, and pray for her fever to go down and that her breathing will improve.
- The mother leaning over her star football player son, who's convulsing because of a concussion and neck injury and is now surrounded by emergency workers . . . or the teammates huddled together nearby.
- The anxious dad waiting for his daughter to get home from college after driving late into the night, and she doesn't answer the phone.
- The woman who was rushed to the emergency room with severe abdominal pain, and the doctor tells her that she has a huge cancerous mass on her ovary.
- You. When are you most likely to turn to God?

The deadly conflict between the Israelites and the Palestinians is still alive today in the West Bank and in Gaza. And after hundreds of generations, it now looks like religion is at its worst, with both sides "defending their faith" and calling upon God to be on their side, giving them the victory. Khaled Mashal, Hamas leader in Gaza, is quoted as saying, "Before Israel dies, it must be humiliated and degraded. Allah willing, before they die, they will experience humiliation and degradation every day."[10]

Though we are not about to debate this issue, we simply want to acknowledge that such events color perceptions of God for individuals all over the world, of Allah and Jesus, of right and wrong, of life and death. And in the midst of it all, every one of us—you and I included—must discern how such seemingly unrelated events influence how and if we personally call upon God in *our* everyday lives.

Hymns and Murder

The faith journey for me (Tim) started a long time ago. I was one of eight children to a circuit preacher in the hills of a tiny central Pennsylvania town, and our family went to church Sundays, Wednesdays, and the special days in between. I watched many of the same people I saw in Sunday morning services come in and out of our home throughout the rest of the week, with sullen faces and distressing stories and looking to my dad for answers. Smiles one day. Tears and heartache the next. Good, churchgoing people trying to get by. People who would sing "Standing on the Promises of God," yet were mostly hurting—and questioning.

One particular Sunday night will forever be etched into my brain. It was church as normal, with my mom and family all parked in our usual pew, singing the old hymns, competing in a "Bible sword drill," and doodling during my dad's closing sermon. Even the guy sitting in the wooden pew way back in the corner was in place—right where he always sat. Shirt. Tie. Bible in hand. I think he even prayed publicly as part of the service that night.

Yet nobody in his or her right mind could have guessed what would happen later that evening to this friend of my father. At home and snug in bed for the evening, we were awakened by a phone call. The phone was out in the hallway, so my dad had to get up and answer it. On the other end of the line was the man in the corner pew. The conversation, as I recalled it, went something like this:[11]

"Preacher, I shot him."

"What? Shot who?" said my dad.

"The man who was fooling around with my wife."

"What do you mean you shot him?" my dad questioned.

"Preacher, I shot him with my rifle. He's dead." Evidently when he got home from church that night the other man was "with" his wife. He got his rifle, loaded it, and then waited for the secret lover to leave. As the lovers stepped out onto the porch, he watched as they embraced. That's when he pulled up the rifle and watched through the scope for just the right moment . . . put his finger on the trigger . . . then shot and "killed him dead."

My dad was an emotionally even-keeled man. But by the cut in his voice, I knew this was different. He was stunned and deeply grieved that his friend had just killed somebody. He was also nervous, trying to figure out what to do and who to call to turn him in to the proper authorities.

Immediately my dad called the state police, and he worked to get his friend surrendered to authorities. I just listened and then began to wonder: how does a man go from church and just flip a switch and commit murder? I had no idea what a crime of passion was. Mouthing off, my buddies on the school bus the next day bantered back and forth that if someone were playing around with their wives, he would be a dead man, too. All the boys laughed, but the real issue lurked deep inside of me: Was it the devil? Was it mental . . . craziness in his head? I started wrestling with questions of right and wrong, evil, and suffering. Why do people act and feel the way they do? Does God affect who we are, the way we live, and how we behave? Does our relationship with him even matter?

When God Doesn't Make Sense

When I was sixteen, we received a call that my fourteen-year-old sister, Candace, had been in a car accident on a dirt road not far from the farmhouse where we live. I was at home that August morning because I had been injured in football practice the day before, and I was planning to go later to the doctor to get my knee checked. I was in bed, dead to the world, when the phone rang. Dad answered and came blowing into my room, shouting "Candy was in an accident, is hurt, and we need to get to her fast." I jumped out of bed like a wild man fumbling around, and quickly Dad and I were down the steps, out, and into the Buick with its 465 wildcat engine. I took off down the lane of our old farmhouse so fast that my dad's car door wasn't even closed yet.

"Where is the accident?" I shouted. He'd told me when I was getting dressed, but I had forgotten in the frenzy.

"By Zion Cemetery, on the curve coming down the hill."

The old cemetery was so far back in the woods that the other girls who were in the car accident had to run almost a mile to get to the nearest house to make the call to get help and reach us. Not many people traveled those old dirt roads. But I knew them like the back of my hand. That's why I drove and Dad started praying. If you can believe it, we arrived on the scene before anyone else. I slammed the car into park, jumped out, and started running toward the demolished new Oldsmobile. Glancing to my right, I noticed Dad kneeling by the car door. I shouted, "You pray, I will take care of her."

As I reached the car, I witnessed my worst fear. I saw Candy lying in the car, lifeless. Panicky and not sure what to do, I painfully crawled through the broken glass and into the backseat to help. There was blood everywhere. A petite young girl sat holding my sister in her arms. With a blood-soaked cloth, she was trying to stop the bleeding from a massive gash in Candy's head. Dad yelled, "Tim, is she alive?" I checked her pulse. It was very slow, but it was there! I choked out, "Dad . . . Dad . . . she's still alive."

Trying to figure out what to do next, I noticed green gum caught in her mouth, sticking all throughout her teeth. Thinking she would choke and that it would block her airway, I reached in and began clearing out as much as I could grab with my fingers. As I cleaned out the gum, I looked up again. Through the window of the car I saw my dad, kneeling along the old dirt road, praying against hope that God would somehow perform a miracle.

Never before had our family been through a major crisis. We were a close-knit, God-fearing, and "had enough to get by" family who always tried to do everything right. Incidents like these don't happen to families in central Pennsylvania, I thought. We are good people. My dad is the pastor.

If the miracle was that Candy would live, after being so close to death, then God answered our prayers, I reasoned. But everything changed for our family after this event. The damage to her brain from the blunt force of the accident left her in a coma for twenty-eight days. She suffered from a traumatic brain injury (TBI) and went through over two years of rehab. She was so wild when she first came to that she would shake and, like an animal, try to bite the person nearest to her. She seemed trapped inside her broken body. My dad was so happy that she was responding in some way that he let her bite him. She really got him bad one time, and the nurses in turn had to take care of him.

The healing process was slow. Candy had to learn how to walk and talk all over again. Later, because scar tissue formed on her brain, she battled epilepsy—life-threatening at times. Because we had such a large family and so many responsibilities, I assumed the role of Candy's caregiver at sixteen years old. I traveled to school many times from a hospital room. I even witnessed a lot of what people called miracles. And disappointments. We called them "setbacks." I even developed my own spiritual rituals . . . that if I did things a certain way, somehow God would smile down from heaven and Candy would heal. But I wrestled with the *why*. We had worked hard our entire lives to do everything right, so if God really cared, then why did this happen to her . . . to *our* family? It didn't make sense to me.

Trying to Make Sense of It All

One of the other boys I grew up with suddenly stopped coming to church. His family said he had "changed." I found out later that he became depressed, and he wound up killing himself. Another family from our church would always sit on the right side and toward the front, closest to the piano. It was Dad and Mother to the left, and then in order from oldest to youngest. They reminded me of the "Cindy Lou" family from *The Grinch Who Stole Christmas*. A gentle family. Kind. Poor. Good people who wanted to know God.

To help pay the family bills, the oldest teenage son started working the evening shift at the local grocery store, restocking shelves. One night while he was working, some "psycho" kid broke out of a local facility, had a knife, walked into the store, and brutally butchered and killed him. Why?

It was totally senseless.

A Personal Journey

Now you probably know why I decided to study theology and counseling. It's interesting to note that many students who enter counseling-related programs do so because of prior life experiences, and they have a desire to help people get through life's challenges. I wanted to study human behavior from a religious and psychological perspective—looking not only theologically at who God is but also psychologically at who we are, as human beings. I wanted to understand what caused people to murder or give up on life, and I wanted to know why such devastating things such as my sister's car accident happened to good people. And I did. Early on in my doctoral studies at the College of William and Mary in Virginia, I read an article by Jeffries McWhirter, psychology professor at Arizona State University, that angered me yet forced me to reevaluate once again what I had been taught growing up and had learned in college. In discussing psychology's influence on the decline of theology and religion in the past centuries, McWhirter said:

> Beyond these, however, are very personal reasons for the rejection of theology and religion by psychologists. Too often our religious ideology has not progressed at the same rate as our physical, intellectual, conceptual, and even moral development. . . . As we compare ourselves now with ourselves in the third grade, we are different in most facets of our being. Too often, this is not true of religious development. My concept of God (and other religious beliefs dealing with the concepts of truth, tolerance, existence, authority, and so forth) worked quite well for me in the third grade. It (and they) do not work now as a middle-aged (or young-old) adult. And yet, my colleagues and graduate students describe their vision of God in what sound like third-grade concepts. No wonder so many of us have given up the religion of our youth, or live compartmental lives, or explore alternative belief/faith systems such as Zen, or the Scripture according to Gibran, or the religion of science![12]

Many of the students in my program did not believe God mattered. At least on the surface. I remember reading about the students

C. Gilbert Wrenn described who had tearstains on their papers when they were asked to "detail their personal assumptions about the meaning of existence."[13] Wrenn writes, "It was an agonizing experience for some students to find that their religious faith was still based on the concepts established in childhood . . . [and] because there was often a loyalty to the childhood faith, there was guilt in even examining it, to say nothing of changing it. Hence the tears."[14] I acknowledged his thoughts, but choked on them.

If you have ever studied psychology, you know that many of the great forefathers of psychology also thought that faith in God was nothing more than a crutch. Sigmund Freud, the founder of psychoanalysis and most known for his insights on the id, ego, and superego, said that believing in God was no different from a boy's riding his bike down Main Street, fantasizing and wishing everything would change, as if all of the difficulties in life could just magically disappear. The psychology of God, according to Freud, was nothing more than a neurotic illusion: "Religion is an illusion and it derives its strength from the fact that it falls in with our instinctual desires."[15]

Carl Rogers, founder of the humanistic approach to counseling, attended Union Theological Seminary and was raised as a Christian, but he and other classmates "thought themselves right out of religious work."[16] Albert Ellis, credited as the founder of cognitive-behavioral therapies, really had a difficult time believing that God mattered. In an interview, he admitted that he had a very hard time believing that God exists. Some Web sites even attribute him to say, "OK, I'll admit that there is a .00000000000000005 percent chance that God does exist, but if he does what makes you think he gives a s**t about you."[17]

As I learned psychological theory and therapeutic practice, I constantly debated with myself and with others if God mattered, only to find that he does. And that a relationship with him is one of the grandest journeys of life.

And without faith it is impossible to please God, because anyone who comes to him must believe that he exists and that he rewards those who earnestly seek him.
—Hebrews 11:6

A Universal Longing

The younger author in this book, I (Josh) represent the Millennial generation (those generally born between 1978 and 1995). Religion aside, I wrestled from an early age with the existence of God—of anything beyond myself. I was, and still am, what Os Guinness refers to as a seeker, "people for whom life, or part of life, has become a point of wonder, a question, a problem, an irritation."[18]

Here's my story. I remember it as if it were yesterday. As a young boy I would lie in my bed watching the sun drift beyond the horizon. On those warm summer nights, I could tell how late it was by the amount of darkness peering through my window. Having just showered from a playful, energy-packed, and likely sweaty day outside, I was usually not too tired come bedtime. On those particular nights I did almost anything to keep myself occupied. It felt as though time stood still.

If I got up to turn on the bedroom light I would have to face the unwelcomed entrance of my parents, who would come in and try to lovingly coax me back underneath the covers. To avoid their intrusion I did what any young boy would do—I got my flashlight. Whether it was playing with my baseball-card collection or drawing a picture of a cartoon character, I kept myself busy until the inevitable grogginess got the best of my fight to stay awake.

Sometimes, instead of getting out of bed to play I lay there and stretched my legs, bending my feet behind my butt cheeks to see how long I could take the strain on my thighs. Other nights, I lay there pretending I was a contestant on *The Price Is Right* and played out in my head as if I had won a fabulous trip or a new car. I didn't care that I was only eight years old.

Those were the good nights.

The bad nights were different. Lying in my bed with Mom and Dad in the next room, I felt safe. Perhaps too safe. I had enough security to know I could explore places an eight-year-old boy surely should not go. But I did. And I'm glad I did.

I was like Lucy, Peter, Edmund, and Susie wandering and wondering through Narnia. Or Frodo and Sam making their way through Mordor. But the land I went to was more frightening. In fact, there was no land. No baseball cards. No new cars. No fabulous trips. No people. No earth. Forever. And ever. And ever. An empty universe. I lay in my bed as an eight-year-old boy wondering deeply about what it would be like if I were alone in a universe where nothing else existed. For eternity.

At least Frodo had Sam with him.

Whenever my thoughts wandered to such a deep dark abyss of nothingness, I could stand it for no more than a few seconds before I had to come out. My mind needed relief. I was engulfed in fear, and my sense of safety felt overwhelmed.

Feeling secure in those moments came not from Mom and Dad nearby or the comfort of my sheet pulled to my neck—that was unthinkable. I was in another land, a place that seemed like hell. Where nobody, or nothing, existed.

The ability to change my thoughts back to the present moment brought me relief. To look forward to the next morning at the creek with my friends brought comfort to my soul and a smile back to my face. The reflection of family, friends, and good times together reassured me.

What would it be like if nothing existed, forever and ever? Or worse yet, if I were alone by myself in the universe for eternity?

As I get older I contemplate the possibility of a reality of nothingness. Someday I will die. Where will I go? Who will I be with?

Many experts agree that those childhood fears of being alone in a universe of nothingness, left with nobody to care for or love them, are innate. Whether we admit it or not, we all want to belong. We crave to know that if we died today, somebody would care. That something or someone beyond us exists. In fact, empirical evidence is now showing that we may be born with a desire for a relationship with a "Transcendent Other" and that that longing begins to reveal itself in children as young as three years of age.[19]

Albert Einstein sought something beyond himself. Here's his take:

> The most beautiful experience we can have is the mysterious. It is the fundamental emotion which stands at the cradle of true art and true science. A knowledge of the existence of something we cannot penetrate, our perceptions of the profoundest reason and the most radiant beauty, which only

in their most primitive forms are accessible to our minds— it is this knowledge and this emotion that constitute true religiosity; in this sense, and in this alone, I am a deeply religious man.[20]

The reality of God and the innate human search for his existence and purpose in our everyday life goes beyond age, race, socioeconomic status, career, IQ, nationality, ethnic group, or era in which we live. The search, the longing, the desire to know that someone bigger and greater than yourself exists is a phenomenon we simply cannot explain away. As a matter of fact, in the next chapter we are going to take a look at how universal this phenomenon really is.

> *[Seekers are] people for whom life,*
> *or part of life, has become a point of wonder,*
> *a question, a problem, an irritation. . . .*
> *It happens so intensely, so persistently,*
> *that a sense of need consumes them*
> *and launches them on their quest.*
> —Os Guinness [21]

A Personal Decision

Forget about your religious background for a moment. We don't care whether you have or have not grown up in church, whether you have or have not believed in God before you picked up this book, or whether you have or have not confessed your faith to any particular religion. None of that matters. The question right now is whether God does matter to you—today?

Be honest with yourself: Do you genuinely believe God exists? If you do, do you believe he understands you and is there for you in the seemingly relentless life struggles and daily hassles you face? Does he care about you? Your relationships? Your job? Your health? Your family? Does he make a difference in your life or in the way you be- have? Does he have the capacity to?

Or is God dead? Is he merely a wish-fulfilling extension of your own fantasy, not real but important for the sense of safety and security that the "God delusion" gives a needy humanity? Is he just a culturally mocked-up idea that has lost significance in the rise of industrialism and technological advance around the world? Is he merely a complex psychological crutch that you must escape from in order to know that exquisite existential angst of freedom and aloneness?

As we were writing and discussing stories for this book, the comic *Pogo* came up in our conversation—the issue called *We Have Met the Enemy, and He Is Us.*[22] It's a fitting thought as we consider God's existence because it highlights the reality of each of our personal experiences and how these experiences can affect whether or not we believe in God, and to what degree. Wrestling with the question of God is intensely personal. And none of us can escape it. You are who you are alone before God. Nothing more. Nothing less. What you do with the question of God shapes and colors everything in and around you.

Does God Matter?

We think this question is better answered with another question: Is the problem God or is it our perception of God? You will find out the answer to this question and more in the next few chapters. You are going to also discover what it means to live in a vibrant relationship with God by understanding why you believe, act, and feel the way you do—in your relationship with God and in your relationships with others. Whether you know it or not, you have a relationship style that impacts how you do—or don't do—intimacy with those you love, and in particular, with God.

That's what the profound invitation of the Bible is all about: to be in a meaningful relationship with God. Unfortunately most of us miss it. But you don't have to.

CONSIDER THIS: Your life experiences have shaped what you believe about God and the way you act and feel in relationship to him. Do you genuinely believe God exists and makes a difference in your everyday life? In your relationships? Your job? Your health? Your family? Does he make a difference in the way you behave? Does he have the capacity to?

Write down a few life experiences that have shaped how you view God and your answers to these questions.

Visit www.godattachmentbook.com to watch interactive videos that will help you further understand how your life experiences have influenced what you believe about God. We have created these videos after each chapter and posted them on the Web site to help you understand more deeply what it means to further cultivate a secure attachment to God.

2

God Obsession

Where am I? Who am I? How did I come to be here?
What is this thing called the world? How did I come into
the world? Why was I not consulted? And if I am
compelled to take part in it, where is the director?
I want to see him.
—Søren Kierkegaard [1]

PEOPLE THE WORLD OVER are obsessed with God. However they define him.

Every year 3 million Muslims visit Mecca to fulfill their call to the once-in-a-lifetime Hajj. Islam now makes up more than 1.2 billion of the world's population.[2]

Every year hundreds of millions of Hindus trek to the Ganges River and surrounding temples to have their sins purified. Hinduism today stands at 828 million adherents worldwide.[3]

And every year the Vatican City, the Holy See for the more than 1 billion Roman Catholics worldwide, is the most visited place on the planet per capita.

If you count the additional 1 billion people who adhere to one of the other "Christian" denominations or groups, you have over 2 billion people worldwide who follow the teachings of the Bible and the story of Jesus Christ.[4]

Take a guess at what percentage of the world's population believes there is no God: 20 percent? 15? 10? In fact, a mere 2 percent of the world's population considers itself atheist—those who do not believe in God.[5]

Regardless of how one tries to define him, and whether one loves him, hates him, denies him, or defies him, it's hard to deny the fascination with God the world over.

God, as we know him, is "in."

The fact that you picked up this book says something about you—about your belief in God, or at least your curiosity. Either you're a seeker or you're a believer. Perhaps both.

But there are questions that linger: Is God dead? Is he nothing more than a figment of our imagination and a crutch for the psychologically weak to lean on for security in life? Or is God real? Can we know him? Believe him? It doesn't take long to understand that "God" changes and separates everything and everybody.

Fascination with God

No matter what you hear on the news about lawsuits on prayer, court battles over the display of the Ten Commandments, nativity scenes, and the separation of church and state, there's no denying the phenomenological existence of God. Consider that *Newsweek, Time,* and *U.S. News and World Report* have featured Jesus on the cover more than two dozen times in the past ten years alone. In addition, Jesus has graced the cover of *Time* magazine twenty-one times since World War II. Apart from the past few U.S. presidents, that's more than any person in history.[6]

What do the American people believe? A 2007 *Newsweek* poll found that 91 percent of American adults claim a belief in "God" of some sort, and 85 percent of Americans say that religion is important in their lives.[7] Gallup's latest study reports that 73 percent of Americans "are *convinced* that God exists." Only 3 percent of the American population identifies itself as atheist, being "convinced God does not exist." For the remaining 24 percent of Americans, the jury is still out.[8]

What this "belief in God of some sort" means in the personal life of the average human being varies. For now, and despite what it may or may not mean, the point is that a phenomenon of God is pervasive. The evidence is found in individuals who are searching not only for who God is but also for their own purpose on this earth.

The fascination with God is also evident in the money we spend and the books we read. Take, for instance, the bestselling book of all time: the Bible. Since the original printing press in 1455, it is estimated that nearly 6 trillion Bibles have been sold in nearly 2,000 languages.[9] Consider the preoccupation with such *New York Times* bestselling books as William Paul Young's *The Shack,* described on Amazon as "a one of a kind invitation to journey to the very heart of God"; Tim Keller's *The Reason for God,* a book that normalizes religious doubt but lays a case for belief in an age of skepticism; or Rick Warren's *The Purpose-Driven Life,* a forty-day daily devotional that helps readers find meaning in their spiritual journey. *The Purpose-Driven Life* is one of America's bestselling nonfiction books of all time, according to *Publisher's Weekly.*[10] From the fictional side, even the Left Behind series, Tim LaHaye and Jerry Jenkins's novels about the end times, written according to the book of Revelation, has become one of the bestselling adult fiction series of all time, having grossed more than 70 million copies sold as of 2009.[11] C. S. Lewis's *Mere Christianity,* a book originally recorded as a radio lecture series in Great Britain in 1943, has proved to be a timeless presentation of the principles of the Christian faith, as it remains a top seller even into the twenty-first century.

Another bestselling book that spent two years on the *New York Times* bestseller list was Dan Brown's *The Da Vinci Code.*[12] If you want to see Christian authors and theologians scramble in defense for God, put out a fictional book that makes claims about Jesus the Bible does not support. Just a quick Amazon browse alone brought up fourteen books in response to *The Da Vinci Code.*

And what about the entertainment industry? In the first decade of the twenty-first century, *The Da Vinci Code* movie raked in over $757.2 million worldwide. Mel Gibson's *The Passion of the Christ* brought in $604.3 million.[13] And the $500,000 budget of the Christian movie *Fireproof,* a story about a firefighter who "fireproofs" his troubled marriage and turns his focus to God for direction, reaped dividends of more than $33.4 million at the box office.[14] Good or bad, agreed or disagreed, there's no denying the phenomenon of God throughout our culture.

But does a cultural fascination with God mean that he actually exists? If he does exist, how important is he in our daily lives? A survey on religious beliefs reveals a very interesting pattern of how important religion is in the day-to-day lives of people the world over. For instance, the median proportion of the world's population who say that religion is important in their daily lives is 82 percent. Americans fall behind in the 2009 Gallup research with only 65 percent claiming religion is important to them on a daily basis.

But Gallup throws out a caveat: There is a strong relationship between the level of religiosity and a country's standard of living. When Gallup surveyed the world's population, they found eleven countries where nearly every dweller (98 percent) said that religion was important in their daily lives. Of those eleven, eight of them are poor nations in sub-Saharan Africa and Asia. Among the ten countries where residents were least likely to report religion being important in their daily lives were: Sweden (17 percent), Denmark (18 percent), Norway (20 percent), Hong Kong (22 percent), Japan (25 percent), and France (25 percent). All of these countries are Western and Asian democracies with the world's highest standard of living.[15]

In the twenty-seven countries known to make up the developed world, only 38 percent of the people on average say that religion is important in their daily lives. Compared to the other wealthy nations, if you will, the 65 percent of Americans who report an importance of religion make the United States look like a country of devoted converts ready to make a difference.[16] Or are they?

Dissatisfied About Religion

In the United States, many postmodern sociologists are ready to resign religion to the museum of cultural history, arguing that in today's technologically advanced age, the idea of a supreme other-worldly being is irrelevant. A lot has changed in America; even leaders from the Southern Baptist Convention refer to the twenty-first-century age we live in as a "post-Christian era."[17]

Other research reveals a growing dissatisfaction with the state of religion in America, with only about half of Americans viewing religion as being "very important," and nearly three-fourths seeing religion as a waning influence. In fact, three out of ten view religion as "old-fashioned and out of date," and that number appears to be growing.[18] Additionally, only 33 percent of psychiatrists and clinical psychologists express a belief in God.[19] In a world of economic and political turmoil, many Americans are asking, "What's the point of religion anyway?" With only four out of ten Americans regularly attending a church or synagogue, religious leaders are rightly wondering what's ahead. Americans, it appears, are losing hope in religion.

And who can blame them?

With religious practices such as liturgical repetition and hymns seemingly out of date or irrelevant, sex scandals and moral failures among major church leaders, and the self-righteous making us feel like we're never good enough, many in the Millennial generation and Generation X feel stuck trying to make their way in a religious world where it seems very few represent the spiritual life they say they follow. In their book *Unchristian*, David Kinnaman and Gabe Lyons explain the results of their research on the attitudes of sixteen- to twenty-nine-year-olds toward Christianity. When those in this age group were asked to identify their impressions of Christianity, one of the most unprompted descriptions was that "Christians no longer represent what Jesus had in mind, that Christianity in our society is not what it was meant to be."[20]

Think about how this has impacted you for a moment. According to Kinnaman and Lyons, the most common imagery of religion among churchgoing and nonchurchgoing young people was that Christianity was too judgmental, hypocritical, too involved in politics, and too old-fashioned.[21] Maybe you've experienced the same thing? Perhaps it's left you feeling weary of going to church, or even trusting in God.

Determined to Find God

On the other hand, just because these attitudes exist toward religion's seemingly waning influence does not mean Americans do not believe in the existence of God himself. In addition to the 80 to 90 percent of Americans who voice a belief in God in general, a 2006 Gallup poll showed that 90 percent of eighteen- to twenty-nine-year-olds also hold a foundational belief in the existence of God.[22] In fact, even 80 percent of professional therapists (psychologists and psychiatrists excluded) claim a religious preference, and 77 percent "try to live according to their religious beliefs."[23] And this is good news, since many clients today want their faith addressed as a part of their counseling experience.

The determination to find God continues in the political landscape, as well. Even the past two presidential elections of George W. Bush and Barack Obama were not without a focus on God. Many believed that George W. Bush was elected because of the "values voter," driven primarily by the religious right. In a January 2009 case that attempted to remove any religious references from the presidential inauguration, U.S. District Judge Reggie B. Walton ruled that President-Elect Barack Obama's choice of words was not in the purview of governmental jurisdiction—he could say whatever he wanted and invite speakers and prayer leaders to do the same. Associated Press (AP) later published a full-length Easter feature on the president's search for a new house of worship, quoting Obama as saying, "It takes time to be a believer. . . . Faith cannot be forced and faith cannot be coerced."[24]

Even though the everyday faith of Americans appears to be waning, it's interesting that God is still a centerpiece of the American culture. Though abstract theology, wooden benches, and dusty hymnbooks appear to be a thing of the past, many Americans today are still searching for something to shake them out of the ruts and mediocrity of so much of their daily existence. With so much change, you may be wondering what is in vogue? Or, shall we say, *who*?

A Universal Longing

Though it's true that only 40 percent of Americans identify with a particular church or synagogue, it becomes quite obvious to the 90 percent who believe in God that he is not dead. And while today's culture appears far less religiously oriented, neither can we seem to quite shake free of the idea of God the world over. People just like you are lying in bed at night, alone, thinking about the meaning of life, their purpose, and why they do what they do. And we're left with more questions than answers.

But as Hugh Ross, astronomer and astrophysicist, contends, this is quite normal. You may not be as out there as you think. Ross states:

Modern man is the only bipedal primate species for which any undisputed evidence of the drive to seek more than physical survival and well-being exists. Thus far, evolutionists have been unable to demonstrate a development or evolution of these drives within the human species. Humans living thousands and tens of thousands of years ago evidently manifested these motivations at the same levels as do people today. Where, then, does this strong desire come from? Why is it that the vast majority of the world's people—regardless of education, economics, politics, technology, and geography—believe in some kind of God? . . . Perhaps the most significant reason of all pertains to the exquisite manner in which the physical laws of the universe serve to limit the expression of human evil and to prepare willing individuals for life in a realm where evil does not exist (heaven).[25]

Ross alludes to a desire that lives in every human soul for something beyond mere physical survival. A yearning that lies sincerely in each of us to address the answers to the deepest and darkest questions life has to offer—questions about the inevitability of death, isolation, and meaninglessness. That we ask such questions is normal. That we persist in these questions beyond simple answers and ignorance is super-normal. And it goes beyond race, religion, and age.

Lao-Tse, a Tao philosopher in ancient China, said, "As rivers have their source in some far-off fountain, so the human spirit has its source. To find this fountain of spirit is to learn the secret of heaven and earth."[26]

Mahatma Gandhi said, "I worship God as Truth only. I have not yet found Him, but I am seeking after Him. I am prepared to sacrifice the things dearest to me in pursuit of this quest. Even if the sacrifice demanded my very life, I hope I may be prepared to give it."[27]

The Koran states, "All men turn their eyes to some quarter of the heavens."

The Bhagavad Gita in Hindu scriptures reads, "The wise, full of love, worship me, believing that I am the origin of all, and that all moves on through me. Placing their minds on me, offering their lives to me, instructing each other, and speaking about me, they live always contented and happy. To these, who are constantly devoted, and who worship with love, I give that knowledge by which they attain to me. And remaining in their hearts, I destroy, with the brilliant lamp of knowledge, the darkness born of ignorance in such men only, out of compassion for them."

In the Bible, Moses tells about a literal face-to-face conversation with God whereby God revealed his name and character. Yet Moses, having seen and talked with God, still didn't know who he was, as he asked him, "Who do I say sent me?" And God chose this particular moment to advance the historic and progressive revelation of himself, by revealing his name: "Say that 'I AM' has sent you."

Christian writers ever since have been writing and asking the question of whether God matters. As she became increasingly aware of her own spiritual impotence, Spanish mystic Teresa of Avila, a Carmelite nun born in 1515, and who would later be declared a Doctor of the Church by Pope Paul VI in 1970, once cried out, "Oh God, I don't love you, I don't even want to love you, but I want to want to love you!"

Tertullian, a creative and controversial author who lived A.D. 160–220, resolved for himself the universal tension that exists between God and man, "There is strife between God's ways and human ways: damned by you, we are absolved by God."

Along these lines, C. S. Lewis once said, "From the moment a creature becomes aware of God as God and of itself as self, the terrible alternative of choosing God or self for the centre is opened to it."[28]

On why we approach God, the Puritans wrote, "Our necessities compel us, Thy promises encourage us, Our broken hearts incite us, The Mediator draws us, Thy acceptance of others moves us."[29]

The Courage to Ask

So, then, what does it mean to believe in God? Does it mean going to church on Sunday morning? Singing about God? Wearing a cross around your neck? Praying every now and again? Reading the Bible? Does it mean that we merely believe he exists? Or, at the last agnostic station on the train toward atheism, does it mean that we entertain the difficult possibility that he might exist, but we can never know for sure?

In contrast, does believing in God mean that our faith affects, even transforms, the way we live every day? Like believing that God loves us and living with peace and contentment inside. Having joy in our hearts. Trusting him for our everyday life. Knowing with certainty that he protects, guides, and cares for us. Knowing that he desires to have an intimate relationship with us—that he desires to call us his friends.

You are about to discover insight into why you believe, act, and feel the way you do about God, and how it's directly and indirectly tied to your core relational beliefs. Whether you know it or not, you have a relationship style that infects and affects the way you do intimacy with those you love and, in particular, God. You will also learn how you can overcome and break free from the lies you believe about yourself, others, and God and how they are hindering you from true intimacy with him. Asking the question of whether God matters is one thing; how you go about answering that question and what you do with the answer is entirely different. And whether you know it or not, you answer the question of whether God matters every day of your life by the way you live.

How Serious Are We?

Have the statistics surprised you? What shocked you the most? If the statistics hold true, we can conclude that people are obsessed with thoughts of God—either killing him, crowning him, or denying his relentless pursuit of a love relationship. But many are conflicted about who exactly this God is, if he's even out there. And our preoccupation is not just theological, political, or even psychological—it's intensely personal.

What's the difference between cognitively believing in God and emotionally connecting, trusting, and walking with him every day? Statistics are just numbers. We are real people. With real questions. Real doubts. Real pain. And real struggle. If you are struggling with your belief in God right now, you may be at the best place you could be in your life. As Os Guinness explains, "The important thing is not the distinction between 'believers' and 'unbelievers'; the vital divide is between those who care enough to think seriously about life and those who are indifferent."[30]

This is the question we urge you to ask yourself at the outset of this book: How serious am I about my own search for and belief in God? Personally and professionally, we believe God exists and "that he is a rewarder of those who diligently seek him."[31] Our prayer for you is that you're dead serious.

CONSIDER THIS: If you are struggling with your belief in God right now, you may be at the best place you could be in your life. What will it take to convince you that God exists? What do you need from him to be able to emotionally connect with, trust, and live for him every day?

Write these needs down on a piece of paper and visit www .godattachmentbook.com to interact with us on the barriers holding you back from connecting deeper with God.

3

Crisis of Belief

*To my shame, I admit that one of the strongest reasons
I stay in the fold is the lack of good alternatives,
many of which I have tried. Lord, to whom shall I go?
The only thing more difficult than having a relationship
with an invisible God is having no such relationship.*
—Philip Yancey[1]

THE CHINESE SYMBOL for crisis is understood to be a sign of both "danger" and "opportunity." Danger in that it represents a time of threat—a threat not only to our sense of being but also that shakes our already established belief system to the core. On the other hand, crisis also represents a time of opportunity—a time when people are most open or susceptible for change. You've heard the phrase, perhaps even said it about somebody, "He won't change until he hits rock bottom." Have you been there personally? You don't have to be an alcoholic or drug addict to hit rock bottom. Many times we reach this place in our lives where we question our meaning and reason for living because of an unexpected relational, spiritual, or emotional crisis. And it's usually during a crisis that we are forced to develop a new way of perceiving, coping, and dealing with life to resolve it and move forward.

Loss and Death Anxiety

As a young boy, I (Tim) always wanted to be like my dad. At seventeen years old, he left the comfort of his family in central Pennsylvania, like millions of other young men and women did at the time, to serve in the U.S. military during World War II. He was a soldier seaman on the *USS Pennsylvania*, spending a lot of time in the South Pacific. He loved the outdoors; he was able to fix about anything on our cars.

What I loved about him (and what many others who loved him felt as well) was how kind and gentle a man he was. He loved to laugh and he always made you feel like you were the most important person in the world to him. When he came home from the war, he sought out his old high school sweetheart and married her. Wrestling with meaning and direction in his life, he decided to give his life to Jesus Christ, and he soon packed up to go and become a minister. What I loved about his faith was that he didn't force it on us as children, he simply lived it. A man who never met a stranger. And a friend to all. The locals called him "a long, cool drink of fresh water." He wasn't a father, he was a dad.

They say that "old sailors can smell land before they see it." Dad could. Late in life, he talked often about heaven and angels, and he loved the book of Revelation in the Bible. He suffered deeply when my mother died; he battled prostate cancer and heart disease, and he fought a gallant war with a cancer of the bone marrow. At age eighty-one, when he went into the hospital with severe complications surrounding the death grip of multiple myeloma cancer, somehow or another he knew it would be his curtain call. God gave him the strength to call all eight of his children one last time. I was in Atlanta on a business trip when I got my call. He wanted to assure me that he was all right, and that he would be going to the "Kingdom of our God." Tearfully, I listened and told him what he meant to me. "Tim, if you serve God, I promise you that you will be blessed. There is no greater joy." He then said, "It's because of him that I will see you again."

I made it home on a late-afternoon flight to be with him, just in time to hold his hand and talk. He was fading quickly, so mostly I just held his hand. Later that next morning, July 11, 2007, at 7:00 A.M., he died, with my brother Tom and me standing at his side. Holding his hands, I prayed Psalm 23 over him. I really hated to see him go.

Nowhere else will you come closer to looking for reasons to believe that God exists and matters in your everyday life than when you're faced with death—yours or that of a loved one—perhaps because believing in God will help relieve the feelings of loneliness when we stare death directly in the face. Alfred Nobel, the man who left his riches for the institution of the Nobel Prizes, and who incidentally was not known for his spirituality, had another view. Read by a friend at his funeral was a letter that Nobel wrote: "Silent you stand before the altar of death! Life here and life after constitute an eternal conundrum; but its expiring spark awakens us to holy devotion and quiets every other voice except that of religion. Eternity has the floor."[2]

Do you see the reality in what Nobel is saying? Think about your own life. It usually takes a calamity, a tragedy, or death to move us. More often than not, the sense of invincibility, youth, intellect, and good health clouds any thoughts or feelings of a need for God or the all-too-soon reality of death. No wonder C. S. Lewis penned that pain "is God's megaphone to rouse a deaf world."[3]

What's even more interesting to this search for divine answers, and what Nobel called a "holy devotion," is that it is now becoming empirically valid. Researchers are finding that we have a system built into the very fabric of our DNA that explains the longing every one of us has for meaning and purpose greater than ourselves—a longing that usually comes alive in times of crisis.

The unexamined life is not worth living.
—Socrates

An Unexamined Life

My (Josh) best friend from college is an atheist who challenged my belief of God's existence. His humanistic rationale for believing went something like this:

JOSH: What if you're wrong? What if there is a God, a heaven and a hell. And in your unwillingness to believe, you go to hell?

BRIAN: What if *you're* wrong? What if, in your leap of faith, you are so convinced God exists that you live your life not having any fun—you miss the parties, the ladies, the drinking, the getting high, and the fun of socializing because you think God is going to somehow bless you and take you to heaven. Meanwhile, I'm out having fun in this life, making the most of it. Then, when we both die, we just die. No heaven. No hell. No God. Then who lived the better life? I'll put my money in that pot.

But as Tim Keller says, "Some will respond [and say] . . . 'My doubts are not based on a leap of faith. I have no beliefs about God one way or another. I simply feel no need for God and I am not interested in thinking about it.' But hidden beneath this feeling is the very modern American belief that the existence of God is a matter of indifference unless it intersects with emotional needs. The speaker is betting his or her life that no God exists who would hold you accountable for your beliefs and behavior if you didn't feel the need for him. That may be true or it may not be true, but, again, it is quite a leap of faith."[4]

From a psychological perspective, this is a profound statement coming from a modern-day apologist and pastor in the middle of New York City. What Keller is saying about those who do not believe in God and hold to this particular viewpoint is that they presume that those who do believe in God are people who actually experience an emotional need for him. (Sounds similar to Sigmund Freud's definition of using God as a crutch, doesn't it?) However, there is truth in this, in that when we come to an emotional crossroads we will at some point have to question the existence and power of God in our own lives. Nobody is immune to the emotional crises of life. We will all *feel* the emptiness and pain of disappointment, loneliness, and eventually death and have to reconcile that with our current belief system. It truly is a moment of threat—or opportunity. The choice is yours.

Going to Church

Think about something for a moment. Do you go to church on Sunday? If so, why? If you don't attend church, why not? If you show up occasionally, why are you not going consistently? Why not just stop going altogether? What would it matter? Seriously take a moment and think about these motivational questions for going to church before you read on. Write down the reasons you do or do not attend church.

The reason we have asked you to do this is that we believe it tells us something about our belief in God. Many of us go to church because we genuinely believe God matters in our everyday life. Others of us go to church saying we believe in God but silently wonder if he matters. Still others of us don't go to church at all because we don't believe he matters, or if we do, we question whether church itself matters. Still others of us have not been disappointed in God, but in church members or leaders who have tragically let us down. Whether you go to church or not, take a moment right now for this self-assessment about your church attendance.

Now ask yourself how your view of church, and even God himself, has been skewed by the disappointments in your life. For many of us, going to church is difficult because when we get back into our cars to go home, our feeling of the way life really is resurfaces. Deep down we feel the tension and the reality that go beyond the beautiful Sunday dresses, slick ties, handshakes, smiles, and "How do you do's." An unsettling sense of disappointment continues in our lives. We continue to wonder, due to the financial pressure, terminal cancer, divorce, domestic violence, job loss, miscarriage, rebellious teenager, abuse, or pain-filled marriage, whether God does actually make a difference in our everyday life and the way we're living it. When our disappointments mount, so do our doubts about God.

Be merciful to those who doubt.
—Jude 1:22

Big-Time Disappointments

It's interesting how pain works in our lives. No one is immune. For most of us, pain brings a lot of confusion and discouragement. Amy, a former client, struggled in her spirit and constantly wondered, "Will anyone notice? Trying to cover up this bruise is so hard . . . too much makeup is even more noticeable . . . my husband said he was sorry . . . but he's said that before. I just wish I knew what to do . . . I'm so scared. Maybe Pastor Jon will help me. . . . No, wait, he doesn't like divorce. How can I share what I'm feeling with my pastor?" If the statistics hold true, disappointments are affecting each and every one of us. In fact, one in every four women reading this book right now is being abused by her partner, or has experienced abuse at some time in her past.[5] An estimated 1.3 million women are victims of physical assault by an intimate partner each year.[6] That is a shocking number of women who are sitting in the pews wondering if they're really worthy of being loved, disappointed that their relationship, and therefore their life, isn't what it is supposed to be.

A father vows to himself, "I'm gonna stop today! I can't go on and keep this secret. It's too hard . . . I just don't know how to quit. I would get rid of my computer, but I need it for work. I need to tell someone, but who? My wife would be so hurt if she knew. What about my kids?"

If the statistics hold true, approximately 40 million Americans are sexually involved with the Internet[7] and 72 million Internet users visit pornography Web sites each year.[8] In addition, 47 percent of Christians admit that pornography is a major problem in the home.[9] And catch this—34 percent of churchgoing women have admitted to intentionally visiting porn Web sites online as well.[10] Intentionally or unintentionally, over half of American teens have looked at those pornographic Web sites.[11] So have 43 percent of pastors who have responded, too.[12] Internet pornography is a big-time secret in the hearts of millions of men—and women. Yet apart from the selfishness and false intimacy of the act, there lies a deep desire for a healthy relationship—to know and be known.

Finally, a teenage girl contemplates, "I'm so fat. If I eat, it will make matters worse. Katie says I need to talk to somebody . . . but I'm not sure. I have it under control. If I just weren't so tired all of the time. I miss going out with my friends. And my mom keeps nagging me to eat. *She*'s the one who needs to talk to someone. But who?" According to the latest research, 81 percent of ten-year-olds worry that they are too fat,[13] 40 percent of nine-year-old girls have dieted,[14] and 75 percent of girls have wished they could surgically change something about their body.[15]

In addition to domestic abuse, pornography, and eating disorders comes the breakdown of family relationships. By age eighteen, one in three girls and one in six boys are sexually abused by someone they were supposed to love and trust.[16] And this morning, 40 percent of America's children woke up in a home where their biological father does not live.[17]

These are the children running by you in church on Sunday morning. The men passing the offering plate. And the women singing in the choir. Maybe you're one of them. What counselors recognize every day is that behind that statistic lies the heart and soul of a disappointed, broken individual who is searching, questioning, yet hoping.

Do you know what it's like to be sexually abused? To be hit by your spouse? To be hiding a secret—adultery, pornography, abortion, abuse—then to go to church and try to hear about a God who loves you? When you're wounded in a relationship, it's hard to hear. It's hard to trust. It's hard to feel safe. Even with God. He seems distant. Unapproachable. Uncaring. And those of us who do believe wonder why we doubt. Those of us who don't believe can't understand why we'd look for reasons to believe.

The Unexamined Life, Examined

Physician M. Scott Peck famously penned the words "Life is difficult."[18] Even the Bible tells us, "In this world you will have trouble."[19] At some point in life every one of us will be disappointed by life circumstances—coming to the conclusion that life is not the way it's supposed to be. But problems are never really the issue. We all will have more than our share. What we choose to do with those problems makes all the difference in our spiritual journey. Often the disappointments quickly lead to doubt. But to refuse to doubt for whatever reason will lead to a failure to understand why you believe. As Henry David Thoreau discovered, "Faith keeps many doubts in her pay. If I could not doubt, I should not believe."[20] Believe it or not, doubting and questioning are the path toward real faith.

In the search for God in our everyday life we will eventually take one of two paths. The first and most healthy journey is that we will allow our doubts to lead us to a deeper understanding of why we believe what we do, whether we choose to believe in God or not. But even then, those of us who choose this route must "doubt our doubts."[21]

The second and more devastating of the two paths is giving very little examination or contemplation to the disappointment we have experienced in life. We talk more about those of us who walk this path later in the book. For now, we would like to describe it as "pseudo-faith."

Pseudo-Faith

There are grandmas. And then, there are Me-maws. I (Josh) had a Me-maw.

As a boy I went to her house often. Special moments were Sundays after church, when my family got together and turned the peaceful ambience of her home into playful chaos. My sister and I wrestled and nitpicked. Dad and I whipped each other with the wet towels we had used to dry the dishes. The real fun was seeing who would end up with the bright orange "Special $.99" sticker from the chip bag on his back. After lunch, we napped, played cards, or watched football.

I lived every kid's dream of being loved.

Me-maw—she personified love. She did anything to help my sister and me mature into respectable adults. We spent many nights over at her house, cooking, creating, and playing with homemade toys, romping around in the huge sand piles situated at the block company next to her home. She taught me that to have little was just enough.

Then, she was diagnosed with ovarian cancer.

Because I wanted Me-maw to live longer, I walked a fine line between denial and faith—denying the permanence of the disease on the one hand, and blaming it on my "faith in God" to heal her on the other. Basically I had to ask myself, was I saying I had faith in God to heal her as a way of denying how real and terminal the cancer actually was? In my mind, I believed. Yet in my heart, I'm not sure how much I did. I know I wanted to, and I told others I believed it, particularly my family. They looked to me for the answers. Saying I had faith at least made me appear emotionally healthy and spiritually strong. I think it was my way of talking myself into believing.

But deep down, I was struggling. And nobody knew it but me. I couldn't blame God because the church tells me it's wrong to do that. But I did it anyway. "This surely isn't God's fault," I told myself. "Why would God take the one person who holds our family together? Why does a woman as faithful and loving as Me-maw have to suffer like this?"

I didn't understand. Me-maw was by far one of the closest people I trusted in life. "Why would God allow this to happen?"

It's the age-old question. The Bible talks about a man named Job who asked it a lot. A wealthy man, he lost everything he owned, including all seven children, his health, his job, and his livelihood. Even his wife turned on him.

Jesus asked it just before breathing his last breath on the cross: "My God, my God, why hast thou forsaken me?" (Mark 15:34—KJV).

When we find ourselves stuck in the gap between the way we think life ought to be and the way it really is, it's easy to doubt God's presence in our lives. He feels distant. We feel alone. Even Jesus felt forsaken. Remember his words on the cross. In the Greek text, the word *forsaken* literally means that Jesus felt abandoned by his Father, yet he called out to him in his pain. We do the same. We feel abandoned, and then we question God's purpose, his plan—even his character.

One of the biggest challenges I faced in my time with Me-maw in her last days was her understanding of suffering. Her ability to place her well-being in the hands of someone else she could trust, and who she thought acted in her best interest, challenged my own faith. Faith, I learned, is my ability to trust my well-being to the care of another who I believe has my best interest at heart. Although Me-maw was the one suffering, I was questioning, "Do I really trust God is looking out for *me*?"

When we trust God for heaven but not for our daily lives, we walk around with a pseudo-faith—faith a mile wide and an inch deep. We live in denial and maintain a false intimacy with God. We say he is there for us. And to some degree we believe he's looking out for us, as long as all is well. But when we hit a crisis, our religious behaviors and super-spiritual clichés are usually not enough to get us through the fire. It's easy to believe God to be the God of the universe, but not so easy to believe that God could be the God of *my* life, today.

> *There are five gospels of Jesus Christ—*
> *Matthew, Mark, Luke, John, and You the Christian.*
> *Most people never read the first four.*
> —"Gipsy" Smith

Hurting, Questioning, Searching . . . Yet Hoping

Let's go back: Can we trust God for today, in the here-and-now realities of life, or are our unanswered prayers vainly cast into nothing more than time plus chance spinning randomly in a purposeless existence? Will God protect my son on the baseball field, so that he doesn't get hit with a line-drive baseball in the head? Is God that big that he cares for the small but important details of my one life? Could it be that he is as much the God of my father as he is the God of the Falls Church Little League team, as he is the God of the nations, even as he is the God of the entire universe?

What's funny is how we all look for ways to bargain with God to see if he actually exists and cares about our everyday life. When I (Tim) was younger my mother made me take piano lessons. Whether it was a lack of skill or just my rebellion, I really learned only two songs. Perhaps it was because I spent most of my time playing only those two songs. I remember believing that if I could play them both flawlessly that God would heal my sister Candy of her brain injury. So I went home nearly every day, sat down at our piano, and played the songs.

Perhaps trying to "earn" my sister's healing was my way of bargaining with God. Gideon in the Bible did something similar; he asked God to prove his guidance. Laying a wool fleece out overnight, he challenged God, "If you will save Israel by my hand as you have promised—look, I will place a wool fleece on the threshing floor. If there is dew only on the fleece and all the ground is dry, then I will know that you will save Israel by my hand, as you said."[22] Not only did God do it for Gideon once, he did it twice.

How often are we like Gideon, putting out fleeces to God, looking for him to show up in our marriages, relationships, our poor health issues, our jobs, and seeking to know his will and his way for our lives? "Prove yourself God, and your method to me." You start asking yourself and wondering (and this is the challenge of faith), where does God come alive and how do I trust him for my present circumstances and my future, versus where do I own personal responsibility for myself?

The Psychology of Meaning

If there is any one story that describes the heroism, if you will, of taking personal responsibility in the depths of mere hopelessness, disappointment, and literal hell on earth, it is that of Viktor Frankl. A well-known Viennese psychiatrist, Frankl survived the Nazi death camp at Auschwitz. Choosing to give up a visa to the United States in preference for staying in Germany and caring for his parents, Frankl along with his wife, father, mother, and brother were all arrested and put in a concentration camp at Theresienstadt, in 1942. Only he and his sister Stella would survive.

Studying under the tutelage of Sigmund Freud, Frankl understood behavior from a deterministic mind-set. That is, in such hellish environments such as a death camp, every individual would be determined to become like a groveling animal. But that wasn't the case. What Frankl discovered in his quest for survival as prisoner number 119,104 was that a few brave souls would rise to the occasion to comfort, love, and share their already insubstantial rations with others who needed them. He would later say that, in all classes, ethnicities, and groups, only two races of people existed—decent and unprincipled.[23]

Frankl stayed alive because he *chose* to grow deeper and accept the suffering he had to endure. Of all he had stripped away from him, even to the point of pure nakedness, Frankl realized that the only thing that could not be taken from him was his will to live, his attitude, and his spiritual freedom. Frankl quoted Nietzsche to describe the only explanation of how he could endure to the very end: "He who has a *why* to live for can bear with almost any *how*."[24]

As you think about your own personal *why* to live for in the midst of your disappointments and crises, consider the prisoner that Frankl described who gave up faith in the future and also lost his inward embrace on spiritual freedom. In his book *Man's Search for Meaning*, Frankl tells the story of a man who had a dream in February 1945 that the war for him would be over on March 30. The prisoner was happy and full of expectation. But as time grew nearer, news of the war increased and the man began to lose the hope he had been clinging to. His physical and mental state rapidly declined, and on March 30 he lost all consciousness. He died March 31, 1945, from what appeared to be typhus, but Frankl knew he had died of a broken heart. The war for him was indeed over on March 30.[25]

When we lose hope and the *why* to live for, at best we resign to mediocrity; at worst, we succumb to suicide. Frankl used to ask many of his patients at the outset of therapy, "Why do you not commit suicide?"[26] Based on the client's answers, he would then create a framework to help the client understand his meaning to live. But as Frankl admitted, many of us do not come to an awareness of what we have to offer because we do not look to the spiritual things. As Frankl asked, "The consciousness of one's inner value is anchored in higher, more spiritual things, and cannot be shaken by camp life. But how many free men, let alone prisoners, possess it?"[27] Do we?

> *The most perfect way of seeking God, and the most*
> *suitable order, is not for us to attempt with bold curiosity*
> *to penetrate to the investigation of his essence,*
> *which we ought more to adore than meticulously*
> *to search out, but for us to contemplate.*
> —John Calvin [28]

The Seeking System

Viktor Frankl understood the search for meaning to be "the primary motivational force in man."[29] Dallas Willard agrees, "Meaning is not a luxury for us. It is a kind of spiritual oxygen, we might say, that enables our souls to live."[30] As we have shown, this spiritual longing, this discontent or existential struggle, if you will, for purpose, meaning, and making sense of who God is in the disappointments of life, is as intrinsic to our souls as the longing for air. Blaise Pascal described it as "a God-shaped vacuum in the heart of every man."[31]

As we mentioned earlier in the chapter, this search for meaning is now becoming empirically valid. New research described in the neurobiological and psychological literature is now suggesting that we have a "Seeking System [that is] experienced as restlessness, longing, or an unformed need state ('thirsting [for God]'), [and] is both a conscious and an unconscious process that has roots in development, leading to an object-seeking relationship with a Transcendent One."[32]

Jonathan Haidt, professor of social psychology at the University of Virginia, has studied moral emotions—in particular, the awe and wonder that's felt when we experience a spiritual high, if you will, a sense of the transcendent. Haidt concludes that these spiritual feelings lie in each one of us, as "relatively hardwired pre-cultural sets of responses . . . built into the central and peripheral nervous system of the human species."[33] The idea that this longing for something beyond ourselves is born in each of us is called "naturalistic spirituality" and has been studied and supported in other research.[34] (For a more thorough understanding of naturalistic spirituality and how the brain functions when we're in relationship to God, see note.)

In one particular study, researchers found support for these innate responses after interviewing children who "had no connection with any religious institution" and had "not yet been socialized into secular ways of interpreting reality."[35] The children in this study were essentially unbiased toward any belief system. And what researchers found is extraordinary—that a "relational consciousness" was linked to these children's spiritual experience. That is, the desire and longing to reach for a relationship with a "Transcendent One" exists in each one of us.[36] So much that the scientific discovery of an intrinsic relational nature when it comes to spirituality has even been found in children as young as three years of age![37] Perhaps this is what Solomon meant when he wrote that God "has also set eternity in [our] hearts" (Ecc. 3:11).

We discuss more about the Seeking System and how it functions shortly. For now, it's important for each of us to realize that the longing we have for a relationship with God comes from God, and has been developing in us since the day we were born. As a result, the longing and journey toward intimately knowing God is not too far out of reach, especially in the midst of life's disappointments.

You Will Make a Choice

Every one of us is going to be disappointed. Every one of us is going to come to a point in our lives where we're lying in bed at night, staring at the ceiling, and wondering why life isn't turning out the way we thought it would—doubting if God cares, yet hoping he does. This wondering, searching, and seeking is innate. We may not see the need to believe unless it intersects with our emotional needs. But the reality is this: there will come a day and a time when each of us will face an emotional crisis, possibly death, and we will have to decide if God is important to us or not.

From the time the psychology of God was first studied until now, researchers have emphasized the importance of the "intense emotional experiences that precede, characterize, and accompany some religious conversion experiences."[38] Studies show that as many as 80 percent of us who make a religious conversion to knowing and believing in God do so after experiencing a period of emotional crisis, particularly relational distresses such as divorce, bereavement, and relationship problems.[39] Thus, as it appears in the psychological research, we all look for ways to manage, maintain, and regulate our emotions in times of relational abandonment and loneliness, and we often turn to the divine for safety.

As recent neurobiological research shows, "A variety of psychological processes are fundamentally involved in the spiritual experience. These processes are founded on conscious and unconscious strivings and on the inherent human need for a relationship with God."[40] As Os Guinness said, "The important thing is not the distinction between 'believers' and 'unbelievers'; the vital divide is between those who care enough to think seriously about life and those who are indifferent."[41] The capacity to choose to think about the existence of God is, therefore, left up to each individual. "Just like neurobiological factors . . . psychological factors alone are not causal chains leading to unthinking deterministic processes, but function in the context of human beings' capacity to make choices and impose these choices on the world, including on their relationship with God."[42]

What these researchers are saying is this: at some point in your life, whether you think seriously about it now or not, you will face your need for something *more*—your need for a relationship with God. And whether you choose or don't choose to believe, and what you decide or don't decide to do with it, is up to you. But the bottom line is this: You will have to make a choice—a choice that will lead you in only one of two ways, either toward God or away from him. We'll look at both avenues.

CONSIDER THIS: Every day you make a choice about God, one way or another. And life will get your attention. It always has a way of constantly bringing you back to the question of who he is in your life. Are you taking him seriously or are you indifferent? God desires a relationship with you: "Here I am! I stand at the door and knock. If anyone hears my voice and opens the door, I will come in and eat with him, and he with me."[43] Call on him and take him seriously while he is yet near.

What does it mean to take God seriously? To learn more, watch the chapter 3 video on the Web site.

PART II
HOW RELATIONSHIP CHANGES EVERYTHING

4

Human Hardware and Software: Made for Relationships

with Dr. Gary Sibcy

God said, "It's not good for the man to be alone; I'll make him a helper, a companion."
—Genesis 2:18 (MSG)

A T NINETY-EIGHT YEARS OLD, she sits for hours each day by her window in the local convalescent home. No one has been by to see her in six months.

Jeff grew up in a minister's home and hated it. Especially the God of his father. Jesus didn't make sense. At twenty he hit the wall hard. Drinking and going 120 mph, he hydroplaned and wrecked, flipping the car at least five times. He walked away without a scratch. A miracle? he wonders. But he knows his dad prayed for him every day. He's now a bartender . . . and often wonders who God is, still hating the "stupidity" of Christianity. He and his dad don't talk.

Consumed with anger, Joey hasn't loved Angela for six years. Nearly every morning Angela sips her coffee and wonders whatever happened to the love they once had. He left her last week for another woman.

Cindy has always been a daddy's girl. She and her mom never really clicked. Last month her dad fell over dead from a massive heart attack. Though her mom is still alive, Cindy feels orphaned.

Eight-year-old Tommy's best friend in the whole world, his dad, moved out last month. The nights really seem long without him around, particularly for Tommy's mom, who is becoming more depressed.

Ed never talked much growing up. He wasn't allowed to. Every time he tried, he was beaten down by his parents. "They just don't get me, never have."

Samantha never has been understood. Her parents loathe the way she dresses and are constantly criticizing her. She connects very poorly with kids at school. Just last night she contemplated a plan for suicide for the first time.

Alone.

It's one of the most powerful and tragic words in the English language. Why? Because we were not made to be alone. It's said that kids really aren't afraid of the dark . . . they're afraid of being *alone* in the dark. Big kids are the same way, especially in the darkness of life. Those fears I (Josh) had as a young boy of being alone in a universe of nothingness, left with nobody to care for or love me, are universal. Whether we admit it or not, we all want to belong. We also crave to know that if we died today, somebody would care. That's because we were made for relationships. To love and be loved. When we're left alone and to ourselves, our hearts eventually grow cold over time as we drift into depression and apathy. And slowly, but surely, we die. At least inside.

But we don't have to. Research in the area of psychology is beginning to show us why and how this downward spiral into loneliness happens, as it increasingly emphasizes the power of relationships. Many of us before picking up this book may have been under the impression that much of this is strictly behavioral. You may have thought, for instance, "My relational problems are because of the way I act. If I can just change the way I behave, things will get better." Of course, that's always easier said than done. And you'll see why.

What you are about to learn is that the way we think, act, and feel in relationships is based on core relational beliefs we develop and maintain literally from the cradle to the grave—beliefs that affect and infect how we do relationships, with one another and with God. Beliefs that are wired into the physical/ biological components of our brain known as the limbic system, and provide us with answers to why we do the things we do.[1] But don't think for a second that because they are wired into our brains that we can't change—because we can! And the answer is found in the context of our most intimate relationships.

Hardwired to Connect

Parenting in the twenty-first century has quite a different look and feel compared to decades past. Those in primitive cultures had to rely on everyone else living around them to survive. Even as late as into the mid–twentieth century, living and interacting in a community was the norm. Front porches, bowling alleys, community gatherings, carnivals, town meetings, and even the family dinner table were the settings for meaningful conversation and connection.

But something has changed. Divorce rates are up. The numbers of single-parent and fatherless homes have increased. And with the poor economy, two incomes are no longer a luxury but a necessity just for most families to stay afloat. As a result, casual daily "I'm there for you" conversations at home, community social events, and visits to the next-door neighbor are things of the past. At the same time, more of our kids are suffering from depression, anxiety, drug abuse, attention deficit and conduct disorders, and suicide, than ever before.

Is there a link? That's exactly what researchers at the University of Dartmouth Medical School wanted to find out. So they brought together a team of pediatric medical doctors and neuroscientists, and combined them with the youth service professionals and scholars who study civic society to conduct a thorough examination of the already existing research. They embarked upon "a serious effort to integrate the 'hard science' of infant attachment and child and adolescent brain development with sociological evidence of how civil society shapes outcomes for children."[2]

What they found is fascinating. They reported that "*all* scientific research now shows that from the time a baby is born, a baby's brain is biologically already formed to connect in relationships." In fact, this study was so huge that an executive report was written to the nation from the Commission on Children at Risk.[3] And others around the country have taken notice:

- "A major report"
  —William Raspberry, nationally syndicated columnist
- "A real wake-up call for America's parents"
  —Diane Sawyer, *Good Morning America*
- "A stunning, must-read report"
  —*NY Post*
- "A fascinating new report"
  —George F. Will, nationally syndicated columnist

Here are some of the main points, taken from the executive summary of the study:

- "In large measure, what's causing this crisis of American childhood is a lack of connectedness. We mean two kinds of connectedness—close connections to other people, and deep connections to moral and spiritual meaning."[4]
- "Much of this report is a presentation of scientific evidence—largely from the field of neuroscience, which concerns our basic biology and how our brains develop—showing that the human child is 'hardwired to connect.' *We are hardwired for other people and for moral meaning and openness to the transcendent.* Meeting these basic needs for connection is essential to health and to human flourishing."[5]
- "For what may be the first time, a diverse group of scientists and other experts on children's health is publicly recommending that our society pay considerably more attention to young people's moral, spiritual, and religious needs."[6]

Two Crucial Questions

In addition to the study at Dartmouth Medical School, a team of researchers at Johns Hopkins Medical School set out on a thirty-year study to find out if a single related cause existed for mental illness, hypertension, malignant tumors, coronary heart disease, and suicide. After studying 1,377 people over a thirty-year period, the single common denominator was not diet or exercise. Not at all. They found instead that the most significant predictor of these five calamities was a lack of closeness to the parents, especially the father.[7]

Why? Stress! When a child grows up in a loving, intimate home, particularly with a father, the child is better capable of handling stress in life.

Each one of us responds to life's stressful situations the way we do for a reason. We are hardwired as human beings—truly created and programmed to:

1. Long for deep, lasting, and satisfying relationships.
2. Seek, search, and live for a destiny that is greater than ourselves.

These traits are part of what it means to be created "in the image of God." Important though this is, that's still not the whole picture.

Another set of factors—this one arising out of attachment theory and research—is understanding what shapes the way we think, feel, and act, creating our basic perception of the world. This perception of self-definition and relatedness develops as early as infancy and continues to progress over time in our life, affecting us every minute of every day. At the heart of these factors are two essential questions that all of us instinctively ask:

1. Am I worthy of love?
2. Are others capable of loving me?

Your answers to these questions, both cognitively and emotionally, are the basis for the formation of your core relational beliefs, and they have a profound impact on how you see yourself and on the way you relate in the closest and most important relationships in your life, including your relationship with God.[8]

Human Hardware and Software: Made for Relationships

Our core relational beliefs are the product of a complex web of experiences and memories. Over time children internalize experiences with their primary caregiver in such a way that they form a prototype, or internal working model, that guides later relationships outside the context of the family.[9] John Bowlby, the founder of attachment theory and primary pioneer of the research on attachment relationships, identifies two key features of these working models of attachment, or our core relational beliefs: (1) whether or not the self is perceived to be worthy of the primary caregiver's—or Mom and Dad's—caring response; and (2) whether or not the primary caregiver is perceived to be reliable and responsive to the child's needs. The intense feelings of stress upon separation, and the subsequent feelings after the caregiver returns, shape that information we attend to and remember, and the attributions and interpretations we make about relational experiences both with others and most importantly with God.[10]

These core relational beliefs begin in infancy with very specific representations of our relationships primarily with Mom, Dad, or both, and whether they are there for us in times of stress, need, or want. As we enter our teen years and young adulthood, these beliefs move away specifically from our primary caregivers and become generalized to other individuals, particularly our romantic partners and even to God. If our primary caregiver is reliable and available during times of stress and duress, we develop positive beliefs about our self-worth. (I am worthy of love and I am capable of gaining love and support in times of emotional stress.) The subsequent response from our primary caregiver then shapes the beliefs and expectations about the reliability and willingness of other people. (Other people are able and willing to help me when I am in need and they are reliable and trustworthy.)

When we use the word *memory* to describe how our core relational beliefs develop, we refer to any past experience that influences the way we think, feel, behave, and relate.[11] Though you may be sitting there thinking about your past experiences with your parents and trying to remember how they treated you, understand that the development of your core relational beliefs does not necessarily require that the experience be consciously "remembered." Understanding the two broad divisions in your memory system may help clarify the difference between implicit and explicit memory.

Implicit memories—memories that we may not be able to consciously recall—begin at birth and continue to develop through our lifetime. These memories are encoded in the brain based on repeated sequences of behavior and include sets of behaviors, feelings, sensations, and perceptions, including our most important relational experiences. Based on these stored sequences of experiences, more general rules are formed about how to do things (e.g., how to put on clothing or how to ride a bicycle). Implicit memories also store patterns of relationship experiences. Developmental psychologist Erik Erikson labeled the first stage of human development *trust and mistrust*. This central developmental task is the foundation for all human emotional and relational growth, and it typically occurs in a child by the age of one. Trust is developed as a child associates crying with being comforted, or develops mistrust when its needs expressed in crying are met with a parent's anger and rejection.

Based on interactions with those who are responsible to care for them (most often parents), children form perceptions about their identities, others, intimacy, and emotions as early as the first year of life. For example, a child may conclude, "I can express my emotions effectively, and my parents will respond in a way that helps me feel better." Interestingly, even at that early age, the parents' response to the child is imprinted onto mirror neurons, and later in life, the child is likely to automatically, almost instinctively, and without awareness, respond to his or her own emotions and behaviors in a manner that reflects the way the parents responded.

Unlike explicit memories, implicit ones are not accompanied by an internal sensation of the event or of being "remembered." In this way, past experiences powerfully influence the way we think, feel, behave, relate, and perceive events today, but without any of our awareness of how the past is influencing the present. Not surprisingly, the perceptions a child develops about life at this early age strongly shape his or her view of God and every other relationship for the rest of his or her life.

Here are two examples of implicit memory:

- As a boy, I (Tim) had a snake fall out of a tree and land on my shoulders. Today when I see a snake, I can feel that snake wrapped around my neck and shoulders. Snakes and I don't get along too well. This is implicit memory.

- I (Josh) remember being at school a few years ago and seeing one of my best friends sitting at his cubicle, working. Being a relatively physical guy, I walked up from behind him and nonchalantly reached my arm out to gently hit him across the shoulder as a way to get his attention and say hello. As I did, he rapidly swung around in his chair with fists ready to fight. As I jumped back I said, "Bro, what in the world are you doing?" Having been physically beaten by his father early in life, his initial reaction to somebody's coming at him from behind was to fight. This is implicit memory.

In contrast, *explicit memories* are those that we typically think of when we think of memory. It's also the type of memory you are most likely using to recall facts about your relationship with your primary caregiver as you read this book. There are many different types of explicit memory, including both factual and autobiographical. Factual memory concerns consciously recalled pieces of information, like what a bicycle is or what a flower is. Autobiographical or narrative memory has to do with memories of ourselves *in* time. For example, memories of our lives that revolve around specific moments in our history, like the joy of getting our first bicycle, our first kiss, or who won the game we watched last Saturday. The capacity to form autobiographical memories does not come online until about age two.

Both factual and autobiographical memories are stored and recalled as verbal information, and they require that we be conscious of them in order for us to properly talk about and understand them.

In many ways, all of our experiences can be encoded as implicit memories and a special part of the brain, known as the hippocampus, takes implicit memories and assembles them like a jigsaw puzzle and transforms them into explicit, verbal memories that can either become factual (you recall what a "bicycle" is) and/or autobiographical (e.g., you remember your dad teaching you how to ride a bicycle).

Autobiographical memory is sometimes referred to as narrative memory. This is a very important part of our lives and represents some of the most complex functions in the brain, as the prefrontal cortex takes our implicit, emotionally charged memories and integrates them with our explicit autobiographical memory to form stories about our lives and relationships. The very essence of secure adult attachment with others and with God is the ability to understand our lives. It's a coherent story that includes *the good, the bad, and the ugly* events and integrates them into an understanding of why we are the way we are.

In an important way, the Bible is the story of God's dealings with humankind, and each of our individual testimonies is our way of understanding how God has worked in our lives and continues to do so even today. Counseling may be seen as our effort to help people develop more coherent narratives as they come to an understanding of their lives.

The Secure-Base System: How Core Relationship Beliefs Develop

We hope you're beginning to understand how our memories of and experiences with our primary caregivers early in life are not just behaviorally but also biologically encoded in our brain. The secure-base system is a powerful way to conceptualize and understand the different components of attachment relationships.[12] In our most important relationships in the first years of life, we form implicit, emotionally charged *core beliefs* about ourselves. We learn which emotions are acceptable and which are off-limits for our parents, and the lessons we learn in those years form our most fundamental assumptions about the reality of feelings, the expression of them, and the validity of emotional needs. The assumptions we develop form a powerful interpretive grid that can determine how we respond to our own emotions and others' feelings for the rest of our lives.

Before explaining how it works, I (Tim) want to illustrate it with a personal example. I remember an incident when my son, Zach, was little. We were at a softball practice for my daughter, Megan. While I was on the field coaching, Zach was playing with his mom off to the side. This particular softball field had a train trestle nearby. When he was a boy growing up, one of Zach's favorite toys was "Thomas the Tank Engine." My, wife, Julie would occasionally tease him about the possibility of the train's coming by while he was playing, and he couldn't wait for it to come over that big bridge. Until the day he got his wish.

In a matter of seconds, a cargo train came barreling down the tracks right toward him. If you've ever been around a train, you know its overwhelming presence. Out of nowhere a look of terror came over Zach's face. And whom did he turn to? His mother! And as he went running into her arms overwhelmed with fear, his actions were basically screaming to her, "Is that a good choo-choo or is that a bad choo-choo?"

When we hit moments of fear or disappointment, or crises in our life, we begin seeking safety. Zach, overwhelmed by the potential of a bad choo-choo, made a beeline for Julie. As she picked him up and their eyes met, without saying anything he was asking, "Are we going to be okay? Or do we need to run?" What's interesting about that moment was that Julie was also responding to his questions without verbally saying anything. Her calming response in the midst of his terror provided the security Zach needed. Once he knew he was safe, he was able to emotionally regulate himself. As soon as Zach felt secure again, even though the train was still going by, he was able to get down and start playing and explore the world around him all over again.

The secure-base system has four core components that unfold in a feedback loop. To illustrate this fourfold process, we'll imagine a mother and her toddler walking into a showroom filled with toys. The mother sits in a chair, and the child initially sits in her lap as he looks around the room. The first component is the *secure-base experience,* which refers to the child's sense of security and is tied directly to his belief that his mother is available, attentive, and accessible. Picture Zach running into Julie's arms as the train came barreling by. Her answer to his screaming nonverbal question of "Am I safe?" made all the difference in his ability to be able to feel secure enough to get back down, play again, and explore.

The second component revolves around the child's *exploration*. The little boy crawls off his mother's lap and explores his surroundings, frequently looking back at his mom to share the experience—and to check to make sure Mom is available if he gets frightened. Exploration is an essential element in building the child's self-confidence. Self-confidence, then, is inherently relational and begins with confidence in the secure relationship with loving parents. Take note that in this model, self-confidence is inherently relational and begins with confidence in the other.

Third, if something threatens the child's sense of security (such as a stranger entering the room, the parent leaving, or a train coming by), the child's desire to explore quickly evaporates and *attachment behavior* is activated. This behavior is the desire to be reconnected with the parent to feel safe again. It is propelled by intense emotion, usually a mixture of anxiety and anger.

There are at least two kinds of attachment behavior: proximity seeking and signaling. *Proximity seeking* is any behavior that helps the child obtain physical closeness to the parent. It can take many forms, including crawling, running, or reaching for the parent. *Signaling* is how the child alerts the parent that there is a problem, including whining, crying, screaming, or pleading. The mom's interpretation of these messages of proximity seeking and signaling plays an important role in how sensitively and effectively she responds to the child's distress. If she doesn't respond with appropriate compassion, the child concludes his mother isn't safe, doesn't care, and possibly that he isn't worthy of her love.

For example, I (Tim) remember having Zach with me one evening at a local Target store. We would always play a friendly game of hide-and-seek. He would hide. I would find him. Until one day I decided to hide and he couldn't find me. As I watched him, peering out through a clothes rack, I noticed how nervous he began to get. And he gently said, "Dad." Then he raised it up an octave and said, "Dad, Dad." Then he took the sound of his voice straight vertical and blew out the store—so much so that the security guard who was nearby heard him and came running. You could only imagine the scene when I jumped out and scared him. (My wife, Julie, wasn't too impressed.)

Finally, the fourth component is when the caregiver and child reconnect and produce a *safe haven* of calm, peace, safety, and love. The threats have been identified and overcome, the connection has been reestablished, and love is reinforced. The loop goes full circle in healthy family environments—it begins with security and ends with security.

The experiences of these early years—including how healthy or not this attachment loop of interactive behaviors and feelings is—become part of the "wiring" in a child's brain. Research shows that a child's core beliefs about relationships are encoded and organized into internal working models that are stored in the limbic system (also known as the emotional brain) as implicit memories. These memories are emotionally charged, preverbal structures that strongly influence a child's behavior long before he or she develops explicit, verbal, autobiographical memories of the experiences that shaped him or her.

This wiring also determines, along with personality and other factors, the person's basic style of relating to others. When children or adults perceive that the answer to the two crucial questions ("Am I worthy of love?" and "Are others capable and accessible of loving me when I need them?") is yes, they feel safe and secure, and they are willing to try new things because they are convinced that failure doesn't bring condemnation or abandonment. But when the answer to either question is no, people invest every ounce of energy to fend off attacks (even when they don't exist), win desperately needed approval, and avoid any risks of failure or rejection.

Develop a Timeline of Your Life

At this point in the journey, we recommend that you take time to draft a detailed timeline of your life that includes all of the major events and relationships you have experienced. At first you will log explicit memories. We hope that as we move on, however, throughout the book and refer back to the timeline, that some of the implicit feelings, thoughts, and behaviors you have had will begin to be realized. For each event or relationship (they should include parents, primary caregivers, siblings, romantic interests, and close friends), describe the moment—your feelings at the time and your behavior during and after the event. Some events were joyous, and they are easy to remember, but some events haunt us, and we have repressed the trauma for years. These occasions may not come to mind very readily.

Developing an accurate and meaningful timeline is a spiritual experience. Schedule an extended time alone, away from responsibilities and distractions. If you're a parent, find someone to stay with the children for several hours, and go to a park or a library where you can think and pray alone. Ask God to bring past events to mind. As you sit quietly, a few events will probably leap to your mind. Jot those down, and then wait for more. Review the significant holidays in your mind—especially Christmas and birthdays when the family was all together. After a while, perhaps another memory or two will come, and then nothing. But wait. Quite often, the Holy Spirit will resurface memories buried for years. You'll think, "Wow, I haven't thought of that for a long time!" Jot it down, and wait again. After a while, you may think of one or two more events that you haven't remembered for many years. Some of the memories may seem obscure and irrelevant, but write them down anyway. Their significance may become clear after you've had time to reflect on them and connect some dots. Days or weeks later, the Lord may bring even more memories back to you, but for now, you have enough to work with.

For each event, describe the wound you experienced, your immediate emotional response, and then your learned response of self-protection, control, distrust, avoidance, and warped responsibility. This is hard work, and it may take conversations with a trusted friend or counselor to fit the pieces of the puzzle together, but the results will usually be dramatic. Now the patterns of your life come into sharp focus. You see the wounds, the environment of distrust, your self-protective and controlling behaviors, and your reasons for acting the way you have acted. Seeing provides us with the opportunity to make new, different choices—decisions that can change our relationships both with others and with God, for a lifetime.

Your Core Relationship Beliefs About God

Understanding more clearly how your core relational beliefs affect and have the potential to infect your relationships now both with others and with God may require more out of you than you bargained for when you picked up this book. What you're about to read may very well change the way you have understood and framed your universe—especially how you have viewed God up to this point. In fact, it may change your life, penetrating and shattering any cynicism, doubt, and skepticism that you have had through the years.

Your specific God attachment and the core beliefs and presuppositions you have about God directly affect the way you relate with him every day. As you discover your personal style of relating to others and to God, our hope is that you are able to be truly honest about and discover your own personal views of God—because they may not be as accurate as you once thought.

In a recent Gallup poll, researchers discovered that 31 percent of Americans view God as "judgmental," 25 percent view God as "benevolent," 23 percent view God as "distant," and 16 percent view God as "critical."[13] On the other hand, those found to have a secure attachment relationship with God are more likely to describe him as "loving," "protective," "not distant," "not inaccessible," and "who gives me comfort," "a warmhearted refuge," and "who is always waiting for me."[14] Lee Kirkpatrick, who was the first researcher to conceptualize and study religion as an attachment process, has since found that not only does God serve the function of an adult attachment relationship but also that earlier attachment relationships are most likely to shape the way we view God in adulthood—and how we ultimately relate to him on a daily basis.[15]

Our core relational beliefs about our self and about others affect, and often infect, how intimate we are with others and even with God. What's interesting is that these core relational beliefs manifest themselves in what we call an *attachment/relationship style*. And you have an attachment style, the discovery of which is the focus of the next chapter.

CONSIDER THIS: How do you view God? Loving? Caring? Accepting? Available? Or is he distant? Judgmental? Uncaring? Write down at least five characteristics of God the way you view him. Begin considering how you have developed these beliefs about and views of God.

For a more in-depth message of how you relate to God, watch the chapter 4 video on www.godattachmentbook.com.

5

Your Attachment Style

Urged by my need, invited by thy promises,
called by thy Spirit, I enter thy presence worshipping
thee with godly fear, awed by thy majesty, greatness,
glory, but encouraged by thy love.
—*The Valley of Vision* [1]

J USTIN AND RACHEL had been married for ten years, and they had
two sons, six and three years old. Most people who knew them
casually believed they had a wonderful marriage. They didn't see the
tension often hidden just beneath the surface. It wasn't that they were
facing catastrophic problems. No one had cancer, and they didn't lose
every penny in the stock market. But gradually, the pleasant patterns
of relating to each other eroded. Anger and fear became the most common emotions in the household, and everybody suffered.

Justin was a typical engineer, very facts-driven and no-nonsense
about everything in his life. His way of showing love to Rachel was to
bring home a nice paycheck twice a month. They had always enjoyed
the freedom his income provided. Rachel was from a broken home,
and she treasured times of closeness with Justin. In fact, she wanted
more of him than he seemed willing to provide. In the early years of
their marriage before the boys arrived, she had all of him, and she
loved it. But recently, the stresses and time commitment of raising two

boys, one now in soccer and football much of the year, were taking their toll on her. Justin was one of the coaches on his son's football team, and he worked out at the gym three times a week as he had done since he was in college. He was only doing what any good dad would do, he believed, but Rachel felt that he was pulling away from her.

In the past year, she asked him several times to spend more time with her. She pleaded with him to be closer to her, but her pleading only drove Justin away. He couldn't stand to feel smothered! And when he pulled away, she became even more desperate and needy, causing him to want to run even farther and faster. This dance continued for months, until Rachel talked to her pastor. After she told him the story, she blurted out in tears, "What's wrong with us? It seems like we're going in opposite directions, and we can't connect with each other anymore!"

As is true of many couples, opposites attracted—at first. Later, under the strains of daily life or the sudden shock of trauma, the personality traits that attracted them to each other when they were dating now drove them apart. They despised the qualities they once admired in each other. They seemed to be coming from two different planets, and in fact, they perceived the world in very different ways. They probably won't find peace and love until they understand why they think, feel, and act the way they do.

Four Styles of Relating

Every single person reading this book right now has a relationship style, whether they know it or not. You have a relational style, and by the time you're finished reading this chapter, you will have discovered yours. But what's important to understand right now is that your relationship style and core relational beliefs usually do not show up until you're under stress or duress, or you experience disappointment in some way.

Four distinct relationship styles are developed based on the way we answer the two crucial questions:

1. Am I worthy of love?
2. Are others capable of loving me?

The way we relate to people, situations, and even God is determined, to a significant degree, by the nature of our relationship with our parents when we were very young. This doesn't mean that what happened when we were little children is totally determinative and we are locked into roles and perceptions for the rest of our lives, nor does it mean that sinful behavior is excusable and should be blamed on your parents. What it does mean is that we do need a clear understanding of the hills some of us have yet to climb along the highway of both emotional and spiritual maturity. Let's look at these four styles.

A Brief Overview

Stemming from the two crucial questions are two dimensions of adult relationship beliefs: view of self (beliefs of self-worth) and view of other (beliefs about whether others are trustworthy and reliable). Researchers have used the answers to these questions to develop a four-category system for understanding your attachment style. These styles are a reflection of the underlying internal working models of how we see and interpret our closest relationships.

There are four primary styles of relating: secure, anxious, avoidant, and fearful.[2]

- *Secure* attachment describes those who hold a positive view of their self and others. Because they believe they are worthy of love, and that others are capable and accessible when they need them, secure people are comfortable with both closeness and independence.

- *Anxious* people hold to a negative view of their self and an unrealistically positive view of others. As a result they are usually anxious in relationships and have an unhealthy fear of abandonment because they believe they are not worthy of love.

- *Avoidant* people are the opposite of anxious people, in that avoidants have an overly positive view of their self, but an excessively negative view of others. People who

are avoidant are uncomfortable with closeness and tend
to become overly self-reliant because they do not believe
others will be there for them.

- *Fearful* people have a negative view of both their self and
others. These adults have a very difficult time with intimacy and closeness, and they often avoid relationships
altogether.

Researchers have also helped us understand these relationship
styles based on levels of attachment anxiety and attachment avoidance
(see figure opposite).[3]

- *Secure* adults experience low levels of avoidance and anxiety, are comfortable with closeness, experience feelings
of positive self-worth, and have healthy means of coping
with stress, particularly by seeking out loved ones.

- *Anxious* adults show increased levels of anxiety and de-
creased levels of avoidance, are insecure in relationship
security, have a low sense of self-worth, are afraid of
rejection, crave closeness, and are obsessively worried,
needy, and clingy in their closest relationships.

- *Avoidant* adults report high levels of avoidance and lower
levels of anxiety, have an overinflated sense of self-worth,
and are uncomfortable with closeness.

- *Fearful* adults experience high levels of avoidance and
anxiety, seek acceptance and self-worth from others, but
fear that others are not capable of meeting their needs,
and therefore are uncomfortable with closeness and
building intimacy.

	SELF	
	Positive View *Low Anxiety*	Negative View *High Anxiety*
OTHER — Positive View	SECURE *Comfortable with intimacy and autonomy*	ANXIOUS *Preoccupied with relationships and abandonment*
OTHER — Negative View	AVOIDANT *Downplays intimacy, overly self-reliant*	FEARFUL *Fearful of intimacy, socially avoidant*

Bartholomew's Model of Self and Other

Source: K. Bartholomew, "Avoidance of Intimacy: An Attachment Perspective," *Journal of Social and Personal Relationships*, 7 (1990):147.

Secure Attachment

Psychotherapist Virginia Satir famously remarked that children don't need perfect parents to grow up emotionally strong and healthy, but they need "good enough" parents. Moms and dads who do an adequate job providing safety, encouraging exploration, and responding appropriately to their child's cries for reconnection enable the child to answer yes to both crucial questions. The child feels worthy of love and is convinced that his parents are fully capable of giving him the affection and encouragement he needs. The parents' attentiveness to the child's needs helps him internalize the conclusion: "My needs are legitimate, and my parents are glad to meet them." He realizes that the most important authority figures in his young life—Mom and Dad— are trustworthy, and since they aren't threatened by his expressions of emotions, he isn't threatened by them, either.

As secure children grow up, they feel equally comfortable with intimate relationships and their own sense of autonomy. That is, they aren't too needy or too independent. They develop wisdom in relationships, perceiving who is trustworthy and who isn't, but they aren't black-and-white thinkers; they are secure enough to look at shades of gray in people and situations. They have emotional integrity, admitting the reality of the full range of emotions—both positive and negative emotions—and they engage in a healthy emotional regulation and aren't dominated by their emotions. Under stress, they have the ability to think clearly, seek advice from trusted friends, and respect authority without engaging in blind obedience. In short, secure people:

- Aren't afraid of emotions, their own or anyone else's.
- Are willing to seek and accept comfort from other people.
- Know that relationships can be safe, and that knowledge gives them courage to engage in love and intimacy.
- Take responsibility for themselves.
- Find the courage to act when action is needed.

Anxious Attachment

The messages some of us have internalized from childhood lead us to conclude that the answers to the crucial questions are "No, I'm not worthy of love," but "Yes, people around me really care." In many cases, their parents were emotionally immature, needy, and unstable, sometimes reversing roles and expecting the child to provide the love the parent desperately wanted. These parents felt threatened by the child's innate desire to explore her world, and instead insisted on the child staying close. The child internalizes this environment and learns to value intimacy at the expense of autonomy. Without a sense of self-confidence learned through exploration, the child learns powerfully negative self-perceptions: "I'm incompetent. I can't do anything on my own. I need others to take care of me." She also believes she has to remain close to her parents at all times, so she develops an inordinate fear of abandonment.

Anxious people haven't developed accurate perceptions about others and don't have enough confidence to be autonomous. For these reasons, they trust too much, often trusting untrustworthy people to come through for them. They are preoccupied with whether people love and accept them, and they experience the constant undercurrent of the fear of rejection. They second-guess things they say to others, fearing they have said "the wrong thing" and harmed their fragile sense of security in the relationship. They crave closeness, but they are seldom secure in any relationship, even when others have proven over and over that they really care. Their longing for love causes them to smother others with attention and affection, eventually driving them away and leaving the anxious person feeling abandoned and confused.

Is it tough being an anxious type? Yes. Because you don't believe you're worthy of love.

Is it tough loving an anxious type? Yes. Because you can never love them enough.

Those whose relationships are shaped by their anxiety:

- Long for intimacy but live in constant, nagging fear of rejection.
- Are too needy, desperately looking for others to make them feel safe and secure.
- Trust too easily and unwisely, overlooking signs that others have not earned their trust.
- Are fragile and vulnerable to any perceived criticism, interpreting it as severe rejection.
- Hope that authority figures will finally come through and fix their problems.
- Experience a deep, controlling fear that they aren't competent to make it on their own.

In the opening story of this chapter, Rachel showed signs that she is an anxious person. Justin was initially attracted to her because he felt he could be her champion, but her neediness began to smother him and drive him away.

The poor view of self characterized by the anxious person can and often will develop in very subtle ways without many of us even knowing it. For example, a child who is pulled between two divorced parents could be made to feel guilty for wanting to spend more time with one parent and not the other. If the parents in turn "punish" the child by withholding benefits or time from her for wanting to be with the other parent, the child will most likely perceive she is not worthy of love unless she does as others want her to.

Avoidant Attachment

Some parents stimulate exploration in their children, but when the kids become anxious and cry out to reconnect, these parents interpret their pleas as weakness or manipulation. In this environment, children develop a strong sense of autonomy but a distrust of authority. They answer "Yes, I'm worthy of love," but "No, these people don't really care about me." Over time, they conclude that they have the skills and competence to make it on their own, and they have to, since no one is there to pick them up when they fail or become afraid.

As adults, those who are avoidant may resist intimacy because it appears to be risky, painful, and smothering. More often, they simply don't see any need for close relationships. They are isolated, but unlike anxious people, they don't mind at all. Those who are avoidant don't feel a lot of angst in strained relationships because they don't believe they need those people to survive and thrive. They are still human with real emotions, but they've repressed them so long that they don't even know many of their feelings exist.

Avoidants tend to devote their emotional energies to competition at work, in sports, and in politics, and they express intense anger over losses and joy in victories. Their spouses (especially the anxious ones) wonder where the emotions go when they are alone at home or in the bedroom. In times of stress, avoidant people become more emotionally withdrawn, more intellectually focused, and more determined than ever to prove themselves at all costs. They seldom, if ever, express any relational needs. Instead, they just plow through life looking for the next opportunity to prove their worth by their successes.

Is it tough being avoidant? Yes. Because you don't trust anybody.

Is it tough loving an avoidant? Yes. Because they never really let you in.

Avoidant people:

- Avoid intimacy because they don't see the need for it.
- Are confident in their abilities and are self-reliant.
- Commonly experience low levels of anxiety in relationships, even when others are very needy and demanding.
- Are very analytical about those in authority, and seldom trust others very much.
- Withdraw from those who express emotional needs.
- Have, in effect, business relationships with others, even close family members, with clear expectations of what each person will do to make a relationship work.

Fearful Attachment

Sadly, some children grow up in homes where the answer to both questions is a resounding "No!" These homes may have been physically, emotionally, and sometimes sexually abusive. Instead of love and stability, the child often experienced parents who exhibit out-of-control rage, fierce demands, or soul-numbing isolation. The child doesn't enjoy a safe haven, the joy of exploration, or the confidence of re-attaching when times are tough. That's because the source of the child's comfort is also the source of pain and hurt!

Without a secure foundation, the child becomes emotionally and relationally frozen in fear. Most days are another quest for survival, and his highest hope is to escape unscathed one more day. Fearful people really don't believe they are worthy of anyone's affection, but they don't have confidence they can make it on their own. They also tend to attract psychiatric diagnoses such as trauma and dissociative disorders, bipolar disorders, psychosis, and borderline and schizotypal personality disorders.

In severe cases, children in abusive families learn dissociative behaviors to avoid the intense pain and overwhelming threats. Researchers are discovering more about how these types of experiences cause disintegration between the circuits in our brain responsible for feelings, emotions, and sensations and the circuits involved in self-awareness, narrative memory, and rational problem-solving.

Children who grow up in chaotic and destructive home environments become relationally disorganized. They often can't figure out whom to trust, where to find safety, and how to gain confidence in their abilities. With these discordant and disconnected perceptions about life, they can't find a consistent style to make relationships work. They might try virtually anything: expressing needs or never telling anyone how they feel, smothering others or remaining isolated, trusting too much or never trusting anyone at all. Every aspect of life, it seems, is up for grabs. They long for acceptance, but they are terrified that people will hurt them again. Not surprisingly, they have a deep, abiding distrust of authority figures, but they may secretly hope those in authority (such as their spouse, boss, pastor, and God) will finally come through for them and give them the love and support they've always wanted.

Fearful people are terribly fragile, but they build a hard shell around their hearts in an attempt to avoid being hurt again. They long to trust someone, but they have difficulty trusting even those who have proven to be loving and honorable. Love and acceptance always seem to be just out of reach, if, indeed, they haven't given up entirely on ever finding love.

Fearful people:

- Feel unloved and unwanted, unworthy of anyone's affection.

- Long for real relationships, but are terrified of being close.

- Lack confidence in their abilities to make life work.

- Are fragile, easily shattered, and vulnerable to any perceived offense.

- Believe they need to trust those in authority, but just can't.

- Sometimes remain isolated, but sometimes launch out into relationships, seeking the connection they've always wanted. Their neediness, though, almost always drives people away.

Relating to God

In the next chapter we begin to look more deeply at how we can connect with God, but before we get there, it's important to see how to connect more deeply on a horizontal level, and how our most important human relationships shape our perceptions of God.

When Rachel understood these relational profiles, and more specifically, her own, she sighed, "Now I get it. Now I understand why I've been so needy in my relationship with Justin. Because of my childhood, I've wanted to be loved, and I've smothered Justin with love—and I've demanded to be loved by him. But I've just driven him away." Sad in the face, she continued, "But it looks like there's no hope—for me, for him, or for us. We've always been this way, and we always will be this way. And God? Oh, my gosh. I've treated him exactly the way I've treated Justin, and I've felt abandoned by both of them." Right analysis; wrong conclusion!

No matter what we've experienced, no matter how defective or deficient our backgrounds are, God can transform us from the inside out. He doesn't make our past experiences go away. Instead, he uses the broken pieces of our lives to reframe our autobiographical stories and make a new, beautiful mosaic of love, hope, and insight. The Scriptures are full of hope. In the gospels, Jesus touched people and made the flesh of lepers clean and pure, gave sight to the blind, enabled crippled people to walk again, cast out tormenting demons, freed people from their evil oppression, raised people from the dead, and in the ultimate demonstration of the love and power of God, paid for our sins on the cross and came out of the tomb three days later to prove that he can change anyone—even you and me and us.

When we feel hopelessly mired in lifelong habit patterns, we need to remember the psalmist's words: "He turned the desert into pools of water and the parched ground into flowing springs."[4] Nothing is too difficult for God. When our hearts feel heavy and the light of hope has dimmed, Paul tells us, "For God, who said, 'Let light shine out of darkness,' made his light shine in our hearts to give us the light of the knowledge of the glory of God in the face of Christ."[5]

The very essence of secure adult attachment is the ability to understand our lives and the narratives we find ourselves in. As we discussed in the last chapter, it's about a coherent story that includes *all of your experiences and memories*—both good and bad—and integrating them into an understanding of where you're at, why you do the things you do, and your relationship to God. In an important way, the Scriptures are the story of God's interaction with the human race, and your testimony is your way of understanding how God has worked in your life and continues to do so even today. Counseling and psychotherapy may be seen as our effort to help people develop more coherent narratives as they come to an understanding of their lives and move toward more secure ways of relating with God and others.

Steps Toward Secure Ways of Relating

God can change us in an instant, but far more often, he takes us through a long process of healing and growth. Life's greatest lessons are learned from facing our deepest wounds. The struggle to make sense of and transform life is like rehab after a major injury. It requires courage and tenacity, but gradually we grow stronger, wiser, and more compassionate toward others who are on the same journey. And like rehab from a major injury, healing and getting stronger take time. Each day is another step of progress. It may come so slowly that we barely notice, but sooner or later, we can look back and see how far we've come.

The first step is rigorous honesty about ourselves and our predicament. We must find in Christ the courage to admit where we are without casting any blame on others or the situation. For those who have been physically, sexually, verbally, or emotionally abused, you are not to be blamed for what happened to you. On the other hand, you are responsible for your life today and the way you live: "Lord, I and I alone have made a terrible mess of my life. I need your love and your forgiveness, for nothing—and no one else—can even begin to save me out of this mess that I am in." Do the surprising and counterintuitive thing (because that spotlight shining on our own sins is so uncomfortable): stay with this a while and let God's spirit dredge up some things that will otherwise have to be revealed and dug up later. It's like cancer surgery—it does no good to cut out 90 percent of the festering mass and leave a little for later. Let God take it all out, because that little that is left can harm you later on.

Furthermore, no one does surgery on themselves unless they are foolish. Do this work with at least one other person—a good friend, counselor, or your pastor. Becoming accountable to at least one other person who is secure substantially increases the odds you will follow through and complete the work that God is doing in you. The Bible says, "Two are better than one."[6]

As to our predicament—to understanding life in its relational context—most of us grew up believing our families were completely normal. We had never experienced another family, so we assumed this was the way life ought to be. Only later did we begin to get a glimmer of insight that our families were messed up—that a long familial and generational history preceded us in our troubles. When we suspected that our families caused us pain, we may have excused them, minimized the hurt, and drifted back into denial to stop the pain. Maybe only in reading the last few pages did some of us realize that our earliest childhood and life experiences have so clearly colored every relationship and habit in our lives.

Now we must face the hard facts. We do not need to run from them any longer. The truth hurts—but it is truly the gateway to real change. In fact, as long as we cling to our denials and excuses, we have no hope for change. When we face the facts we can grieve our wounds, forgive those who have hurt us, and learn new skills of relating to others.

Here is another core truth of this book: We were wounded in relationships, and we are healed in them, too. We won't make much progress on our own. We may want to remain isolated so we can read and study on our own, but we won't take many steps forward that way. Certainly, we need time alone to think and pray, but we also need time with people to let them speak truth, affirm us, let us explore new concepts, and reconnect with them when we feel threatened.

Does this sound familiar? It should. Those are the same components a child needs to find security and gain a sense of confidence. Find a secure support group, some wise friends, a pastor, or a counselor to help you take those steps. These people won't be shocked that you have attachment struggles. They probably have been working through their own. When you were a child, you looked into the mirror of your parents' faces to discover if you were loved and safe. Now, find some new mirrors. Look into them, and believe what their reflections tell you: you are loved. The reason so many of us often turn to the Bible when we hurt is that it is filled with the story of a sacred romance—of God's love for us.

As the Bible says, "Though my father and mother forsake me, the LORD will receive me."[7] It starts with God.

Even pain we've buried for years need not keep clouding our lives. With the love of God and a few trusted friends, we can overcome anxious, avoidant, and fearful patterns in relationships. By God's grace and the warm love of our friends, we can become loved, secure, creative, independent, and caring people.

Your past is not your past if it's affecting your future. Though the past is a reality for each of us, it doesn't have to haunt us any longer or dictate our future . . . especially in our relationship with God. By God's wonderful design, our past hurts and disappointments become part of our story of hope. In his book *The Healing Path,* psychologist Dan Allender describes the spiritual perception we can have about even the most painful events in our lives. He wrote:

> If we fail to anticipate thoughtfully how we will respond to the harm of living in a fallen world, the pain may be for naught. It will either numb or destroy us rather than refine and even bless us. . . . Healing in this life is not the resolution of our past; it is the use of our past to draw us into deeper relationship with God and his purposes for our lives.[8]

No matter how painful your past might be, and no matter how distorted your relationships have been, don't run from them. Look squarely at them, and trust God to do what he does best: turn a desert into a fountain of life.

The following survey is meant to help you discover your primary attachment, or relationship style. Once you have finished the survey, use the results as a guide throughout the book as you journal about your relationship with God and how you relate to him.

Discovering Your Relationship Style[9]

It's helpful to think about relationship styles as four distinct categories, and it's natural to ask, "What style am I?" In reality, however, only some people are clearly just one relationship style. Most folks are different shades of all four styles. You may, for instance, discover that you are predominantly one style, but that you have a few traits from each of the other three styles.

It is also important to note that your relationship style can change depending on the relationship you are in. In fact, your relationship style is not always in operation. It appears only in more intimate relationships, such as close friendships and romantic relationships. But your style with your best same-sex friends can be different from your style in your romantic relationships. Also, your style can change as a relationship changes.

Despite all that we've just said, the following survey can help you get to know yourself a little better. As you take the survey, consider how you typically feel about and relate to people you're in relationship with. We know it's tempting to answer these questions according to how you *would like* to relate to people rather than how you *actually do* relate. So you must really work at being honest with yourself as you read through the checklists.

Circle the numbers next to those statements that generally describe you. Go with your first instinct; don't overthink the statements.

The Avoidant Attachment Style

1. I don't like sharing my feelings with others.
2. I don't like it when my partner wants to talk about his/her feelings.
3. I have a hard time understanding how other people feel.
4. When I get stressed, I try to deal with the situation all by myself.
5. My partner often complains that I don't like to talk about how I feel.
6. I don't really need close relationships.

7. I highly value my independence and self-sufficiency.

8. I don't worry about being alone or abandoned.

9. I don't worry about being accepted by others.

10. I tend to value personal achievements and success over close, intimate relationships.

The Anxious Attachment Style

1. I really like sharing my feelings with my partner, but he/she does not seem as open as I am.

2. My feelings can get out of control very quickly.

3. I worry about being alone.

4. I worry about being abandoned in close relationships.

5. My partner complains that I am too clingy and too emotional.

6. I strongly desire to be very intimate with people.

7. In my closest relationships, the other person doesn't seem as desirous of intimacy and closeness as I am.

8. I worry a great deal about being rejected by others.

9. I tend to value close, intimate relationships over personal achievement and success.

10. When I get stressed, I desperately seek others for support, but no one seems as available as I would like them to be.

The Fearful Attachment Style

1. My feelings are very confusing to me, so I try not to feel them.

2. My feelings are very intense and overwhelming.

3. I feel torn between wanting to be close to others and wanting to pull away.

4. My partner complains that sometimes I'm really needy and clingy and other times I'm distant and aloof.

5. I have a difficult time letting others get close to me, but once I let them in, I worry about being abandoned or rejected.

6. I feel very vulnerable in close relationships.

7. Sometimes I feel very disconnected from myself and my feelings.

8. I can't decide whether or not I want to be in close relationships.

9. Other people can really hurt you if you let them get too close.

10. Close relationships are difficult to come by because people tend to be unpredictable in their actions and behaviors.

The Secure Attachment Style

1. I find it easy to share my feelings with people I'm close to.

2. I like it when my partner wants to share his/her feelings with me.

3. I am comfortable getting close to others, but I also feel comfortable being alone.

4. I expect my partner to respect who I am.

5. I expect my partner to respond to my needs in a sensitive and appropriate way.

6. Building intimacy in relationships comes relatively easy to me.

7. I let myself feel my emotions, but I'm rarely, if ever, overwhelmed by them.

8. I am able to understand and respond sensitively to my partner's feelings.

9. I do a decent job balancing my need for intimacy with my need for achievement and success.

10. When I get stressed, I feel comfortable seeking comfort from my partner and/or close friends.

Now that you've finished the survey, note the distribution of your circled numbers. What styles do you exhibit two or three traits from? Does one style emerge as dominant? What about your results, if anything, surprised you?

CONSIDER THIS: What relationship style do you see yourself fitting into? On the continuum of anxiousness and avoidance below, place an X on where you see yourself. How has your relationship style affected the way you interact with those you love? Your spouse? Your children? Your closest friends? God?

◄ – – – – – – – – – – – – – – –|– – – – – – – – – – – – – – – ►

High Anxiety   Secure   High Avoidance

HIGH ANXIETY: Highly preoccupied about abandonment; extremely anxious in relationships

HIGH AVOIDANCE: Highly avoidant in relationships, overly self-reliant, downplay intimacy

Visit www.godattachmentbook.com for a message on your specific relationship style.

6

Meeting God One-on-One

I went to a psychologist friend and said if 500 people claimed to see Jesus after he died, it was just a hallucination. He said hallucinations are an individual event. If 500 people have the same hallucination, that's a bigger miracle than the resurrection.
—Lee Strobel [1]

L OVE HIM OR HATE HIM, there's no denying the singer Johnny Cash lived with passion. Though his journey was packed full of arrests, affairs, and addiction, he battled through it all to become one of America's most legendary singers of all time. In the award-winning movie about him, *Walk the Line,* there is a gripping scene that brings to light what it means to live (and sing) from the heart. With meaning. Purpose. And passion.

Having scored an audition with record producer Sam Phillips, Johnny Cash and his band chose to sing a gospel tune originally sung by Jimmy Davis, a song describing the moment that Jesus saved his soul and forgave him.

No more than a few verses into the song, Phillips stopped Cash and asked if he had something else to sing. Cash was offended. He asked Phillips, "Is it the song or the way I sang it?"

Phillips said, "Both."

Cash, noticeably irritated all the more, piped back, "What's wrong with the way I sing it?"

Phillips replied, "I don't believe you." Though Johnny Cash sang a song of belief in God, that he had peace within, and that God had saved him, Phillips called him out, saying that what he sang and what he felt were diametrically opposed. He sang with his mouth, but not his heart.

Do those around you believe you have what's real? Have you ever been in church singing a hymn or praise song and were just merely going through the motions?

We have.

Perhaps that's why this story resonates so much with us.

Who, Not What, You Know

Her noticeably frazzled look and despondent demeanor had me (Tim) questioning every ounce of confidence I'd gained in graduate school. With hopelessness staring me directly in the eyes, my mind began filtering through every counseling theory I could remember. Rogers—unconditional positive regard. Erickson—intimacy versus isolation. Ellis—adversity, beliefs, consequences.

I tried to convince myself that this, one of my very first clients, could be helped if I just used the right formula. "Surely I can figure this woman out," I thought.

Then out of nowhere, with disheveled hair and full of energy, my client stood up, walked directly around my desk, inches from my face, and in a raspy, almost demonic voice said to me, "Say Jesus."

After a brief silence, I said what any confused counselor would: "What?"

She got noticeably louder: "I said, *say Jesus*!"

"Um, Jesus," I said.

Young and fresh out of graduate school, having memorized every counseling theory known to man, I thought I had everything I needed to be a good counselor. But this client put me in my place—quick. Unbeknownst to her, she reminded me in that moment that what was really important, at least to her anyway, was God. She didn't necessarily care what or how much I knew. She cared about *who* I knew. She wanted to know that I believed in the transformative power of Jesus Christ to change her.

> *I would rather live my life as if there is a God*
> *and die to find out there isn't, than live my life*
> *as if there isn't and die to find out there is.*
> —Albert Camus

The Real Thing

We were created by God and for God. At the core, our hearts long for a real relationship with him, and we can smell a fraud a mile away— even if that fraud is wearing our own skin.

People will try almost anything to connect with God. Some try ancient Indian techniques of hunkering down in sweat lodges for days at a time to have a mystical experience. Others use yoga, meditation, and other Eastern methods of spirituality. In the Christian realm, the Protestant Reformation broke down walls in churches that separated the "haves" (the priests) from the "have nots" (everyone else). Later, denominations created unique forms of worship to point to God's unapproachable holiness or celebrate his nearness. Some still use pipe organs, but many today have bands that sound as good as professional groups. Grand cathedrals in our major cities stand as monuments to the glory of God, and in the hills of Appalachia, some people pass rattlesnakes to each other in obedience to, as they see it, God's command.

Some pastors yell; others whisper. Some church services last for several hours, but worshippers in most churches are checking their watches if the pastor preaches five minutes too long. Twenty to thirty years ago, we experienced a movement away from traditional worship styles, but the last five years or so have seen a resurgence, especially among young people, of the use of candles, quiet reflection, and soft music. There is a style of worship for almost any taste, and every one promises the same thing: an authentic connection with the God of the universe.

Does an Authentic Relationship
with God Really Make a Difference?

Before we get too far into this chapter and introduce God as an attachment figure, many of you may be wondering whether or not an authentic connection with God makes a difference anyway. Besides, many psychological theorists throughout the past century, including Sigmund Freud, have used words like *regression* and *dependence* to negatively characterize a believer's relationship with God.[2] And though we certainly understand how spirituality and religion can be harmful and unhealthy when they are abused or otherwise wrongly practiced, research has consistently shown the positive effect of religion and religious coping when applied in a healthful way.

Dr. Harold Koenig, founder and former director of Duke University's Center for the Study of Religion, Spirituality, and Health, and founding co-director of the current Center for Spirituality, Theology, and Health at Duke University Medical Center, and his colleague Dr. David Larson, the former president of the National Institute for Healthcare Research, found that spirituality and religion have very positive effects on our mental health. Take a look at some of the findings of their life's work:

- Spirituality helps to safeguard against the effects of stress and depression.[3]
- Religion is associated with "the prevention of mental illness and substance abuse."[4]
- "Religious involvement is more strongly related to mental health outcomes than to physical illness and mortality."[5] That is, being involved at church, in religious practices, or with the spiritual disciplines has shown to have more positive effects on mental health even than on physical health and death rates.
- Personal involvement in spiritual practices and a religious community is related to a lower likelihood of anxiety disorders, depression, and alcohol and drug abuse and dependence. According to the research, being involved in a

public religious community "is most strongly predictive of better health."[6]

- Religious involvement in a faith community is also linked to a faster and more likely recovery from mental illnesses and substance abuse/dependence. The findings on substance abuse come primarily from studies on the efficacy of twelve-step programs like Alcoholics Anonymous.[7]

Think about these findings for a moment in light of your attachment style and how you view yourself and others. Think about whom you would run to when you're stressed or otherwise living under a lot of pressure—at the end of a long, hard workday; after you hear bad news; when you're overwhelmed with life and everything going on around you. Write the name of that person down. Now look at that name for a moment and picture a time when you were stressed and that person came through and was there for you. What feelings do you have when you think of that person? Especially the assurance of knowing the person will be there for you no matter what happens in life—that he or she has your back. Perhaps you feel safe? Comforted? Secure? Confident? According to attachment theory, when we feel safe and secure our stress and anxiety levels decrease and our desire for exploration increases. With the overwhelming research pointing to the positive effects of religion on mental health, an authentic relationship with God may be just what the doctor ordered.

But what about those of us who can't really think of a safe person we could turn to? Perhaps when we were growing up, the source of our comfort was also the source of our pain; therefore, we have never experienced what safety in a relationship is really like. Or we were extremely hurt or otherwise harmed by a church leader or religious fanatic. Now we're more hesitant than ever to even think about turning to or trusting a God we hear is safe, yet we can't see, feel, or touch.

Though Koenig and Larson in their research have found no evidence that religion can harm health, there is evidence that unhealthy forms of spirituality and religion, such as the religiously motivated medical neglect we mentioned earlier in the book, are harmful, leading ultimately to death.[8] Dr. Kenneth Pargament, in his pioneering research on religious coping styles, has found that "positive" religious coping styles, such as viewing God as a benevolent, caring God and seeking social support, are linked to better health. On the other hand, "negative" religious coping styles, like interpersonal or shared dissatisfaction with religion and viewing God as a punisher, actually predict poor health.[9]

What does this ultimately mean to you? Koenig, Larson, and their colleagues sum it up:

> We believe that the state of the evidence probably reflects reality. That is, there are undoubtedly specific subgroups in the population who have been harmed by religious involvement, which has led to either direct or indirect negative health effects. Identification of those subgroups is an important area for future research. Nonetheless, the dominant pattern is one in which religious involvement either has no effect or has positive effects on health.[10]

Why is it that most of the 1,200 studies reviewed by Koenig and Larson show that religion has a beneficial and invigorating effect on health? Perhaps it's because God really does function as a safe haven and secure base in our lives, someone we can turn to in times of need and stress.

God as an Attachment Figure

Connecting with God is about experiencing him as a safe haven and secure base in both good times and bad. And the level at which you're able to connect with him may be based on the way you turn to him as an attachment figure in your life. In the last few chapters we showed the components of the attachment behavioral system and explained the four styles of relating, particularly and beginning with our primary caregivers. But can God actually function as an attachment figure in our lives as well? And if so, how can we lean on him to experience the safety we need for an intimate relationship? That's what attachment researchers have been looking at since the early 1990s, and it has been a focus of our own study the past few years.[11]

In order for God to function as an attachment figure he must serve each function that characterizes an attachment relationship. Our ability to seek proximity to God, turn to him as a safe haven, experience him as a secure base so we are free to explore, and grieve over perceived loss or brokenness in our relationship with God can be the difference between cognitively believing in God, as many of us do, and emotionally connecting, trusting, and walking with him every day.

Proximity Seeking and God as a Safe Haven

Research supporting the claim that people seek God as a safe haven during times of stress is the most studied area of attachment theory in the context of religion.[12] Lee Kirkpatrick, one of the pioneering researchers in the area of God attachment, suggests that in times of distress persons of faith seek proximity to God in ways similar to that of an infant who seeks closeness to his parent. John Bowlby, who originally developed attachment theory, suggested that "Whether a child or adult is in a state of security, anxiety, or distress is determined in large part by the accessibility and responsiveness of his principal attachment figure."[13]

We mentioned earlier that the imagery and language used in regard to Christianity is extremely representative of attachment relationships. Coping with stress and troubling times in life is much easier when Christians speak of Jesus being "by one's side," "holding one's hand," or "holding one in his arms."[14] Bible verses like the ones below are what Christians cling to when they seek God as a safe haven:

- "Even though I walk through the valley of the shadow of death, I will fear no evil, for you [God] are with me." (Ps. 23:4)
- "Cast all your anxiety on him because he cares for you." (1 Pet. 5:7)
- "Never will I leave you; never will I forsake you." (Heb. 13:5)
- "God is our refuge and strength, an ever-present help in trouble." (Ps. 46:1)

- "The LORD is close to the brokenhearted and saves those who are crushed in spirit." (Ps. 34:18)

Other research supports the safe-haven function God plays in the life of a believer. For instance, it has been found that in times of emotional distress, people turn to prayer even more than to the church; grieving persons tend to increase their faith and religious devotion during times of loss, even though their fundamental beliefs do not change; and soldiers pray more frequently in combat. Times of death and divorce; fears associated with serious illness, emotional crises, or relationship problems; and other negative events have also been found as stressful activators that send one to seek God as a safe haven.[15]

These findings show how our relationship with God is similar to our other attachment relationships—and that our idea of God can ultimately determine how safe God is in our life.[16]

God as a Secure Base

With the convincing theory and evidence showing God as a safe haven and emotional comfort, a core aspect of understanding God as an attachment figure is how he functions as a "secure base." Incredible research has shown that those who believe they have a relationship with a stronger, wiser nonphysical deity report higher levels of global happiness.[17] When individuals feel secure they experience positive emotions such as joy, gratitude, and contentment. Such feelings allow people to explore the world around them; they become more creative, engage in increased times of recreation, and are more likely to serve others or repay kindness.[18] Secure attachment to God provides contentment in the here and now and assurance in future challenges.[19]

Feelings of Loss or Perceived Abandonment by God

Finally, feelings of loss or perceived abandonment by God often elicit feelings of grief and anxiety in the person of faith. This is difficult to determine, however, because in many cases, separation from God is by choice. Either they stop believing God exists or they have no conviction about sin in their lives and are therefore indifferent to whether God is there or not.[20]

Doubts about whether God exists in reality can produce anxiety, especially among people who come from a religious upbringing.[21] In fact, one study showed that college students who are going through the life transition of moving away from home experience higher levels of stress, more daily hassles, increased rates of depression, and more doubt about God. There are other reported instances where a person of faith felt abandoned by God, and the feelings were most often overwhelming, especially if the perceived abandonment came at a time of particular need.[22]

God as My Attachment Figure

Take a moment and make four columns on your paper, then top each with one of the following functions of an attachment figure: proximity seeking, safe haven, secure base, and grief over loss or perceived abandonment. Now, under each category, begin jotting down how God has functioned as an attachment figure in your own life.

- *Proximity Seeking:* Do you seek him? And if so, when? What circumstances or events make you most likely to turn to God? When are you not turning to God?

- *Safe Haven:* Do you feel safe with God? When are you most likely to feel safe with him? Under what circumstances have you not felt safe with God? Why? What was going on in your life at that time? How safe do you feel with him now? Rate that on a scale of 1 to 10, 10 being extremely safe, 1 being extremely unsafe. Write down a few phrases that describe your experience with God when you feel safe with him (e.g., by his side, holding his hand, in his arms, etc.). If you have a hard time with this, write about your difficulty with it and begin thinking of why you have a hard time feeling safe with God.

- *Secure Base:* Do you feel secure in your relationship with God? Do you really believe that he has your best interests in mind? On a scale of 1 to 10, 10 being extremely secure, 1 being extremely insecure, rate how secure you feel in your relationship with God. Are you feeling insecure with God during difficult times? Are you disappointed in God? Do you blame him when life is hard? Are you afraid of facing death? Be honest with yourself as you note down how God may or may not function as a secure base in your life.

- *Grief over Loss or Perceived Abandonment:* Do you get sad or afraid when you feel like God is distant? Write down the times in your life when you felt most abandoned by God. What was the most prevalent feeling you had during those times? How afraid are you of God's walking away from you? Rate that on a scale of 1 to 10, 10 being extremely worried and 1 being not worried at all. Why do you think you worry so much about God forsaking you? If you don't worry about God abandoning you, why not? Have you ever wondered about God's presence or absence in your life?

Attaching to God

We may say we believe almost anything, but our true beliefs are revealed in the crucible of troubles. Even here, we see how the components of secure attachments function. Theologian Gordon Kaufman was the first to connect attachment theory to our relationship with God. He observed, "The idea of God is the idea of an absolutely adequate attachment figure. . . . God is thought of as a protective parent who is always reliable and always available to its children when they are in need."[23]

In the same way that we relate to our parents, we relate to God in a feedback loop. If we believe that we are secure in his love, we venture out to explore new ideas, opportunities, and relationships. Sooner or later, when we experience failure, criticism, or other kinds of threats, we look to God for reassurance and reconnection. At this moment, if we believe God loves us and is there for us, we reconnect with him and enjoy him as a safe haven again.

The moment of trouble, however, is when the faith of many of us evaporates. Perhaps because we have had poor models when we were children, we make the colossal but wrong assumption that, in our difficulties, we aren't lovable or worthy of love or God isn't capable of caring for us. When this happens, we exhibit anxiety, avoidance, or fearful responses to God, and our relationship with him breaks down.

Everybody looks pretty normal when things are going well. But when the chips are down and we're thrown into the trenches of heartache and stress, that's when relationship styles and character surface, and we truly see people for who they are. Soldiers may be friends before the battle, but after it they are blood brothers for life. A marriage may be fine before the child got cancer, but husband and wife grow to depend on each other more than ever as they struggle to find hope each day.

Of course, not all of these stories end well. Too often, many of us distance ourselves instead of supporting each other, or we viciously blame those we claim to love instead of hugging and speaking words of affirmation. These responses often reflect the experiences we had with our attachment figures. As Lee Kirkpatrick suggests, in times of distress, people of faith seek proximity to God in ways similar to that of an infant who seeks closeness to his parents.

The goal of parenting isn't protecting children from stress. It's to prepare them to handle stress by giving them confidence and security based on consistent love. Children don't grow healthy and strong if they aren't allowed to experiment and explore the world they live in, which necessarily involves successes and failures. Times of threat, however, are the most crucial moments in the relationship. It is then that the child cries for help and realizes whether the parents are there to respond.

In the same way, God doesn't protect us from all harm. In fact, he allows us to enter into the dark places of life from time to time, and he "prunes" us so that we'll grow stronger and bear more fruit. It is a tragic misconception to assume that God's job is to make life easy for us. Author and psychologist Larry Crabb observes that many of us think of God as "a specially attentive waiter."[24] When we get good service from him, we give him a nice tip of praise. When we don't get what we want, we complain.

When we try to avoid pain, we may miss God's purpose for it. Author and professor J. I. Packer observed that God has a higher purpose for our struggles. God's purpose, he notes, is to deepen our relationship with him. He wrote:

> This is what all the work of grace aims at—an even deeper knowledge of God, and an ever closer fellowship with him. Grace is God drawing us sinners closer and closer to him. How does God in grace prosecute this purpose? Not by shielding us from assault by the world, the flesh, and the devil, nor by protecting us from burdensome and frustrating circumstances, nor yet by shielding us from troubles created by our own temperament and psychology; but rather by exposing us to all these things, so as to overwhelm us with a sense of our own inadequacy, and to drive us to cling to him more closely. This is the ultimate reason, from our standpoint, why God fills our lives with troubles and perplexities of one sort or another—it is to ensure that we shall learn to hold him fast.[25]

Back to Johnny Cash. Later in the conversation, producer Sam Phillips looked at Cash and said, "If you were dying, you're telling me you would sing that song . . . about your peace within . . . or would you sing something different . . . something real . . . something you *felt*?"

Our prayer is that, as you journey with God, you will find him as a safe haven, a secure base; and in times of stress, you will turn to him and trust him for your everyday life. Why? Because he changes everything.

CONSIDER THIS: There's no safer place to be than in the presence of God.

Is he safe to you? Go to www.godattachmentbook.com and watch the chapter 6 video.

7

When It's Hard to Connect

*What else does this craving, and this helplessness,
proclaim but that there was once in man a true
happiness, of which all that now remains is the empty
print and trace? This he tries in vain to fill with everything
around him, seeking in things that are not there the
help he cannot find in those that are, though none
can help, since this infinite abyss can be filled only
with an infinite and immutable object;
in other words by God himself.*
—Blaise Pascal[1]

WEDNESDAY NIGHTS were prayer meeting nights. Every week. As part of the evening service, church people would take time out to pray for missionaries, the needs in the church, personal problems, and the sick. I (Tim) don't remember a lot about those nights except for the moment when time seemed to stand still, the time my dad taught me a hard lesson about prayer.

During prayer time people would gather in groups, so I always went to the front of the church and would kneel beside my dad. As my time came to pray, I wanted to impress him, so I would recite my own little "Now I lay me down to sleep" prayer about missionaries in some faraway land that I had no idea even existed and about keeping us all safe and in good health. A prayer I had memorized and quoted, week after week after week.

By the way he looked at me after I had finished, I could tell he wasn't impressed. "Tim, why do you always repeat the same prayer?" I looked at him stunned that he would even say anything to me about it. And then he said, "Prayer is about sharing with God what is in your own heart, your heart to his, one on one. It's not about repeating the same thing to him." I'm usually a slow learner, but not that night.

How often have you prayed and felt as though your prayers bounced off the ceiling, that you had no real connection with God? Difficulties in our lives, whatever the cause, surface our true beliefs about ourselves, our sense of safety, and our view of God. Like a child who feels threatened and cries out to be reconnected with his mother or father, we need assurance that God is available, attentive, and accessible. There may be dozens of reasons people have trouble connecting with God, but we want to focus on three:

1. Our preconceptions of God based on our attachment patterns learned in childhood.
2. The invisible nature of God.
3. The reality of sin that separates us from God and clouds our perceptions.

Presumptions

Our presumptions about God often start with how we've viewed our parents as we were growing up. In fact, studies have shown that a girl's view of her mother and a boy's view of his father are likely to have a direct effect on how they perceive God.[2]

Research shows that, with two parents present, girls possess both a strong maternal perception of God and a more moderate paternal God perception (influenced by both male and female parenting), while boys identify God almost exclusively with masculine characteristics such as justice, fairness, power, and moral laws.[3] That is, girls tend to maintain attributes of both power and nurturance (i.e., compassion, caring, empathizing, and comforting) in moral reasoning. This study also found that the paternal view of God, held by male children, is one of power and authority, and the view of God characteristic of the maternal image is of one who is caring and welcomes the child.[4]

Also, if parents were perceived differently from what traditional roles would predict—that is, the father as the nurturing parental figure and the mother as the powerful maternal figure—children were more likely to view God as both powerful and nurturing. Cultural messages that teach children traditional roles the father and mother should or should not play, whether it be through television, church, or school, greatly affect the child's subsequent view of God later in life. By exhibiting behaviors that oppose the traditional mind-set and surpassing the expectations, fathers who show nurturance and mothers who show power greatly impact their child's view of God in a more positive way.[5]

Through emotional involvement with his children, a father plays an indirect role in his child's view of God as nurturer. When fathers are absent, they are more likely to be idealized.[6] This is important to note because the God image has been found to be determined more by the idealized parent than the actual parental figure. Thus, if the father is present, the child develops a more balanced view of God as both powerful and nurturing than if the father were absent.[7] In cases of absent and emotionally distant fathers, God can become a more perfect parent as a "substitute attachment figure."[8]

Presumptions of Secure Attachment

As we saw earlier, those of us who enjoyed "good enough" parents felt secure as kids, and when we felt threatened during forays of exploration, we learned that our parents were safe havens of love and security even in some of our darkest moments. It's not very hard for us, in most cases, to connect the dots between our parents and God. We naturally assume that the ultimate authority figure in the universe is, if anything, even more loving, more powerful, and more supportive than our parents. We aren't surprised or angry when God doesn't protect us from all harm and give us everything we want. We are convinced that good parents—both human and divine—understand, balance, and know that overprotecting children doesn't help children grow strong.

Presumptions of Anxious Attachment

Many of us, however, come to God with very different presuppositions about his nature and the way he wants to relate to us. Those of us who are anxious feel insecure in the relationship. We dance for God, hoping he will be pleased and, in turn, bless us. We sing (sometimes at the expense of the poor eardrums around us) and pray and study with all our hearts because we long so deeply to find security in knowing that God is pleased with us; we can quote dozens of passages about his love and acceptance, but deep in our hearts we just don't believe it. When we miss a church service or quiet time, we're overwhelmed with guilt and anxiety that God is surely mad at us. Sound familiar?

We thirst for God, but demand that he protect us from being hurt ever again; and we are bitterly disappointed when he doesn't come through as we're sure he should. We are very active in pursuing God and trying to please him. In fact, we are probably the most active of any of the relational styles—reading books, listening to messages, praying for hours, and going to meetings. We hope we can do enough to win God's approval and feel connected to him. Occasionally, we feel very close to God. Those times may almost be ecstatic, and we want the feeling of closeness to last forever—but it doesn't. When those feelings of intimacy wane, we wonder what's wrong with us, and we may redouble our efforts to win God's approval again. When a new teaching promises marvelous healing and a deeper relationship with God, we eagerly buy the books and attend the seminars. When a new service opportunity arises, we're the first to volunteer. The challenge to connect with God really isn't about him, it's about us—never feeling like we measure up. With knots in our stomach, we are just waiting for the other shoe to fall. Anxious. Afraid. So we try anything to feel affirmed and loved by God.

Presumptions of Avoidant Attachment

Those of us who have developed an avoidant attachment usually have an arms-length relationship with God. We tend to appreciate the facts of our salvation, but focus much more on our duty as believers than on the relationship we have with God. The more committed of us devote our time and energies to making the church function effectively, and more often than not our efforts make a big difference. When others talk about God's love, however, we aren't as inspired and are rarely moved to desire it, too. We just acknowledge that it's nice that others feel close to God, but a deep, rich relationship with God is not even on our personal radar screen. When other people express a heightened level of emotion, either about their needs or their experiences with God, our avoidance causes us to drift away because it makes us feel uncomfortable.

When we're avoidant in our relationship with God, it's easy to say we're dependent on him, praying and reading the Bible—until things fall apart. When that happens, we close God out and wonder if he's really capable of loving or being there for us, because he seems so distant.

Presumptions of Fearful Attachment

Then there are those of us who suffered chaotic, abusive home environments. For many of us the source of our comfort was also the source of our pain. If you didn't know whether you were going to be loved or smacked as a child, your heart still cries out for love, but eventually you "wall" everyone out. You have to. People and relationships aren't safe. This pattern so easily spills over into our relationship with God as a fearful type, and we view our relationship with God the same as we view our earthly relationships with those who were supposed to love us.

Unfortunately for us, we never really feel safe—because all we have known is chaos. We thus carry this over into our adult relationships and subsequently feel disconnected and out of place in every relationship and every environment. In our fearful relational style, we may try almost anything to connect with God, but we seldom feel close to him because we have learned to attribute the chaos to him. It's kind of a "gun-shy" approach to God. Our lack of self-confidence makes us vulnerable to the claims of teachers and preachers who profess to offer the solutions to life and happiness. But we're soon disappointed again when the promises aren't fulfilled, and we drift back into emotional and relational isolation.

• • •

The three painful patterns of attachment certainly shape our perceptions of God in a negative way, but they aren't the only reason we have trouble connecting with him.

God Is Invisible

When we talk to a friend face-to-face, we see the person's expressions and hear his or her voice. We can tell by nonverbal communication, too, whether someone really means what is said. Even when we talk on the phone, the digital signal is translated to sound remarkably like our friend's actual voice. Every human-to-human relationship has a physical quality to it. Even our memories of those who are away from us by distant decades or a brief trip to the store are based on physical interactions. But God, as Jesus told the Samaritan woman, "is spirit." We can't see him, but we can see definite signs of his existence. The whole creation, from the vastness of space to the intricacies of the body's genetic code, tells us that God is great, he is creative, and that he is attentive to every detail of our lives.

In his book *Reaching for the Invisible God,* Philip Yancey says that one of the characteristics of God is that he hides. If God were a physical being, Yancey reminds us, God's body would fill every space in the universe because he's omnipresent. He hides to protect us from harm, but also because he values faith as the connection point between us and him. It is part of his plan for us to pursue him (even as he pursues us). Yancey writes:

> Does God play hard to get for the sake of discovery? . . . The Bible sometimes portrays God as the initiator, the Hound of Heaven in pursuit. Yet just when we think we have God, we suddenly feel like Isaiah searching for the One who absconds, *Deus absconditus,* Now you see God, now you don't. We do know that in his relationships with people God places a premium on faith, which can only be exercised in circumstances that allow for doubt—circumstances such as God's hiddenness.[9]

Some people, like my (Josh) friend Brian mentioned earlier, refuse to believe until they can see and feel God. And they are in good company. Thomas, a disciple of Jesus, had been with him every day for over three years, and he had heard Jesus' predictions that he would be killed and then raised from death back to life. After the crucifixion, others reported to Thomas that they had seen Jesus and talked to him, but Thomas would have none of it.

"Unless I see the nail marks in his hands and put my finger where the nails were, and put my hand into his side, I will not believe it," said Thomas.

Can you relate to Thomas? *God, show me some tangible results here.* You, too, are one of those people who must see it to believe it? Notice what happened next.

About a week later Thomas was hanging out at the house with the rest of the disciples and Jesus showed up. Having no regard for the locked door, Jesus just appeared out of nowhere and said, "Peace be with you!" Then he looked at Thomas and said, "Put your finger here; see my hands. Reach out your hand and put it into my side. Stop doubting and believe."

Obviously perplexed, yet enlightened by what happened, Thomas responded, "My Lord and my God!"[10]

Jesus replied, "Because you have seen me, you have believed; blessed are those who have not seen and yet have believed."[11]

Remember, this is the same disciple who earlier in Jesus' ministry had had enough courage and belief to stand beside him even in the face of impending death. When Lazarus had died and Jesus wanted to go "wake him up," the disciples said it would be too dangerous to go to Bethany. But Thomas challenged the rest of the disciples, "Let us also go, that we may die with him."[12] Even after having been with Jesus, he was still skeptical.

Unlike Thomas, we don't have the opportunity to have Jesus bodily appear to us to show us his wounds, but we have plenty of evidence to stimulate our faith. The stars, rivers, oceans, and mountains "declare the glory of God"; the Scriptures clearly teach about the nature of God; and the history of the church shows us how people throughout the centuries have found God to be trustworthy. Though he is invisible and "hides" from us, we see evidence of him all around us every day.

The Barrier of Personal Sin

The primary problem between us and God isn't the way our parents treated us when we were children, and it's not that God is invisible, either; our greatest barrier to experiencing an intimate relationship with God is our selfishness, sinfulness, and rebellion against him. And that's true for every human being on the planet. Though most of the secular world and news media shudder at the word *sin,* let's start by considering its very definition. According to the dictionary, *sin* is "an offense against religious or moral law; a transgression of the law of God; a vitiated state of human nature in which the self is estranged from God." When we sin, we turn our backs on our relationship with God, ultimately distancing ourselves from him.

From a biblical perspective, "Everyone who commits (practices) sin is guilty of lawlessness; for [that is what] sin is, lawlessness (the breaking, violating of God's law by transgression or neglect—being unrestrained and unregulated by His commands and His will)."[13] Jeremiah says that "the heart is deceitful above all things and beyond cure. Who can understand it?"[14] Solomon, the wisest man to live, said "There is not a righteous man on earth who does what is right and never sins."[15] Paul confirms our wretched human condition by writing that "all have sinned and fall short of the glory of God."[16] For "If we claim to be without sin, we deceive ourselves and the truth is not in us."[17] And the punishment for sin? Paul writes that "the wages of sin is death, but the gift of God is eternal life in Christ Jesus our Lord."[18] Herein lies the great divide between death and salvation. But "if we confess our sins, he is faithful and just and will forgive us our sins and purify us from all unrighteousness."[19] Those who are saved by accepting and believing the promises of God through Jesus Christ as Lord will have their sins forgiven and will live with God for eternity.

In his insightful book *The Prodigal God,* pastor Timothy Keller says that the familiar story of the prodigal son in Luke 15 has a few surprises that help put the understanding of sin and salvation into perspective. The word *prodigal,* from Greek (ἄσωτος), doesn't mean "wayward"; it means "wastefully extravagant." In the story, the father's love for both sons was extravagant, just as God's love is for us. That's the reason for Keller's book title; the father in the story represents God and his gracious, extravagant love for us. The very same

God who leaves ninety-nine sheep to go after the one he has lost. The extravagant God who rejoices in heaven more "over one sinner who repents than over ninety-nine righteous persons who do not need to repent."[20] Remember, God wants to be in relationship with us, but when we sin we deliberately turn away from it.

Keller tells us that there are two errant ways to try to find meaning and purpose in life apart from God. One, illustrated by the younger brother, is rampant self-indulgence. This son wanted the cash from his inheritance, but he asked for it before his father was dead. In that culture, his insistence on getting the money before his father died was an incredible insult. But imagine the love his father had for him, selling one-third of his property and giving it to his son anyway. This young man ran to a distant country and wasted it all on "wild living." He didn't care about his father at all. He only wanted his father's things so he could spend them on his own pleasures.

The elder brother stayed home to work on the family farm, but when we see his response when his father welcomed the younger brother back into the family and threw a grand feast, we discover his motives for doing the right things for all these years. He, too, only wanted the father's things. He didn't care about the father. Though he lived under the same roof and worked hard in the father's fields, he was doing it all for selfish reasons. All of his work was just to earn points to prove himself and gain leverage over his dad.[21]

All of us are represented by one of these brothers (or perhaps both at different times in our lives). At the core of our hearts is the evil of selfishness. We care only about our pleasure, our success, and our reputation, and we will use anything to get what we want. Why do people *feel* far from God? Because they *are* far from God's heart.

The solution to sin isn't to fill the void with even more self-indulgence or to check off "good Christian" boxes to prove that we should be acceptable because we've done so many good things for God. No, the solution is the extravagant grace of God who "made [Jesus] who had no sin to be sin for us, so that in him we might become the righteousness of God."[22] When we recognize our sins—either self-indulgence or self-righteousness—we need to repent, turn from our sinful behaviors, and trust in Christ's sacrifice to forgive us. Without the process of forgiveness, sin creates brokenness and separation from God. As Oswald Chambers asked, "Are you drawing your life from any other source than God himself? If you are depending upon anything and anyone but him, you will never know when he is gone."[23]

When we're living a life of repentance and forgiveness, God's light and love shines in our hearts, and we are born into the family of God. Spiritual intimacy, a true attachment to God, begins by accepting Jesus Christ into our heart because "he is the atoning sacrifice for our sins, and not only for ours but also for the sins of the whole world."[24] It is "in [Jesus] we have redemption through his blood, the forgiveness of sins, in accordance with the riches of God's [extravagant] grace."[25] "Yet to all who received him, to those who believed in his name, he gave the right to become children of God."[26] That is what the great invitation of the Bible is all about!

Those of us who are just beginning this spiritual journey need to connect with a trusted friend, pastor, or mentor to help disciple us and teach us how to develop a deep spiritual intimacy with God. This book is also a great start! Those of us who have been believers for a while need to remember that staying close to God isn't a continuous self-improvement project (the elder brother) or a "get out of hell free" card by which we can now behave any way we want. Every step of spiritual growth is based on remembering our forgiveness. A deep memory of God's extravant grace always produces the twin traits of true faith: gratitude and humility.

> *Little children, keep yourself from idols.*
> —1 John 5:21 (KJV)

In God's Place

When we fail to identify and address the hindrances to a genuine connection with God, we try to fill our hearts with something—anything!—that promises to make us happy and fulfilled. God has made us so that only he can fulfill our deepest longings. Saint Augustine wrote, "You have made us for yourself, O God, and our hearts are restless until they find their rest in you."[27] The great calamity of life is to reach for something or someone other than God to fulfill the deepest longings of our hearts. And reach we do. For all of history, and certainly today, men and women's hearts are terribly restless because they are trying to fill them with almost anything but God. Dallas Willard alluded to this in his book on spiritual disciplines: "Obviously, the problem is a spiritual one. And so must be the cure."[28] We spend billions of dollars on pleasure and comfort, hoping we can have enough fun, great sex, relaxation, and enjoyment to compensate for the stress and emptiness we feel. These things are filling for a while, but before long we need more, and we need them to be even more thrilling to satisfy us.

Some of us crave power over others to prove that we are superior and valuable. We are driven to win at all costs, and we don't care who we walk over to get to our goals. When we face any obstacle, we become furious, and we use people instead of loving them.

When our lives feel out of control, some of us compulsively try to control people and situations in the hope that we'll feel safe if everyone and everything is in place. We become demanding and rigid. When we face situations or people we can't control, we become anxious and even more demanding.

Many of us long to feel loved, so we become approval addicts. We live to please people around us, and we are terrified of losing their affection or respect. We think about every word we say and everything we do to see if others are impressed with us.

To be sure, there's nothing in the world wrong with enjoying fun moments with family and friends, being promoted or winning a game, keeping a semblance of order in our lives, and knowing others love us—as long as these are seen as gifts from God. When they occupy first place in our hearts, the Bible says they have become idols, and they have a destructive effect on every aspect of our lives. Though there may be many different variations for individuals, it's easy to see that anxious people often are addicted to approval, and pleasing them becomes an idol. For avoidant people, success, pleasure, and control can become idols in their hearts. And fearful people feel their lives are so chaotic that control might be their main pursuit in life.

Pursuing something other than God as our primary focus in life takes our attention away from him. When we miss or we don't embrace the connection with God, our heart searches to fill the void and our Seeking System ultimately goes awry. Instead of feasting on his love and strength, we are left to our own resources, and we become easily stressed and empty. Idols can't give us the love and joy we long for, but in our blindness we think that we need just a little bit more success, pleasure, control, or approval to make us really happy. Ah, the addictive pattern erupts. And when we use people to meet our selfish needs, we certainly aren't loving them. They feel used and confused as they try to relate to us.

Authentic Affection

Some of us need to be re-parented because our concept of God and our identity have been distorted by our earliest relationships, but all of us need to be forgiven for our sinful self-absorption. Thankfully, the message of the Gospel addresses both of these crucial needs. In this life-changing message, we find that God is a safe haven, the protector we need when we feel threatened, and the source of forgiveness for our sin. Christ, then, addresses both our wounds and our sins.

There is a difference—an enormous difference—between intellectual assent to the truths of the faith and actual faith in God. The first one leads to theology and interesting arguments; the other leads to intimacy with God. Jesus said that in his day, many people called him "Lord," but their hearts were far from him. Today is no different. Countless people file in and out of church services each week, but their hearts aren't warmed and they don't sense God at work in their lives during the week at home, in school, or at work. As we've seen, the experience of pain surfaces our true beliefs. No wonder Yancey called it "the gift nobody wants." C. S. Lewis called pain "the megaphone to rouse a deaf world." We discover authentic faith when we realize that God is the initiator, and he went to incredible lengths to prove his love for us. In one of the most beautiful passages in the Bible, Paul quotes an early hymn describing the humility and love of Christ. He wrote:

> Who, being in very nature God,
>   did not consider equality with God something to be grasped,
> but made himself nothing,
>   taking the very nature of a servant,
>   being made in human likeness.

And being found in appearance as a man,
    he humbled himself
    and became obedient to death—even death on a cross!
Therefore God exalted him to the highest place
    and gave him the name that is above every name,
that at the name of Jesus every knee should bow,
    in heaven and on earth and under the earth,
and every tongue confess that Jesus Christ is Lord,
    to the glory of God the Father.[29]

To show us his love, Jesus stepped out of heaven where he enjoyed perfect union with the Father and the Spirit, as well as fabulous riches as the creator of the universe. He gave all of that up to become a helpless infant, live in poverty, and live in the shadow of the cross. Why? To make us fabulously rich by his grace. Though he lived a perfectly sinless life, he took all of our sins on himself when he was on the cross. There, he didn't pay some money to ransom us from spiritual death; he gave his life. If the measure of love is what it gives, there has never been love like this. To describe Christ's humility in suffering for us, Saint Augustine wrote, "Man's maker was made man that he, Ruler of the stars, might nurse at his mother's breast; that the Bread might hunger, the Fountain thirst, the Light sleep, the Way be tired on its journey; that Truth might be accused of false witness, the Teacher be beaten with whips, the Foundation be suspended on wood; that Strength might grow weak; that the Healer might be wounded; that Life might die."[30]

How do we experience his love?

I (Josh) remember speaking to a group of eighteen- to thirty-year-olds at a church where I used to pastor. I'll never forget Anthony, a sharp but seemingly depressed twenty-something who approached me after the service.

"Josh, I have been praying and reading my Bible, no different than before, and God just feels so distant. It's like I can't feel his presence or his love for me anymore. What should I do?"

Have you ever had one of those Southwest Airlines, "Wanna get away?" moments? This was my moment. Looking to buy time until I could think about what "pastorly" advice to give him, I asked him to explain his predicament to me once more, trying to discern if what he was experiencing was just a spiritual dry spell or if depression itself was beginning to take over every area of his life. It wasn't too long into the conversation that it dawned on me.

"Are you wrestling with anything in your life?" I said.

After fumbling through some words he finally admitted how pornography was beginning to take over his life. That's something we as counselors have seen time and again take away the spiritual intimacy and connection in people's relationship with God.

The Bible tells us that we need to repent. We acknowledge that our hearts have been far from God—either in self-indulgence like the younger brother in the story in Luke 15, or in self-righteousness like the elder brother. We tell God that we have given up on filling our hearts by ourselves. Sinful attitudes and behavior have only brought us more pain, as well as brokenness in our relationship with him and those we love. And we accept his sacrifice, not just as a fact of history but also as the payment of our own sins in our personal story. The words we say aren't magical. God knows our hearts and responds to us by throwing the biggest party in heaven we can imagine!

The marks of an authentic connection with God are gratitude (we are amazed that God would forgive us and love us like he does), an awareness of the Holy Spirit's presence in our lives (in our hearts he confirms the fact that we are now God's children), the desire to help others (especially those who can't pay us back), and a heart longing to please God (which is simply love responding to love).

But what about those who responded to God's invitation of grace years ago but still feel distant from God? Our hearts are not static things. After we accept Jesus as our Savior and enter a relationship with God, we tend to drift back toward the sins of either the younger brother (which often lead to addictions) or the elder brother (religion). Our heart's default mode isn't to love God more; it's toward selfishness and sin. Because sin is something we do, we must constantly "count the cost" and seek God's grace and forgiveness.[31] We need to continually come back to the heart of the Gospel and let it sink deeper and deeper into our souls. Whenever we get bored with the thought of God rescuing us from sin and shame, we are drifting far away. Martin Luther observed, "The truth of the Gospel is the principal article of all Christian doctrine. . . . Most necessary is it that we know this article well, teach it to others, and beat it into their heads continually."[32]

The Gospel of Christ is the source of hope, light, and love for many people. Those who have doubts about authority figures and naturally distrust them because of early childhood trauma can recognize in Jesus an authority who proves his love by his kindness and sacrifice. When we begin to grasp the amazing truth of God's grace (and we won't understand it all until we see him face-to-face, if then), we reach out in faith, and we discover that he's there. Others may have been absent when we needed them, but he's always there. Others may have been cruel when we were hurting, but he is tender and compassionate. Others may have ridiculed us for having needs and feeling afraid, but he says, "I know exactly how you feel because I've been ridiculed, abandoned, mocked, beaten, and even murdered." We don't have to earn his love, and in fact, we can't. If we try we only create distance between us and him. Instead, we notice how much he loves us, and we gladly accept his kindness and forgiveness.

Knowing God may begin in the head as we explore concepts, dispel myths, and uncover truths about God, but a real relationship with him is from the heart. Perhaps it may be what the Psalmist meant when he wrote, "Taste and see that the LORD is good; blessed is the man who takes refuge in him."[33]

CONSIDER THIS: What is your God-attachment style? How has your relational style with God been a barrier for you in connecting with him more intimately? What are other personal barriers in your life that prevent you from turning to or connecting with God? What are you going to do to overcome these barriers? Write down at least three to five practical steps you can take today to begin to strengthen your attachment to God and visit www.godattachmentbook.com to understand how to implement them into your life.

8

Exploring Your Seeking System
and What Happens
When It Goes Awry

*Modern man is drinking and drugging himself
out of awareness, or he spends his time shopping,
which is the same thing.*
—Ernest Becker[1]

THE FIRST TIME I (Tim) met Jake, I was impressed. Everything in life was going his way. Family. Prestige. Big-time money. Influence. And the truth was, he was a lot of fun to be around. But some of our initial discussions took quick, sharp turns to what wasn't okay. This upright, good-standing man had a private side to him that he had kept masked for years. Even those he was closest to figured everything was all right, but they didn't understand what was really going on inside of him. He didn't, either.

Until the night he was arrested for his third DUI (having previously buried the first two, getting off scot free). On this third occasion he was also caught packing a gun with no permit and making threats about people. No permit. Threats. Alcohol. It didn't make sense to me. It certainly didn't seem like him. But it was. It was all everybody could do to keep it from hitting the papers, because if it did, it would be pure scandal. Why? Because it didn't make sense. A loving family. Great esteem in the community. But lost in the abyss of emptiness. Driven to drink. Doing drugs. And being with people who didn't represent him in any way, shape, or form. Somewhere, somehow, something had gone awry.

When life's not the way it's supposed to be, we tend to reach for anything to calm or soothe the emptiness, or fill the hole in our soul. Jake eventually said that he was empty, angry, and tired of trying to prove that he measured up. What I realized in the end was how mad he was at his family, God, and especially himself.

The Spin of Belief

If you've made it this far into the book, the assumption is that you are not, as Os Guinness says, "indifferent" to thinking about who God is in your personal life. As we have already mentioned, from Teresa of Avila, to Viktor Frankl, to the neurobiological and psychological research of the present day, we have the freedom and innate ability to make a choice concerning our attitudes and beliefs about God. And as we mentioned, it's often the disappointments, losses, and emotional crises that lead us on a journey of doubting God's character and even his existence, thus bringing us to the crossroads of a decision—a decision either toward God or away from him.

What follows is how easy it is to turn from God to someone or something else to calm and soothe the stress, emptiness, and existential longing in our hearts for something greater than ourselves and to fulfill the deep longing in our souls for God. In psychology, the early stage of this pattern is best described as abusing a substance. It's not that we're necessarily addicted; it's that we're turning to our drug of choice for some type of temporary relief. Unfortunately, if the problem goes unresolved, as it usually does, we move further down a pathway of dependence, believing it's the only way to anesthetize the pain in our life. But it never satisfies.

Whatever you do, do not skip over these chapters too quickly, thinking you've already chosen God and therefore don't need to read them. For perhaps in doing so you are blithely assuming you don't fit the context for what we're about to say. That very act in and of itself could be a dead giveaway as to why you actually don't have a relationship with God in the way you think you do.

The Need for More

I (Tim) remember meeting with a pastor who really changed the way I thought about disappointments in life. I had no doubt that he was a kind and caring man, a family man who loved his wife, kids, and his congregation. But as the people came and the church grew, so did the pressures of maintaining the constant demands of his role, and the longer hours. With his wife working her own job to help pay the bills, and busy running the kids from school to practice and back home for dinner, homework, and bedtime, he figured it would be best if he didn't burden her yet with his concerns, too. Welcome to the widespread conundrum I often see in too many ministry leaders around the country.

Working long hours and having no one to confide in, he was alone. And as the pressures to perform in ministry mounted, he increasingly began to isolate himself. The more he drew inward, the more lonely he became. Before long, the alluring and seductive message of a naked woman figuratively shouting from the computer screen "I want you" had him falsely feeling affirmed and validated. Not wanting to "click" through it, he told himself one peep wouldn't matter, and if it did, he'd be able to stop. But he didn't and then seemingly couldn't. Wrestling internally with feelings of guilt, conviction, and increasing loneliness, he pressed in even more. If his wife or the congregation found out, he'd probably lose his job and maybe his marriage. So he trusted nobody. And like a cancer consuming his liver, he was dying inside and became emotionally numb to what he was doing.

Thomas Merton, in his book *No Man Is an Island*, says, "There is a false and momentary happiness in self-satisfaction, but it always leads to sorrow because it narrows and deadens our spirit. True happiness is found in unselfish love, a love which increases in proportion as it is shared."[2] Simon and Garfunkel, in their song "I Am a Rock," sing about the downward path toward aloneness, a picture of how self-gratification can lead to isolation, like a rock, or even an island—chilling descriptions they conclude that lead to feelings of apathy, where islands never weep and rocks never hurt.[3]

With nobody around him to talk to, his struggles at work, his loneliness, and his feelings of worthlessness led him into further isolation. And deeper into the pornography. He needed more. The pictures he was viewing before were no longer bringing the same level of excitement. What had started as infrequent quick fixes with women on the computer screen had turned into an everyday addiction of looking at everything the Web had to offer. Sadly enough, this man of God had grown lonely on the outside and hard on the inside; and to continue to anesthetize his pain, he needed more and more of the substance to get the same effect.

When I got the call to help, this pastor had been arrested for exposing himself to a group of minors—a charge that put him on the sex-offender list for the rest of his life. "Tim, that is not me!" he pleaded. "I would have been the last person you would have thought would do anything like this!" And he was right—before the addiction.

Gerald May, in his book *Addiction and Grace,* wrote that "Addiction is the most powerful psychic enemy of humanity's desire for God."[4] Just a few quick glances on the computer for this pastor led to a felony. And the same path to addiction can start just as easily for every one of us. It begins by knowing whom or what we turn to when we're feeling hurt, wounded, and like nobody in the world cares about us. When we're sitting around and realize that life really is not the way it's supposed to be.

Right here is where we can say we trust God for eternity but live like we can't trust him for our everyday lives. We're not sure he will actually pull through for us in our disappointments and "momentary troubles."

"How could God really care about me?" we tell ourselves. "If he is here with me, then why am I feeling so alone and isolated?"

Idols of the Heart

When we're feeling alone and broken, it's easy to turn to someone or something else to soothe the stress and anxiety. But when we reach for anything in our lives to fill the void, these things can quickly become *idols* that consume our thoughts, time, and devotion—and are the very seeds of addiction.

Whether the quick fixes, or idols, are pornography, drugs, alcohol, or promiscuous sex, we start reaching for anything to feel better. "But I don't do any of these things!" you may be saying. That's great. But the danger is that these idols do not necessarily have to be bad things. In fact, a lot of times they are good things—good things that are more likely to become addictive substitutes for God than the bad things. Why? Because the more honorable and incredible the "someone" or "something" is, the easier it is to take the place of God in your life.

Perhaps you're depending on work, career, marriage, kids, golf, shopping, social standing, or money to achieve the happiness and life fulfillment we in America are taught that we deserve. Either way, once you turn to something else to fill the void in your life, that something begins to require more time and attention and can deafen everything else around you. Anything or anyone that diverts you from God and living according to his ways is an idol.

Solomon knew this well when he wrote, "All man's efforts are for his mouth, yet his appetite is never satisfied."[5] But as most of us soon figure out, these good and bad things cannot fully satisfy the emptiness in our hearts, leaving us feeling emptier than we were before, which ultimately leads us on the path to despair—as in the case of the pastor above, or into a deeper search for more.

The Seeking System

One of my (Josh) best friends in graduate school was a former heroin addict. Though I didn't know him then, he would tell me stories about his poor relationship with his father, how he ended up on the streets of Jersey selling drugs, and how he became addicted to heroin at a very young age, narrowly escaping death on a number of occasions.

Though John died in a car accident a few years ago at just thirty-three years young, the last years of his life were spent ministering to those caught deep in drug and alcohol addictions. Having come clean of his addiction, John's relationship with God was richer and deeper than anybody else's I had known. If he wasn't talking about God, he was thinking about God. If he wasn't thinking about God, he was worshipping God. The John I knew became intoxicated with God. I envied the relationship they had together.

Much of my own counseling experience has been helping juvenile delinquents and addicts come off the streets and into drug-rehabilitation programs. Some of my closest friends are former addicts. And the one common denominator I have seen in those who turn away from their drug of choice is an ever-growing deep love and passion for God. It's as if their motivation to fight for and do anything they could to get the drug of their choice is replaced with the same longing to know God more intimately. Many have told me, "I know what I am capable of without God. And I never want to experience that again." The brain research and psychology behind why we turn to or away from God reveals a possible link.

Your Seeking System—that is, the longing you have to know of God's existence and your meaning in this life—is actually engaged by a process called dopamine neurotransmission. Dopamine is a neurotransmitter that generates passion, energy, joy, and a drive to seek rewards and thrilling adventure. Anthropologist Helen Fisher refers to it as the "endogenous love potion."[6] It, along with norepinephrine and serotonin, is the motivating force behind the early stages of romantic love and is what has been found to cause the focused attention and giddiness that allows two young lovers to abandon all of their other friends, spend every waking moment together, and obsess about everything that they have in common, including their tastes in music, food, and hobbies. It's the chemical in the brain that makes two individuals think that, because they both like black beans and peas, they "must be made for each other."

However, that's not all. In addition to the dopamine system being the primary motivator behind the drive for exhilaration, joy, and unrelenting focused attention, researchers are also alluding to dopamine as a core chemical involved in the longing and "search for higher meaning." As researcher Jaak Panksepp states, "The desires of the human heart are endless. It is foolish to attribute them all to a single brain system. But they all come to a standstill if certain brain systems, such as the dopamine (DA) circuits arising from the mid-brain nuclei, are destroyed. . . . These circuits appear to be major contributors to our feelings of engagement and excitement as we seek the material resources needed for bodily survival, and also when we pursue cognitive interests that bring positive existential meanings to our lives . . . seeking spiritual heights and philosophical insights that may not even exist."[7]

Though we are certainly not drawing any conclusions here, we are highlighting the interesting link that seems to exist between our brain's innate drive for seeking pleasure, joy, reward, and exhilaration in connection with another individual and our pursuit of existential meaning in our lives. In fact, research is increasingly making the connection between the dopamine system and one's experience of God.[8] One particular study traced the activation of the dopamine system in committed Christians who were praying the Lord's Prayer. Those conducting the study suggested that the expectation of the person praying the prayer *may have been one of receiving back from it both reward and relationship.*[9]

But as we said earlier, anything that has that much predictive value for good also has that much predictive value for bad—for leading us in a different direction.

The Downward Spiral

Brain researchers have found that a hormone called oxytocin is biologically responsible for promoting feelings of connection and bonding, and it is released throughout our brain when we hug our spouse of many years, when a mother nurses her newborn infant, and during sexual intercourse. These oxytocin receptors are known to be located in the same parts of the brain as dopamine, meaning that oxytocin is rooted in our reward circuitry.

To explain this further, two groups of people were asked to look at pictures of both romantic loved ones and nonromantic friends. The brain activity in these people was completely different depending on the type of face the person looked at. What functional magnetic resonance imaging (fMRI) scans showed was that the brain activity of a person looking at his or her romantic partner was extremely similar to brain activity of new mothers listening to their infants' cries. What's more, fMRI scans showed these brain images to bear striking resemblance to scans of those addicted to cocaine.[10]

When someone like my (Josh) friend John, who was addicted to heroin, needs larger and larger doses of the substance to get the same high, this is called the tolerance effect. The same thing happened in the case of the pastor described earlier, who went from pornography to public indecency with a minor. Panksepp, the same researcher who defined and described the Seeking System, believes that oxytocin actually reduces the tolerance effect. What Panksepp showed is that the brain develops a similar tolerance for naturally occurring opiates. Though dopamine may be the hormone that creates the instinctive pleasure of love and attachment, it is oxytocin that makes it possible for that pleasure to last for a longer period of time.[11]

Unfortunately, though drugs like heroin, cocaine, alcohol, and the viewing of pornography provide the pleasure and reward of seekers looking for relief from life's disappointments, they also "hijack the neural circuitry of love" and further damage "the brain chemistry that regulates the bonds of love."[12] It's why close family and friends are so devastated when their loved one turns his or her back on them to seek the drug of choice.

What or Who Are Your Idols

Anything that has potential for good in our life has equal potential for evil. Take a moment and make a list of the things in your life right now that give you meaning, a sense of purpose, and feelings of affirmation. Now, ask yourself if God is the primary focus for each of the relationships or things you listed. How do you measure this? Ask yourself what or whom you're turning to in times of stress. Are you living your life vicariously through your children? Are you holding your spouse to the same standards as if he or she were God? Or are you making your own financial and career successes the primary motivator of your life, even more than God?

Once our heart is divided between God and our idols, we come to find out how powerful the addiction is. As we mentioned earlier, addictions consume more and more of our time and attention and they pull us away from our closest attachment relationships.

When it's a full-blown addiction, it is nearly impossible to control. It leads to behaviors that leave us saying things like the pastor said earlier in the chapter, "This is not me! I don't do things like this!" Chemically, we now need more and more of the substance to feel the same high, and in doing so we'll do anything to get it. Addicts will steal, cheat, and lie to get more of what they need.

When we set up idols in our lives and become addicted, we often have the following characteristics. We:

- Live in a state of denial about our problem.
- Refuse to take responsibility.
- Blame others for our problems (my husband won't communicate, my boss makes me work too late, the kids never listen, my dog ate my homework).
- Fail to effectively balance our life.
- Mismanage our use of the idol or substance.
- Demand more of the substance to maintain the same effect.
- Increase our addictive behaviors in both intensity and frequency.
- Use the good or bad idol or substance to feel pleasure and find meaning in life and to avoid negative feelings such as loneliness, anxiety, depression, and anger.

When we are feeling the pressures of life, evil loves to get us alone and isolated, and make us feel as though God doesn't love us. It's no wonder, then, that evil would give us quick fixes. Things to pour ourselves into when we're feeling hurt, wounded, and like nobody in the world cares about us—things that give us affirmation, identity, and a sense of pleasure.

But the Bible tells us to not lose our hearts. To not give ourselves and our feelings over to the things in this life that do not matter, both good and bad for you. Because though you will have disappointments in life (disappointments that often feel like hell in the moment), they are achieving for you an eternal glory that is much bigger than all of your disappointments combined. "Therefore," the Bible says, don't fix your eyes "on what is seen, but on what is unseen. For what is seen is temporary, but what is unseen is eternal."[13]

Though it's not easy to turn to God and the eternal when we're hurting, we must—because the consequences of not doing so are also eternal. The more and more we turn to idols and substances in this life, the further and further we move ourselves away from God. It's not that God is not near; it's that we move on to the things we trust in more than God himself.

Tim Keller says that every one of us is a spiritual addict to the core, seeking and searching for pleasure and identity. He says, that in

[s]eeing ourselves as spiritual addicts apart from the inter-vening grace of God, [we must ask ourselves] "Who are you really? Have you got a core identity? Based in what God has done for you in Jesus?" And that no matter what adversity you face, you know you can stand it because you know who you are?

   Or are you just a businessman? Business woman? Just a father? Just a mother? Just an artist?[14]

Honest questions we must all ask. Whom or what have you turned to in times of stress and disappointment? In whom or what have you placed your identity? There are seekers and believers. Some seekers simply turn away.

Tim Keller gives a chilling description of the spiritual conse-quences of addiction in his book *The Reason for God*:

In short, hell is simply one's freely chosen identity apart from God on a trajectory into infinity. We see this process "writ small" in addictions to drugs, alcohol, gambling, and pornography. First, there is disintegration, because as time goes on you need more and more of the addictive substance to get an equal kick, which leads to less and less satisfaction. Second, there is the isolation, as increasingly you blame oth-ers and circumstances in order to justify your behavior. "No one understands! Everyone is against me!" is muttered in greater and greater self-pity and self-absorption. When we build our lives on anything but God, that thing—though a good thing—becomes an enslaving addiction, something we *have* to have to be happy. Personal disintegration happens on a broader scale. In eternity, this disintegration goes on forever. There is increasing isolation, denial, delusion, and self-absorption. When you lose all humility you are out of touch with reality. No one ever asks to leave hell. The very idea of heaven seems to them a sham.[15]

Do you want to turn to God for intimacy, safety, and identity in this life and the next? We do.

CONSIDER THIS: What are you giving your heart to?
This is a very delicate topic and is described in more detail in the chapter 8 video on the Web site.

9

The Grand Delusion

I tell you that unless your righteousness surpasses
that of the Pharisees and the teachers of the law,
you will certainly not enter the kingdom of heaven.
—Jesus[1]

IN GRADUATE SCHOOL, I (Josh) would wake up at 6:00 A.M. during the week and meet my friend John (from the last chapter) at the gym. Since he worked behind the desk every morning, it was the perfect opportunity for us to talk as I worked out. Most mornings we used it as a kind of conversational devotion across the gym, discussing the writings of A. W. Tozer, to Oswald Chambers, to Jesus. Though I have many memories of these particular mornings, there is one that has stuck with me like it was just yesterday.

As I was sitting up on the bench catching my breath in the sixty seconds between sets, John yelled over to me, "Josh, listen to these two passages, 'The way of a fool seems right to him, but a wise man listens to advice,'[2] and 'Do not drag me away with the wicked, with those who do evil, who speak cordially with their neighbors but harbor malice in their hearts.'"[3]

John continued, "Josh, always remember, brother, that you are both. You are the fool and the wise. The one who is righteous, but also the one who does evil."

As I sat there on the weight bench, ready to do another set, the power of John's words fell on me harder than if the weights had slipped out of my hand. What John was saying was what he had learned as a result of his drug addiction and recovery: until you understand your own capacity for foolishness and evil, your ability to care for and have compassion for others is extremely limited. Or put it this way: an awareness of your own evil thoughts, foolish attitudes, and subsequent behaviors leaves no room for self-righteousness and feelings of superiority toward others because of the compassion you develop for others in light of your own sinful nature.

This chapter is about awareness and relationships—or how the lack of awareness leads to poor relationships, first with God and then with others. The reason this chapter is so important to every one of us is that we often are unable to trust God for the here-and-now needs of our lives. When disappointments and momentary troubles happen, having the faith that God is going to pull through for us can be difficult, so we instead turn to someone or something else—another relationship, pornography, drugs, alcohol, work, family, kids—to soothe the stress, emptiness, and anxiety we feel inside.

Why is it so easy to do this? Because in the moment, "it" calms us, and "it" can mean everything, at least in the here-and-now. It's about reward and pleasure. That's why it's so hard for us to give up our bottles. And nowhere do we see this happen more than in religious circles.

Religion That Trumps Relationship

Can religious behavior become all-consuming and unhealthy? Let's look at a story from the Bible where Jesus, who was teaching in the temple at the Mount of Olives, was rudely interrupted. "The religion scholars and Pharisees led in a woman . . . [and] they stood her in plain sight of everyone and said, 'Teacher, this woman was caught redhanded in the act of adultery. Moses, in the Law, gives orders to stone such persons. What do you say?'"[4]

Have you ever been caught in the wrong—and then ridiculed and judged in front of everybody? A black sheep? Just as Jesus would do, right?

Wrong.

The Pharisees "were trying to trap [Jesus] into saying something incriminating so they could bring charges against him. [Just then] Jesus bent down and wrote with his finger in the dirt. [And] they kept at him, badgering him. He straightened up and said, 'The sinless one among you, go first: Throw the stone.' [Then] bending down again, he wrote some more in the dirt. Hearing that, they walked away, one after another, beginning with the oldest."[5]

Let's stop for a moment and examine this passage. The Pharisees were known for their rigid adherence to rules. They believed that moral behavior meant God would be pleased with them. Never mind their despicable attitudes; it's no wonder they quickly became adversaries of Jesus' message of grace.

In Matthew, Jesus called the Pharisees "whitewashed tombs"— pretty on the outside but dead and stinking on the inside.[6] "You're hopeless, you religion scholars and Pharisees! Frauds! You're like manicured grave plots, grass clipped and the flowers bright, but six feet down it's all rotting bones and worm-eaten flesh. People look at you and think you're saints, but beneath the skin you're total frauds."[7]

Religious? Yes. Frauds? To the core.

The motive of the Pharisees in this particular situation was to incriminate Jesus, not to bring this woman to justice. They didn't care about her or the law. So Jesus used the law against them and demanded that the witness to this woman's adultery step forth and cast the first stone.[8] But he required something greater of that witness— that the witness himself had to be without sin. The Pharisees knew they were trapped. So they dropped their stones and walked away.

After the Pharisees left, "the woman was left alone. Jesus stood up and spoke to her. 'Woman, where are they? Does no one condemn you?'

"'No one, Master.'

"'Neither do I,' said Jesus. 'Go on your way. From now on, don't sin.'"[9]

This is a clear picture of religion trumping relationship—a caricature of how such religious behavior brings about death, not life. Isolation, not relationship. Bondage, not freedom. And not only does it bring about death, isolation, and bondage in the heart of the one being accused, but it also brings about death to everybody else who comes in contact with it.

Why? Because religious behavior is like a drug that hijacks the circuitry of love. At the root of it is the desire to feel good about yourself and have a "right standing with God." As a result, moral behavior, not grace, becomes the means to heaven. Which is precisely why the Pharisees rejected Jesus' message of salvation by grace through faith. Salvation by means of grace meant their own self-effort was in vain— their drug had been taken from them. Just as one needs more and more heroin or cocaine to get the same high, so do the religious need more and more moral behavior to feel good about themselves—hence they set up more laws and judged others.

Whenever salvation becomes about moral behavior and self-effort, we isolate ourselves from "the immoral sinners" who aren't "living up to par." Doing so leads to feelings of superiority, judgment, and oppressive, shunning behaviors. Just as the heroin addict turns his back on his family to pursue his drug, so too will the religious fanatic turn his back on his own children in the name of religion. Religious behavior can become a drug that hijacks the circuitry of love.

> Later when Jesus was eating supper at Matthew's house with his close followers, a lot of disreputable characters came and joined them. When the Pharisees saw him keeping this kind of company, they had a fit, and lit into Jesus' followers. "What kind of example is this from your Teacher, acting cozy with crooks and riffraff?"
>
> Jesus, overhearing, shot back, "Who needs a doctor: the healthy or the sick? Go figure out what this Scripture means: 'I'm after mercy, not religion.' I'm here to invite outsiders, not coddle insiders."[10]

Jesus Freaks

I (Tim) have always enjoyed some of Elton John's music. He is a fine artist. But I'll never forget growing up listening to the song "Tiny Dancer" and shaking my head every time I heard him sing about "Jesus freaks" marketing God in the public square. When I was growing up, tracts were often used as a big part of telling others about

Jesus. People would leave these little "tickets" out there that posed the question, "Are you going to heaven or hell?" I'm not sure if it was my conservative traditional upbringing or if Elton John was really making fun of the Jesus freaks—probably both—but it bothered me. I didn't understand why he would make fun of people who claimed to know Jesus.

Maybe the "Jesus freaks" were too embarrassed to tell their story face-to-face. I can see where people would make fun of that. On the other hand, these people were trying to share a message. Were they weirdos? Or did they really have something that maybe Elton John didn't have?

Some of them were probably religious fanatics and frauds. I have met a few of those. But there were certainly others who were sincere. The fine line between the two is something I've wrestled with through the years, especially as I began studying the pioneers of psychological thought and theory who believed religion was oppressive and irrational. The zeal of the religious fanatic was particularly challenging: were they truly odd and off-base, as they often looked and seemed, or were they simply people who were sold on Jesus and living a whole different reality?

I remember the time when a zealous member of one of my dad's churches challenged him for allowing my sisters to wear makeup to church, calling him a hypocrite. For a central Pennsylvania boy, those were "fightin'" words. My dad wasn't a fraud. He genuinely loved God, loved his wife, and loved every one of his eight children. As a kid I was just trying to figure it all out.

As I look back, rules and personal preferences, not necessarily truth, ruled a lot of what we called Christianity. I began to see more clearly that this man making the accusations knew little to nothing about relational ministry. The way he treated his own family was more about rigid rules than grace and love. J. P. Moreland said that "in the actual practices of the Evangelical community in North America, there is an over-commitment to Scripture in a way that is false, irrational, and harmful to the cause of Christ, and it has produced a mean-spiritedness among the overcommitted that is a grotesque and often ignorant distortion of discipleship unto the Lord Jesus."[11] In all of it, we feel superior to anyone who isn't as committed, loyal, obedient, and intense about doing all the right things.

What Does This Have to Do with Pleasure and Reward?

That's a great question. The answer lies in what or whom we turn to for life. If you're a believer, start by honestly asking yourself why you gave your life to God. If you're a seeker, ask yourself why you haven't.

Our hunch is this: if you are truly honest with yourself (and there is initially nothing wrong with this, by the way), the pure motivation for believing or not believing in God stems from a selfish desire to seek pleasure and reward, and to avoid pain. If you've heard the story of Jesus and made the choice not to believe (which we have heard from a countless number of clients and friends), perhaps it is because doing so would require you to give up the things of this life that give you pleasure and make you feel good now.

Many believers, on the other hand, believe in God initially out of a desire to not go to hell. We take the "ticket" Elton John sings about and choose heaven, not because God really matters to us so much as knowing he is going to keep us from going to hell, burning in the fiery pit forever. The difference in motives is slim. Beneath the surface is a drive to escape pain and seek pleasure.

St. John of the Cross, a Christian mystic who lived in the sixteenth century, wrote that when seekers become believers, the first stage of spiritual development they experience is a love of God for pleasure's sake. In likening it to the infant-mother attachment, he wrote:

> It must be known, then, that the soul, after it has been defi-
> nitely converted to the service of God, is, as a rule, spiritu-
> ally nurtured and caressed by God, even as is the tender
> child by its loving mother. . . . The loving mother is like the
> grace of God, for, as soon as the soul is regenerated by its
> new warmth and fervor for the service of God, He treats it
> in the same way; He makes it to find spiritual milk, sweet
> and delectable, in all things of God, without any labor of its
> own, and also great pleasure in spiritual exercises, for here
> God is giving to it the breast of his tender love, even as to a
> tender child.[12]

John of the Cross's description of a path toward a deeper love for God in the 1500s is not far from what we see today scientifically and experientially. When we come to know God, we do so with the same selfish hang-ups we had prior to believing. But it's the Holy Spirit's working in our hearts and lives that ultimately removes the selfish motives and desires to move us toward a deeper relationship with him— one that is more focused on serving him, not ourselves.

This is why Jesus likens his relationship with believers to that of marriage.[13] Truly loving your spouse is about moving from a selfish love based on passion and romance to a purely *selfless* love based on intimacy and grace. It's as if God nurtures our spirit and allows us to experience the pleasure of knowing him for a while before taking us deeper into our understanding of his grace and our love for him.

The Bible says that once we are saved we are gifted and blessed "with every spiritual blessing in Christ."[14] Salvation is not the end, but many a good believer treats it as such. And in so doing, he or she fails to nurture a level of relationship with God that is ever-growing love, away from love for pleasure's sake and toward a love for God's sake. Picture David's desire for a relationship with God: "As the deer pants for streams of water, so my soul pants for you, O God. My soul thirsts for God, for the living God. When can I go and meet with God?"[15]

Talk about a prayer of pursuit, Moses' conversation with God is the perfect example of a growing maturity for love of God: "If you are pleased with me, teach me your ways so I may know you and continue to find favor with you . . . [and] if your Presence does not go with us, do not send us up from here. . . . Now show me your glory."[16] Moses wanted to learn from God. He wanted to be in his presence at all times. And most important, his desire was for the glory of God. Period.

> *Unhappy, let alone angry, religious people provide more persuasive arguments for atheism and secularism than do all the arguments of atheists.*
> —Dennis Prager[17]

Paths to God

The Bible outlines two different ways that people seek salvation and make sense of life. One is the constant pursuit of grace. Grace is the complete responsiveness to God that flows out of our recognition that we can't possibly make it on our own. Our sins are too big and dark and innumerable, and our resources are far too tiny to matter. We turn to God and plead, "God have mercy on me!" And, amazingly, he does; for justice in our matter would call for a searing punishment as the necessary judicial price for our overwhelming sinfulness. This path, no doubt, is the narrow one that very few people choose consistently and completely.[18]

The second way is far more popular; it is, in fact, the broad way that seems to be chosen by many confessing Christians,[19] and was the way chosen by the Pharisees. In our path to knowing God we believe that we still have some duty or ability to make life work on our own. So we launch a spiritual self-improvement program and try to work our way to heaven.

We haven't completely left God out of the equation, though. We use him to give us additional resources. To prove that we are truly worthy, we get him on our side, go to church, pray, read the Bible, and serve others—doing all these good behaviors as leverage to demand God's blessings. Relations with God are like some business exchange theory: when we do these things, we think he owes us. It's not a genuine love relationship; it's still all about our happiness, our success, and our popularity. We're just using God to get what we want. And the result is devastating: guilt, aloneness, and eternal separation from God. The Lord says: "These people come near to me with their mouth and honor me with their lips, but their hearts are far from me. Their worship of me is made up only of rules taught by men."[20]

So why, then, is this seemingly joyless path of religion chosen over the path of grace? Because the path of grace is often a path of suffering and brokenness, and rarely do we feel the pleasures of reward in the midst of pain. Those of us who choose to live out our faith through grace remember what it was like before we were redeemed. It's when we experience the pain, suffering, and heartache of losing our selfish desires that we are often transformed into the most forgiving, loving people on the planet. We build strong, resilient relationships that last and don't gloss over differences and difficulties. Instead, we are committed to both grace and truth. We seek to resolve problems with honesty, love, and understanding.

Both grace-filled, relationship people and religious people obey, but they do it for diametrically opposing reasons. Those of us who have experienced God's love and forgiveness realize how much God cares for us, and we obey because we want to please and honor him with every fiber of our being. When we're coldhearted, self-righteous, angry, and "religious," we do religious things for the wrong reasons. We obey to twist God's arm to give us what we want or to impress those who are watching us. But we can never do enough. Religion then becomes an all-consuming force to establish our sense of emptiness, give us meaning, and satisfy our desires. Religion is an idol.

"Grace will save a man but it will not save him and his idol," wrote A. W. Tozer.[21] Idolatry began with external, tangible objects that people bowed down to and worshipped. Today, though we have moved away from towers and statues, idolatry is not much different. Instead of physical objects, we have erected gods out of money, careers, power, status, and religion—all of which anesthetize our pain but often at the sacrifice of our relationships.

The spiritual journey toward maturity and a deep love relationship with God must rid the believer of anything he or she is putting identity into other than God. As Paul Vitz, professor at New York University and an expert on the study of atheism, said, "The very painful burning away of defense, projections, and other 'comforts' eventually permits a love of God in the absence of rewards for the self. This process can cause serious pain, as in the suffering of Job, the point of whose 'test' was to show that even when all rewards were taken away from him he still loved God."[22]

A relationship with God is about purging yourself of anything and everything that prevents the relationship from growing—so that, in the face of adversity and disappointment, in spite of the reward or satisfaction, you love God anyway. Just because he is God. A. W. Tozer said, "To have found God and still pursue him is the soul's paradox of love, scorned indeed by the too-easily-satisfied religionist but justified in happy experience by the children of the burning heart."[23]

*And without faith it is impossible to please God, because
anyone who comes to him must believe that he exists and
that he rewards those who earnestly seek him.*
—Hebrews 11:6

One Last Caveat: Atheism

The emotional damage from exposure to religious people and environments lingers long after the events. When we're wounded we're reluctant to trust anyone again, especially anyone who claims to speak for God. Delusional religious fanatics who commit terrible crimes and wield absolute control over their followers provide a key indictment against the Christian faith—and are argued as *prima facie* evidence against belief in God, especially by such noted atheists as Richard Dawkins and Christopher Hitchens.

Hitchens, in his book *God Is Not Great,* explains:

> Imagine that you can perform a feat of which I am incapable. Imagine, in other words, that you can picture an infinitely benign and all-powerful creator, who conceived of you, then made and shaped you, brought you into the world he had made for you, and now supervises and cares for you even while you sleep. Imagine, further, that if you obey the rules and commandments that he has lovingly prescribed, you will qualify for an eternity of bliss and repose. I do not say that I envy you this belief (because to me it seems like the wish for a horrible form of benevolent and unalterable dictatorship), but I do have a sincere question. Why does such a belief not make its adherents happy? It must seem to them that they have come into possession of a marvelous secret, of the sort that they could cling to in moments of even the most extreme adversity.[24]

This book helps Hitchens understand exactly that: that even in the most extreme adversity, those saved by grace understand their faith is not about the reward of *feeling* happy; it's about the reward of knowing a God who loves them so much that he himself was willing to endure death on a cross, cosmic abandonment from his Heavenly Father, and the torment of hell, so we wouldn't have to. Jesus Christ in his free will *chose* the way of suffering and died on a cross on Calvary so that you would never have to experience the eternal abandonment (hell) or sting of death that he went through for you. He redeemed you, by his overwhelming grace and love for you, to be in relationship with him—for eternity.

Would the god you're serving now do that for you? Or are you serving a god who loves you conditionally—a god who will leave you still feeling empty at the end of the day, the god of money, career, drugs, alcohol, kids, marriage, religion?

And this is precisely what we've been telling you: that God wired you for this type of relationship with him. Looked at from another perspective, it is also why only 2 percent of the human population considers itself to be atheist, especially when you would think there were so many more, considering the amount of ink and TV time given to the subject. Truth be told, it seems that nothing on earth—and no place in the heart and mind of every human being—can escape the idea of God. In fact, "no society in history has attempted to live without a belief in the sacred, not until the modern West."[25] Yet today the message of atheism in the modern West has become "unoriginal" and "has lost value." In fact, among scientists, university scholars, psychiatrists, psychologists, the mainstream media, and the arts, the more outrageous and radical belief system today is to choose to believe in God.[26]

Atheism and Father Relationships

Dr. Paul Vitz has studied atheism extensively. He has found in his studies of many well-known atheists throughout history a consistent, common denominator: a poor or absent relationship with the father. Vitz says that Sigmund Freud was, in fact, correct to fret over his claim that "once a child or youth is disappointed in or loses respect for his earthly father, [his] belief in a heavenly father becomes impossible."[27] Vitz concludes, in what he calls the "defective father hypothesis," in his book *Faith of the Fatherless: The Psychology of Atheism*, that many of the factors that determine atheism include absence of a father through death or abandonment; or, while remaining present and even nice, a father who is passive, fragile, or unworthy of respect; or, a father who is physically, emotionally, sexually, or psychologically abusive.[28]

In addition to these poor relationships with the fathers, Vitz also found a significant level of "ambition and intellectual arrogance" among these atheists. For example, Voltaire was described "as seldom trying to conceal his intellectual superiority. . . . His passion was for fame; he was certainly not much motivated by his love for others."[29]

Additionally, Ludwig Feuerbach, a German philosopher, "has been described as a lonely figure whose loneliness 'was the product of an unsatisfied intellectual vanity.' Feuerbach considered himself a 'philosopher of outstanding importance,' an attitude that 'rested firmly on the intellectual arrogance of the man.'"[30] Friedrich Nietzsche's "pride and his arrogance, often to the point of pathos, are widely acknowledged." Psychoanalyst Sigmund Freud himself has repeatedly been criticized for his "ambition and his intellectual overconfidence."[31] And Bertrand Russell, most commonly known to be the most prominent English atheist, was recently described for his "arrogance, intense hatred, psychopathic coldness, and his frequent lies," which are discussed in a major recent biography by Ray Monk.[32]

Defective fathers, arrogance, intellectual pride, ambition—in spite of these characteristics, there is one final personal factor that Dr. Vitz says lies at the core of each of the atheists he describes: free will. He says that no matter the historical, personal, cultural, or family background in which they grew up, they had the freedom to choose to believe or not. As we mentioned earlier, based on the Seeking System, each of us, though wired for connection and seeking answers to our spiritual longings, has the freedom to choose. This is a real decision—and it is yours.

Vitz's psychological critique of atheism shows us the importance of understanding how easy it is to fall into the trap of idolizing and worshipping something other than God. Atheists and religionists are alike, in that they align their identity with something other than God—they choose "a mere projection of the self—a kind of psychological idol."[33] From the atheist's intellectual capacity, ambition, and

drive to be right that there is no God, to the legalist's or religious fanatic's ambition for moral superiority, the root of this stance is a form
of selfishness and self-worship, an identity found in something other
than God.

*But he knew that Jesus was more than an explanation.
He's what we really need. If your friend is sick and dying,
the most important thing he wants is not an explanation
but for you to sit with him. He's terrified of being alone
more than anything else. So God has not left us alone.*
—Peter Kreeft[34]

What Matters Most

In Luke's story about a dinner party, he tells of a self-righteous Pharisee
named Simon who invited Jesus and his men to have dinner. Not wanting to identify with them too closely, Simon didn't have the decency to
show them even common courtesy. In the middle of dinner, a woman
crashed the party. But not just any woman—she was a prostitute who,
we can assume, had encountered Jesus earlier and had experienced
his unconditional acceptance—hence, her intrusion. In an extravagant
display of affection, she wept in gratitude, wet his feet with her tears,
and wiped them with her hair, pouring a bottle of costly perfume on
his feet.

Simon was flat-out angry about the invasion, especially by such a
despicable, nasty person! He didn't "get it"—and he remained unwill-
ing to allow God's love to soften and change his hardened heart. In response to his sneers, Jesus told him a story and asked a question:
"Two men owed money to a certain moneylender. One owed him five
hundred denarii, and the other fifty. Neither of them had the money to
pay him back, so he canceled the debts of both. Now which of them
will love him more?"[35]

Simon answered, "I suppose the one who had the bigger debt
canceled."[36]

Then Jesus delivered the punch line to penetrate the Pharisee's
hardened resistance:

[H]e turned toward the woman and said to Simon, "Do you see this woman? I came into your house. You did not give me any water for my feet, but she wet my feet with her tears and wiped them with her hair. You did not give me a kiss, but this woman, from the time I entered, has not stopped kissing my feet. You did not put oil on my head, but she has poured perfume on my feet. Therefore, I tell you, her many sins have been forgiven—for she loved much. But he who has been forgiven little loves little."[37]

What's wrong with a toxic, rigid, rules-driven, self-righteous heart? Jesus' diagnosis is that it has little love for God or others because it hasn't experienced God's cleansing, transforming love. Why not? Because when we're defined by a toxic, self-righteous heart, we can't or won't admit how broken and needy we really are. Instead of saying, "Lord, have mercy on me, a sinner," we insist, "I'm sure glad I'm not like those sinful people!"

Religious people and environments give misleading and distorted answers to the most important relational questions we instinctively ask: "Am I worthy of love?" and "Are others capable of loving me?" All of us desperately need good and true answers to those questions. Empty religion and self-improvement programs can't provide the emotional connection we long to experience.

The next chapter begins to provide the answers and a process to help us enjoy genuine love, safety, and unconditional acceptance. As Vitz so truthfully admits, "All children want to love their fathers—and to have fathers who love them in return."[38] Especially their Heavenly Father.

CONSIDER THIS: "But small is the gate and narrow the road that leads to life, and only a few find it" (Matt. 7:14).

To understand more about what it means to live from the heart, visit www.godattachmentbook.com and watch the interactive video for this chapter.

PART III
IN PURSUIT
OF INTIMACY

10

The Risk of Grace

*For it is by grace you have been saved, through faith—
and this not from yourselves, it is the gift of God.*
—Ephesians 2:8

B ROKENNESS BEGS FOR HEALING. Bondage begs for freedom. Addiction is only satisfied by grace.

From the opposite ends of the literary spectrum, we find observations about our relationship with God. Irish playwright and Nobel Prize winner George Bernard Shaw noted with wry wit, "God created us in his image, and we decided to return the favor." It is impossible for flawed, finite human beings to truly grasp the transcendent nature of Almighty God. Some of us, it seems, don't even try. In *Talledega Nights: The Ballad of Ricky Bobby*, Ricky prays, "Dear Lord baby Jesus, lyin' there in your ghost manger, just lookin' at your Baby Einstein developmental videos, learnin' 'bout shapes and colors. I would like to thank you for bringin' me and my mama together, and also that my kids no longer sound like retarded gang-bangers."

We can laugh at the absurdity of Ricky's prayer, but our laughter may have an edge of irony if we realize that we, like Ricky, try to make God into someone we can relate to—someone we can control and use for our benefit. To the extent that we "dumb God down" and create our own image of him, we miss out on the joy and the adventure of having a relationship with the real God. One of the most poignant moments in C. S. Lewis's *Chronicles of Narnia* is in the first book of the series, *The Lion, the Witch, and the Wardrobe*. Mrs. Beaver tells Lucy about Aslan, the elusive lion of Narnia, who is a symbol of Christ in Lewis's stories. Mrs. Beaver tells the little girl of Aslan's power and majesty, and how he sometimes appears just in time when people need him most desperately. Little Lucy feels overwhelmed with the thought that she might someday actually face the awesome beast. She asks timidly, "Is he safe?"

"Oh no, dearie." Mrs. Beaver laughs at the thought. "He's not safe. But he's good."

When Jesus stepped onto the planet, he didn't make everybody feel warm and comfortable. He accused his enemies of hurting the people they were supposed to protect, and these leaders were often furious with him. And Jesus challenged his followers to give up their selfishness and devote themselves more fully to God than they ever thought possible. They were undoubtedly inspired, but often, also quite perplexed.

Jesus' goal wasn't to win a popularity contest. His message was at the same time the most comforting and the most threatening ever heard. Wherever he went, no one took him for granted. He was—and still is—the dividing point of history. Paul says that he came to bring freedom.[1] Jesus said it was his mission to bring life.[2] However, we have to take up our cross and follow him.[3] To devote ourselves leads to life. And to experience his grace changes everything. Knowing him risks everything we thought we could control in our lives. Amazingly, it is the best and highest risk that we should ever take, for it is the difference between life and death, now and for all eternity. A God-centered life is soaked daily with an understanding and awe of grace.

Above all the grace and the gifts that Christ gives
to his beloved is that of overcoming self.
—Francis of Assisi

Grace Defined

Grace. It's a beautiful word. Definitions include: (1) elegance or beauty of form, manner, motion, or action; (2) favor or good will; (3) a manifestation of favor; (4) the freely given, unmerited favor of God in the hearts of men and women.[4]

Grace truly is a gift of God in Christ, and its power is expressed throughout scripture:

- "For it is by grace you have been saved, through faith." (Ephesians 2:8–9)
- "Be strong in the grace that is in Christ Jesus." (2 Timothy 2:1)
- "My grace is sufficient for thee: for my strength is made perfect in weakness." (2 Corinthians 12:9)
- "As every man hath received the gift, even so minister the same one to another, as good stewards of the manifold grace of God." (1 Peter 4:10)

Yet unfortunately we often misunderstand the story.

Mistakes About Grace

Modern culture and human nature conspire to confuse us about God's grace. False beliefs about God, self, and others often sound perfectly reasonable, but they have devastating consequences in our desire to connect with God. Let's look at three common misconceptions about grace.

We Are Basically Good People
Who Need a Little Help from God

In the late nineteenth century, Darwin's theory of evolution was all the rage. Gradually, social scientists began to apply it to human development and relationships. They were convinced that because animals and plants were evolving into higher forms, surely man was getting better and better, too. They began to teach that man is basically good; sin and evil were unnecessary illusions. The events of the twentieth century should have disabused all of us of this notion. Not only WWI but WWII and afterward have regularly shown us the ugly reality of sin and evil. Under the dominance of just three men—Hitler, Stalin, and Mao—an estimated 200 million people have perished by mass murder. More recently, the history of smaller wars, ethnic strife, and religious terrorism should have closed the book on any belief that man is naturally good, but it hasn't. Our culture, especially our schools, still contains this humanistic germ that blinds people from seeing the painful truth about ourselves.

Even in psychological theory, a common core belief is that human beings are basically good. If you have some core facilitative conditions, people will make the right choices. Most of the people who believe this are probably the same ones who keep their doors locked at night, too.

The Scriptures tell us that humans were created in the image of God, but selfishness and sin have seriously tarnished that image. We aren't "good people who make mistakes from time to time." We have set ourselves up as our own gods, living for our own success and pleasure, and not caring about what God wants for us. Even more, we live our lives apart from God and we sin against him. The apostle Paul said that we are helpless, hopeless, enemies of God, desperately in need of a savior.

And that's exactly who God sent. Jesus didn't come just to be a good example for nice people to follow. He came to ransom prisoners from the cells of their own sinfulness, and to find those who were lost and restore them to the family. God's grace teaches us that he doesn't love us *because* we are good, but *in spite of* the fact that we're not. That's the incalculable measure of his grace.

I Can Do Enough to Earn God's Acceptance

In the gospel story of the prodigal son we mentioned earlier, the younger brother's selfishness and sin is obvious. He wasted all he had on "wild living." The elder brother, though, did everything right. He worked hard, sweated in the fields, and "never disobeyed" his father. At the end of the story, however, the younger brother was enjoying his father's love and acceptance at a lavish feast, while the elder brother bitterly remained outside.

Obedience, then, isn't the highest virtue for a believer; it's faith. Throughout the Scriptures, we find people who did the right things but for the wrong reasons. In their self-sufficient pride, they didn't want to admit that they needed a savior. Instead, they tried to be their own saviors, giving until it hurt, attending services all day every day, praying for hours on end, and sacrificing time, energy, and resources to prove that they were "good and acceptable to God." However, it is not a performance quest. All of their good actions became barriers to a real relationship with God. Their obedience and hard work only fed their pride and pushed them further from God's heart.

This is the great paradox of grace. Sooner or later, we have to realize that we can never measure up to God's standard of perfect holiness. He is holy. We're not.

Life with God is a pure gift, not a grind that we have to endure day after impossible day. We may do a lot better than "that other guy," and that measure of comparison makes us feel good about ourselves—but that's not the way of grace. Genuine humility flowing from our recognition of how impossible it is for man to earn his way to God is the first step in grasping God's grace. To illustrate this point, Jesus told a story:

> To some who were confident of their own righteousness and looked down on everybody else, Jesus told this parable: "Two men went up to the temple to pray, one a Pharisee and the other a tax collector. The Pharisee stood up and prayed about himself: 'God, I thank you that I am not like other men—robbers, evildoers, adulterers—or even like this tax collector. I fast twice a week and give a tenth of all I get.'
>
> "But the tax collector stood at a distance. He would not even look up to heaven, but beat his breast and said, 'God, have mercy on me, a sinner.'
>
> "I tell you that this man, rather than the other, went home justified before God. For everyone who exalts him-

self will be humbled, and he who humbles himself will be exalted." (Luke 18:9–14)

Jesus' point wouldn't have been lost on his audience. Tax collectors were some of the most despised people in the land. They were Jews who worked for the hated Romans to collect taxes from their countrymen. In addition, they often extorted more than the tax owed for themselves. They were considered to be collaborators, traitors to their own people, just one rung above the ladder from a thief.

In stark contrast, the Pharisees were the respected and empowered leaders of the community. In the story, the mark of grace is seen in the tax collector's humble confession of sin, but the hard-hearted Pharisee believed he was better than everybody else because he had done so much for God. Jesus' listeners that day would have been astounded. The prostitutes and tax gatherers were thrilled that God's grace extended even to them, but the Pharisees would have been furious that all their good deeds, loyalty, and giving amounted to nothing. To experience God's grace, we have to give up on ever trying to earn it. It's a gift—nothing less and nothing else.

> *Faith is a living, daring confidence in God's grace,*
> *so sure and certain that a man could stake his life*
> *on it a thousand times.*
> —Martin Luther[5]

My Sins Are So Enormous, God Couldn't Possibly Forgive Me

The first false belief suggests that we don't really need God's grace because we're already good people; the second one teaches that we merit God's blessing because we can earn it; but the third pushes grace away in abject hopelessness. Those of us with anxious and fearful attachment styles can become so overwhelmed with personal failures that we can't imagine God ever really loving us. Perhaps we have committed a single sin that haunts us, or maybe we have long fought—and lost—a battle with an addictive behavior or secret sexual sin.

When we were children, the message from our parents, whether real or perceived, was, "You aren't valuable," or "If you ever mess up, I'm through with you," or "If you fail at anything, I'll beat you to a pulp." To us, personal failure isn't a minor, temporary obstacle. It's a disaster! We feel awful for what we've done, and we have few if any past experiences of forgiveness we can apply to our sins today. Judgmental counselors and pastors only reinforce our worst beliefs about ourselves. Healing comes when someone shows us unconditional love and acceptance regardless of what we do wrong.

A Hard and Glorious Truth

Throughout the Bible, we learn that we aren't "pretty good people who need a little help," but people who are separated from God with no hope for restoration unless God does it for us—and he did. Similarly, in attachment relationships, children feel secure when their parents assure them that they are loved, not just when they are good but also when they misbehave and when they feel threatened. The hard truth about us is that we are separated from God because of our sin, but the glorious truth is that God loves us so much that he sent Christ to reassure us of his love. The amazing thing is that God loves and restores us right in the midst of our sinful ways.

The story of exile and homecoming is a common one in the Scriptures. The first couple was exiled from the garden when they turned their backs on God, and we've been longing for home ever since then. The children of Israel had been slaves in Egypt for over four hundred years, but God sent Moses to bring them home to the Promised Land. Today, we still have a sense that we're not home yet. Author and psychologist Larry Crabb observed, "Ever since God expelled Adam and Eve from the garden, we have lived in an unnatural environment—a world in which we were not designed to live. We were built to enjoy a garden without weeds, relationships without friction, fellowship without distance. But something is wrong and we know it, both within our world and within ourselves. Deep inside we sense we're out of the nest, always ending the day in a motel room and never at home."[6]

When my (Tim) daughter, Megan, graduated from high school and moved to college and lived in the dorms, it didn't sink in for me until after she was out of the house for a few days. I remember waking up for an early flight one morning, about a week after she was gone. Heading out the door, all I had yet to do was go upstairs and kiss the kids good-bye, just like I had for the last eighteen years. But as I approached the bottom of the steps I looked up—and stood stunned. I knew something wasn't right that morning. Zach was there, but Megan's room was empty. The night-light was out. Megan was gone.

Recently she came home and decided to stay the weekend. She said, "Dad, I am staying home tonight."

I said, "Good, I love it when you are home."

"Me, too!" she said. "My bed. My pillows."

I interrupted, "You could move back in." She just smiled and batted her eyes at this old dad.

She has me right where she wants me.

Our longing for God and for home is a sure sign of God's grace making a dent in our hearts. We recognize that something in our lives is terribly wrong, that something is surely missing. You know why? Because we were made for Eden. We may have tried to fill our hearts with everything we can get our hands on, and have countless toys to entertain ourselves, but nothing has worked. Some of us take a long time to come to the end of ourselves, but sooner or later, we are like the tax gatherer in Jesus' story, and we cry out, "God, have mercy on me!"

The Spirit of God imparts assurance of God's love and forgiveness, even to the hearts of our insecure attachments. We may struggle terribly to resist it, and it may take a while before it sinks in, but as we respond to our heart's longing by pursuing God, we find him to be present, loving, and strong. In a beautiful depiction of God's nearness to us, the prophet Isaiah reported that some accused God of forgetting them, but God responded with tender reassurance. Isaiah wrote:

> But Zion said, "The LORD has forsaken me,
> 　　the LORD has forgotten me."
> "Can a mother forget the baby at her breast
> 　　and have no compassion on the child she has borne?
> 　　Though she may forget,
> 　　I will not forget you!
> See, I have engraved you on the palms of my hands;
> 　　your walls are ever before me." (Isa. 49:14–16)

How near are we to God? Our names are written on the palms of his hands as a constant reminder of his love and our needs. In another powerful description of the truth of grace, Paul tells us there has been a "cosmic swap": when we trust in Christ, he takes all our sins and pays for them on the cross. In exchange, he declares us righteous before God. Paul wrote, "God made him who had no sin to be sin for us, so that in him we might become the righteousness of God" (2 Cor. 5:21).

The grace of God isn't just a nice feeling. It's based on a person's making the ultimate sacrifice for us—and it's simply amazing.

The Paradox of Grace

Grace brings freedom, but in the grand paradox of grace, it also makes us willing slaves of God. Paul compared sin to a Roman debtors' prison. In his letter to the believers in Colossae, he said that Christ took our "certificate of debt, consisting of decrees against us" (the list of every sin we ever commited) off our cell door, and he nailed it to his cell, the cross, where he paid for it in full.[7] We've been set free! We no longer obey to twist God's arm so that he'll bless us. Now we obey because we want to please the one who rescued us. The motives are diametrically opposite. In the grace of God, we make ourselves his willing, indentured slaves. Because we appreciate his sacrifice for us, we are loyal, dedicated, and committed to love him and serve him.

Our motive to obey God is seen in graphic form in the directions Moses gave after he brought the Ten Commandments down from the mountain. In those days, Israelites sometimes became indentured servants to pay off debts. Moses gave instructions about freeing the slave and his family after the debt was paid, but he outlined a provision: "But if the servant declares, 'I love my master and my wife and children and do not want to go free,' then his master must take him before the judges. He shall take him to the door or the doorpost and pierce his ear with an awl. Then he will be his servant for life" (Exod. 21:5–6).

Can you picture this scene? The indentured servant has been working for his master for several years, but because his master is so loving and kind, he wants to stay with him after he could be set free!

As a sign to the whole community that he has stayed voluntarily, the master pokes a hole in the flap of his ear for everyone to see. This tells everyone about both people: the master's love and the servant's glad obedience.

God's grace makes a dramatic claim on our lives. We have been rescued, but we are no longer our own. As Paul told the Corinthians, we've been "bought with a price."[8] We are completely free, but we are then to be completely his. This is where the exchange too often breaks down. Too many of us, after we have tasted of God's grace and goodness, consider his gift as being no more than "fire insurance"—a "get into heaven free" card that we'll show someday to whoever mans the pearly gates. When we buy into this idea, becoming a slave to the one who saved us is not an attractive deal; we'll take the gift, for sure, but we also want to retain the freedom of living our own lives. Tragically, what we fail to understand is that true freedom results from being a slave to God, and the road that seems like freedom, in fact, leads to slavery. The paradox operates at every level of the exchange.

The risk of grace is that we turn our lives over to God. Abandoned. Surrendered. We no longer have to defend ourselves because we are convinced that he loves us so much, but we no longer try to run our own lives. He is our lord, our master, and the one we follow. We don't know where he will lead, but we are willing to go there because we are convinced that life in him is truly the Grand Adventure. We don't know what he'll ask us to do, but we're willing to do it because we're sure he knows best. We respond to him like a loved child responds to his mother. We may not understand everything, and we may ask a million questions, but when we don't get answers, we still trust our Heavenly Father because he has proven himself to us.

Cheap Grace

Throughout the centuries, some people have had a fundamental misunderstanding about God's grace. Since God's acceptance is complete and free, they assumed, they were free to do anything they wanted—no restrictions and no guilt to hold them back. Only decades after Christ, Paul was already battling this error of understanding in numerous places in the young and new church. He told the believers in Rome that this line of logic simply doesn't make sense. Yes, we're free, but we're free from sin so that we can gladly serve God. This concept of belonging to God is found in virtually all of Paul's letters. We've been adopted into God's family, and we imitate the Father who loves us. In one of his letters to the Corinthians, Paul reminded them, "For Christ's love compels us, because we are convinced that one died for all, and therefore all died. And he died for all, that those who live should no longer live for themselves but for him who died for them and was raised again" (2 Cor. 5:14–15).

That's the dual and paradoxical nature of grace: it frees us and it compels us to responsive action at the same time. We are gloriously forgiven and unconditionally accepted, but to grasp that truth motivates us to please the one who gave himself for us. The deeper we dig into the price Christ paid to rescue us, the more we'll be amazed by his love, and we'll delight in honoring him all day, every day.

Those of us who see God's grace in only one dimension may offer a distorted version of it. Dietrich Bonhoeffer, the German pastor, called this "cheap grace." In the 1930s, the church in Germany faced terrible choices. Adolf Hitler had galvanized the nation and gave them back a sense of empowered Aryan/Nazi identity after losing the First World War. Many pastors and church members became intensely loyal to Hitler, in spite of his obvious hatred for the Jews and his intention to conquer the rest of Europe.

In those difficult days, many in the church said they were free to make their own choices because God's grace gave them complete freedom. In all the confusion and noise, one pastor, Bonhoeffer, called believers to avoid the emptiness of "cheap grace" to make the hard choices to follow God and resist Hitler. To Bonhoeffer, God's grace didn't make it permissible to do anything people wanted to do. Instead, God's grace drives us to seek God and find courage to do what he wants us to do—no matter what. After Germany invaded Poland and began the Second World War, Bonhoeffer worked tirelessly to undermine his own government—efforts that eventually cost him his life.

Even after he was arrested, however, Bonhoeffer never regretted his commitment to God and to God's cause, and he never became bitter that his life didn't turn out to be easy and pleasant. He knew that God's grace brings comfort, but it's much more than that. It gives us direction and courage to follow wherever God might lead, even to

death. Thankfully, most of us will never face the challenges Bonhoeffer faced, but we all have choices each day to be loyal to God or give
in to the desire for comfort and popularity. We may not face Panzer
tanks or brown-shirted SS goons, but we will face the insidious drift of
selfishness and self-reliant living. Bonhoeffer faced the risk of grace
with incredible courage.

Sorrow and Restoration

To a dad, there is nothing more wonderful than hearing your kids,
when they have done something wrong, say "I'm sorry, Dad," and fall
limp in your arms. And likewise, as a parent to say "I'm sorry," and
ask forgiveness with your children, when you know you've wronged
them. And to know that you have forgiven each other.

The grace of God gives us freedom and enables us to be adopted
into God's own family as his beloved children, but we are still flawed
people with mixed motives. Our default mode isn't gratitude and righteousness; it's self-absorption, resentment, and a sense of entitlement
that God (and others) owe us. As believers, we live between those difficult zones of "already" and "not yet." God has already forgiven us
and made us his own, but we won't experience the fullness of our relationship with him until we meet him face-to-face.

For now, we are involved in a fight for our hearts and minds each
day. On our best days, we cling to God, rivet our thoughts on his
truth, and trust him to use us in others' lives. On our worst days—
well, we don't need to go there. But while we are flawed people in a
fallen world, we'll drift to our default mode from time to time. When
we sin in attitude or actions, our conscience and the Holy Spirit tap us
on the shoulder to get our attention and bring us back. This is the feeling of guilt, the sting of conviction.

When we're secure, we aren't likely to be overwhelmed by guilt. In
fact, we can welcome it as a sign of God's loving presence and gracious discipline. In his book *Rumors of Another World,* Philip Yancey
writes a chapter called "The Gift of Guilt." When we're insecure, we
think that guilt is anything but a gift! We want to get rid of it, deny it,
or grovel in it to do penance. Yancey writes, "Guilt is the early warn-
ing sign of danger, the first rumor of something wrong."[9] Mark Twain

said, "Man is the only animal that blushes. Or needs to."[10] Uniquely in creation, humans have a complex method of registering moral failure. "The guilty conscience presents itself as an inner voice, a most personal form of communication, and can proceed to have a powerful effect on both body and psyche."[11] When we're anxious, we are terrified of guilt because it signifies failure that leads to rejection. We may deny it, minimize it, or excuse ourselves and our bad behavior, or we may become consumed by an oppressive sense that we are losers with no hope of relief. When we're avoidant, we typically blame others for our problems. When we feel the pangs of guilt, we immediately find someone else and point the finger there. Those of us who are fearful have great difficulty grasping the concept of love, so guilt threatens us to the core. We aren't sure what to do with it, so we either deny it, blame others, or become weighed down by shame—sometimes all within a few minutes.

Paul told the Christians in Corinth that there are two kinds of guilt: one leads to grace and restoration, but the other brings a kind of death. He had written them a strong letter to tell them they were sinning, and he hoped they would turn back to God. When he got word of their response, he wrote, "Even if I caused you sorrow by my letter, I do not regret it. Though I did regret it—I see that my letter hurt you, but only for a little while—yet now I am happy, not because you were made sorry, but because your sorrow led you to repentance. For you became sorrowful as God intended and so were not harmed in any way by us. Godly sorrow brings repentance that leads to salvation and leaves no regret, but worldly sorrow brings death."[12]

At the point that we realize we are sinning, we can choose one of two paths: sorrow that leads to genuine change of heart and produces gratitude, or oppressive shame that robs us of joy and leaves us feeling empty—a kind of emotional and relational death. At their heart, guilt and repentance aren't merely a rhetorical matter; yet in the cosmic scheme of things, Jesus paid the juridical demand of the cost of our sinfulness. We don't just turn from our selfish attitudes and actions to godly ones. Though a genuine change of heart toward God includes a move away from sinful behavior, true transformation is more than just behavioral modification—it's about an intimate relationship with God.

Sin is turning our backs on God, and repentance is often the restoration of that communication and closeness. When a secure, loved child does something selfish and is reprimanded by his mother, the mother doesn't just want the child to do the right thing. The relationship needs to be restored, so she speaks words of reassurance, forgiveness, and love. The process of reprimand, repentance, and restoration actually strengthens the bond between them. An anxious, avoidant, or fearful child, in contrast, has little assurance that repentance will result in a delightful restoration, so he denies he did anything wrong, hides from his mom, lies when she confronts him, and when caught red-handed, feels inconsolable or defiant.

The grace of God is an amazing attachment force that connects us with the heart of God. It communicates his love to those who feel unlovable and forgiveness to those whose sins seem overwhelming. One of the most beautiful and powerful depictions of God's grace in the Bible is found in John's account of Jesus' relationship with Peter. At his last meal with his men, Jesus told them he was going to be killed. Peter assured Jesus that he would gladly die for him, but Jesus replied, "Will you really lay down your life for me? I tell you the truth, before the rooster crows, you will disown me three times."[13]

A few hours later, Jesus was arrested, and he was taken to the first of the sham trials. As Peter waited, he kept warm next to a charcoal fire. Three times, unassuming people asked if he was one of Jesus' disciples, but each time in fear, Peter denied it. After the third time, a cock crowed, and Peter wept bitter tears of shame.

After the resurrection, Jesus appeared to many different people on different occasions. After a week or so, however, Peter gave up on Jesus and his mission. *Maybe Jesus could influence others to inaugurate his kingdom*, Peter may have thought, *but not me. I denied him, and it's over for me.* So Peter took some others to go fishing. After a long night with no fish in the boat, the men saw someone on the shore. The man told them to cast their nets on the right side, and immediately they brought in a huge haul of big fish. Peter had seen this years before, and he now realized the man on the shore was Jesus.

Peter didn't wait for the men to row the boat to shore. He jumped in and swam! When he walked up, he saw that Jesus was cooking fish and bread on a charcoal fire. After they ate, Jesus asked Peter three piercing questions: "Do you love me?" Undoubtedly, Peter vividly remembered his three denials, and now he was being asked to affirm his love for Jesus in a corresponding way. But that's not all. The charcoal fire is significant. As they ate breakfast and as Jesus asked the three questions, the smell of the fire that morning reminded Peter of his worst sins of betrayal by the fire that night when he denied he even knew Jesus.

The significance is that God doesn't overlook or minimize our sins. His Spirit reminds us of our worst sins, even as he assures us of his forgiveness and restores us to enjoy our relationship with him. Toward Peter, Jesus did more than restore relationship; he revealed to him that he would be a critical linchpin in the ministry of the church to come. In so doing he let Peter know that his denial would never come between them—it would never be a source of rejection by him who rose bodily from the dead.[14]

Like Peter, when we feel pangs of sorrow and guilt, we don't need to deny them or try to medicate them with food, drugs, sex, shopping, or other addictions or diversions. The sorrow we feel is God's hand reaching out to bring us back. It's the smell of the charcoal fire to remind us of our worst sins, even as he assures us that he has completely forgiven us. That kind of sorrow restores life, frees us from shame, and inflames our love for God more than ever. That's the healing and restorative functions of the gift of guilt.

Letting Go

When we feel insecure, not safe, we feel compelled to control ourselves, others, situations, and even God. Keeping our clamps on any threats, we are convinced, is the only way we can protect ourselves. The grace of God is the ultimate statement of God's incredible love. The more we grasp it and let it sink deep into our hearts, the more we will be willing to let go of our death grip on ourselves and everything around us. The compulsion to control seems to promise safety, but it brings only heartache, self-absorption, and distrust. God's grace lets even anxious, avoidant, and fearful people relax, enjoy God's love, and find the security and significance they've always wanted.

Instead of control, the true believer is enabled to relax and let go of events and situations that are impossible to control anyway. *To relax* literally means to drop the hands of self-protection. He or she is set free to enter God's good rest—to "be still" and know the mighty

presence of the God who makes peace in our troubled heart. Just listen to the many safe-haven and secure-base references to our Refuge
God in Psalm 46 (NKJV):

God is our refuge and our strength (1a)

A very present help in trouble (1b)

Therefore we will not fear (2a)

There is a river whose streams shall make glad the city of
God (4a)

The holy place of the tabernacle of the Most High (4b)

God is in the midst of her, she shall not be moved (5a)

God shall help her, just at the break of dawn (5b)

The LORD of hosts is with us (7a)

The God of Jacob is our refuge (7b)

Be still, and know that I am God (10a)

I will be exalted among the nations (10b)

I will be exalted in the earth (10c)

The LORD of hosts is with us (11a)

The God of Jacob is our refuge (11b)

True experience of grace, though, doesn't happen in an instant for
most of us. The process of growing in grace involves flashes of insight
as well as long periods of gradual realization. Our hike of faith requires courage and tenacity. We'll often face our doubts, and sometimes we'll want to quit. As we find a friend or two to walk with us,
we'll be willing to take another risk, and then another, to live in grace
instead of fear. Is it worth it? There is nothing better. We're still on the
journey ourselves, but we've seen countless insecure people experience
God's amazing grace—a love that has made them know they are finally secure in God's arms.

CONSIDER THIS: Your idols and addictions will only be satisfied by grace.

And the beautiful part is that you can make grace an expression of your everyday life. To learn more visit the book Web site to watch the chapter 10 video.

11

Spiritual Oxygen

If you are not as close to God as you used to be,
who moved?
—Anonymous

THERE'S NOTHING WORSE than when you feel like you can't breathe—like you can't get air. I (Tim) remember before both of my parents died how hard they labored, trying to breathe. We all know there is nothing better than just clean, fresh air.

In some of my younger, crazier days I liked to "hot dog" a little and show off when we were working out. We got stupid one day and had a leg-press competition without warming up.

In the middle of the push, I felt something burst inside. All of a sudden I got really warm on my side, and a growing pain began to settle in. Concerned I might have ruptured my spleen, I went immediately to the doctor for X-rays and scans in every direction. The good news: the spleen was fine. The bad news: enlarged lymph nodes.

That always makes for a good Friday.

Through a series of tests to determine whether I had non-Hodgkin's lymphoma, I wound up being diagnosed with sarcoidosis, a disease that consumes your lung capacity and makes it very difficult to breathe. Left untreated and if it doesn't go into remission, it can be life-threatening. But not nearly as much as a lack of spiritual oxygen.

There's a story about a student of Socrates who wanted to learn wisdom. The story goes something like this:

Socrates said, "Come, follow me." As he walked him down by the beach, Socrates led the young man waist-deep into the water. Immediately, Socrates took the lad and dunked his head in full submersion. The boy struggled to come up for air, but Socrates continued to hold him under. As the student lost energy and began to give up, Socrates brought the boy up for air and left him on the beach as he returned to town. As soon as Socrates' student came to, he walked to town and approached Socrates about why he held him under.

"When you were under the water, what was the one thing you wanted more than anything else?" Socrates asked.

"I wanted air," the boy replied.

Then Socrates said, "When you want wisdom as badly as you wanted air, you won't have to ask anyone to give it to you."

Put yourself in this story. When you need God more than you need air, you'll turn to him.

At what point in your life have you needed God more than air? Every one of us is going to run out of air at some point. Remind yourself of this often and ask: "When life is difficult, and I am struggling for air, is there anything I turn to for oxygen instead of God?" Think through this for a while. Perhaps the answer is affirmation of others, or power, or control over your life, or financial security. When your air runs out, these things will pass with it. Think of the condition of your soul today, realizing that it will live for eternity. What condition is it in today? Is the oxygen you're getting drawing you closer to God, or driving you further from him?

James and Karen had been childhood friends through most of their school years. They lost touch a year or so after they went away to college, but after a few years they both moved back to their hometown. When they reconnected, they picked up where they had left off, with wonderful, honest conversations about things that matter in life. For years, Karen had tried to help James find God, but he had always resisted. He seemed to want to know God, but when they talked about him, James always became intense. To Karen, he appeared eager, even desperate, to know God, but without any hope of finding him.

Now, years later, their conversations were an exact duplicate of the ones they had before. Karen never pushed her beliefs on him, and she never demanded that James respond in a certain way. He appreciated that, and it made their friendship even stronger.

In one of their conversations about God, James sighed, "To be honest, I'd really like to have what you've got."

"What do you mean?" Karen asked with a wry smile. She knew exactly what he meant, but she wanted him to share more of his heart with her.

"Oh, you know. I want to have confidence in God, that he's there and that he wants to know me. That kind of stuff."

She laughed. "That's what I've been trying to tell you since we were in the fourth grade!"

His mood darkened, and he told her solemnly, "Yeah, but it's just not me. And I can't fake it."

"Do you think I'm faking it?"

He hurriedly reassured her, "No, no. That's not what I mean at all. I can tell your faith is genuine, but if I sing the songs, raise my hands at church, and try hard to feel warm toward God, it seems too contrived. I just can't do that."

"Nobody is asking you to," Karen assured him. After a pause, she remarked, "James, you're an honest person. I appreciate your desire to have authentic relationships. You've always been that way. Sometimes, though, people have a hard time relating to God because they don't understand who he is; and sometimes, the problem isn't with him or with songs or people holding up their hands at church. The problem is that they push God away. People like that have to look inside and clear away the things that keep them from having a relationship with God."

The Beginning Point

Is it possible to know God, to really know him and have an authentic rather than a contrived relationship with him? To genuinely turn to him for the air we need, trusting in his goodness and love for us? In the last chapter, we saw that he calls us his friends, but you may be wondering how that works, since all of your other friends are physically present.

How could I really be friends with a transcendent God, who dwells "in unapproachable light"? Granted, the nature of God certainly presents challenges, but the message of the Bible persuades us not only that it's possible to know him, but that God longs for us to know him.

The prophet Hosea assured the people of his day. "So let us know, let us press on to know the LORD. His going forth is as certain as the dawn; and he will come to us like the rain, like the spring rain watering the earth."[1] In his prayer before his arrest and execution, Jesus prayed to the Father, and he told him, "Now this is eternal life: that they may know you, the only true God, and Jesus Christ, whom you have sent."[2]

Paul captured the paradox of what it means to know a transcendent being when he wrote a prayer to the Ephesians: "I pray that out of his glorious riches he may strengthen you with power through his Spirit in your inner being, so that Christ may dwell in your hearts through faith. And I pray that you, being rooted and established in love, may have power, together with all the saints, to grasp how wide and long and high and deep is the love of Christ, and to know this love that surpasses knowledge—that you may be filled to the measure of all the fullness of God."[3] Paul's words aren't just impressive prose; they are the expression of true hope that people would genuinely experience the incomparable, and in fact, indescribable, love of Christ for them. That's the promise, and that's the hope for every person who longs to connect with God.

We might assume that relating to the infinite, invisible God is unlike anything we've ever imagined, but think of it like connecting with others in our lives. Philip Yancey compared relating to God with his relationship with Tom, the UPS driver who delivers packages to his home in Colorado.[4] When he went to the door, Yancey's eyes recognized the features of Tom's face and his blue eyes, and he heard the familiar tone of his voice. He was wearing the right uniform and doing the work that reassured Yancey that it was, indeed, Tom. To relate to any intelligent being, we recognize his or her traits, take steps to connect, and if all systems are "go," each subsequent step to communicate and connect builds more trust between us. We find out more about each other as we see the responses to good times and bad. Appropriately shared celebrations and comfort in times of trouble further build trust and strengthen the bond.

Many of us, though, think that a relationship with God should work in a completely different way.

How do you think a relationship with God should look? Take a moment and circle the feelings you have of God below. Don't think too hard about it. Answer with your first instinct.

1. My relationship with God should work like magic, meaning that it should just happen.
2. I should always feel enthusiastic, even overjoyed at the thoughts of God.
3. God should immediately be there to help me out of any trouble.
4. When something goes wrong in my life, God is to blame.
5. When something goes wrong in my life, I am to blame.
6. I shouldn't have to explain how I feel to God. He already knows.
7. God should be more available to me than he is.
8. I shouldn't be anxious when I feel like God has abandoned me.
9. I shouldn't feel as though God isn't going to be there for me.
10. I shouldn't have to work so hard to build a relationship with God.

Now that you have answered the questions above, understand that each one is a myth we tend to hold about God or our feelings toward him. Statements 1, 2, 5, 8, and 10 suggest that perhaps we have an *anxious* relationship with God, especially if you circled more than three of them. Statements 3, 4, 6, 7, and 9 suggest an *avoidant* relationship with God, especially if you circled more than three of them. If you answered more than four of any combination of them, it can suggest a *fearful* attachment with God.

When we believe that something *should* or *shouldn't* (that's a key word) happen in our relationship with God, we are overgeneralizing. When have you not felt one of these ways in a relationship with your friends? Many of us, however, come to believe that our relationship with God should work more by magic than by the common traits of building relationships. We think we should feel warm, even ecstatic feelings about God whenever we think of him, and we are sure he should bail us out of any trouble immediately and completely. When these things fail to materialize, we either convince ourselves that these things actually happened or we become deeply discouraged. After all, we surmise, "Other people claim they relate to God this way, so what's wrong with me?" You can then see how any feelings of anxiety or avoidance we have in our relationship with God make it look as though we don't have real faith compared to others. So secretly, and sometimes subconsciously, we decide that if God really does love us and is all about having a relationship with us, it shouldn't be this hard. So we keep going through the motions, or just resign ourselves completely.

The beginning point of connecting with God, however, is to realize that developing a genuine relationship with him takes time, intent, and the risk of trusting him—like most relationships. People who enjoyed security as children usually don't have much trouble understanding the dynamics of building relationships, but the rest of us suffer from myriad misconceptions.

Developing any relationship is a journey down a long and sometimes rough road. When we're anxious, avoidant, and fearful we need clear vision and strong legs to take the steps toward trust, love, and joy in any relationship, including our relationship with God. Our perception has been clouded by false beliefs about the way life works, about authority figures, and about ourselves, and our relational muscles are weak and bleeding from the effects of past wounds.

When we're wounded, the path to build a rich, strong, meaningful relationship with God doesn't begin by walking up a mountain of joy. Instead, it's more like hiking in the Grand Canyon: to get from the North Rim to the South Rim miles away, hikers have to go down into the canyon, along steep walls and staggering cliffs. Going down is the only way to get where they want to go, but even along the dusty trail down to the river, there are spectacular vistas and transforming moments of peace and pleasure. It's not all a grind, and those who hike almost always go with a friend.

For us, too, the path of pursuing God involves going down into our wounds, wrong perceptions, and compulsive, controlling behaviors to experience healing and find hope. Most important, we don't have to travel alone; in fact, we cannot. We need to find a trusted friend to walk with us—someone who has been down that path before, who will point out the dangers, raise our sight to the beauty of the trail, and keep us moving when we want to quit.

What can we expect as we take steps along this path? Some promise that we'll experience complete "freedom," and certainly we'll eventually find more peace than we ever imagined. But what we'll find is even better than freedom. We'll discover that God doesn't wipe away our past; instead, he uses every element of it—the wonderful, the horrible, and the senseless—to weave a new, beautiful, strong fabric of our lives. For the rest of our lives, we'll remember the events of the past, but they won't threaten us any longer. We'll be deeply grateful that God used them—even them—to teach us life's richest lessons and draw us closer to him.

Steps Along the Path

When a counselor explained the process of resolving past wounds and compared it to a difficult hike, Alicia responded, "I've spent my entire life trying to avoid looking at all the crud in my past. Now you're asking me to willingly walk into it? Everything in me is screaming to run the other way! How can I do this simply because you want me to?"

Her counselor explained that it's "one step at a time," and that she didn't have to walk that way alone. And she also told Alicia that if she'd find the courage to follow this path, she'd connect with God in a fresh, real way; she'd learn valuable skills in relating to people; and the past wouldn't haunt her any longer. That, Alicia decided, sounded pretty good. The steps into the healing process follow one another in a logical progression, but they aren't quite like boxes to check off along the way. Sometimes we go backward, retracing our steps in order to find a new way forward. These steps, though, have proved to be tremendously helpful for all kinds of people, no matter what attachment style they have developed throughout life. The first step is to grasp an understanding of your own God-attachment style.

Paul described this process in Romans 5:3–5:

Not only so, but we also rejoice in our sufferings, because we know that suffering produces perseverance; perseverance, character; and character, hope. And hope does not disappoint us, because God has poured out his love into our hearts by the Holy Spirit, whom he has given us.

Recognize Patterns of Self-Defense, Distrust, and Control

The principles of healthy, secure attachments and the unhealthy ones we communicated in earlier chapters form a framework of insight for all of us. When we've grown up with secure relationships we experienced reassurance when we felt threatened during times of exploration. Our experiences taught us that relationships can be strong, healthy, and safe. As we watched other children and their parents, we gained insight about patterns of insecurity, and we learned to appreciate our parents even more. As we grew up, we believed that God is much like our parents, only even more loving, strong, and safe.

For many of us, however, the story is different. Discovering the patterns of self-protection, distrust, and control helps us put the pieces together. We recognize that we respond to an unsafe environment in a particular way, but perhaps a sibling responded in a different (but just as unhealthy) way. As we study the principles of attachment theory, the lights come on and we realize, "So that's the reason I've felt and acted that way all my life!"

Remember the Payoffs and the High Costs of Your Story

As you think more deeply about your life's story and the events and circumstances you have written down as you go through this book, we hope that you're remembering the details and are beginning to put puzzle pieces together. We realize that a lot of who we are, and how we think, act, feel, and relate, has a link—a reason. We may not have understood before, but the picture is getting clearer. Some of us have pushed people away in an attempt to feel safe from harm. We believed that nobody is safe, and we even distanced ourselves from those who really love us. Others among us were driven by the need to connect with somebody (anybody!), but in our neediness, we inadvertently drove people away. Some of us trusted too little; some too much. We developed a warped sense of responsibility, compulsively caring for people who should have taken care of themselves, or avoiding people because we were afraid they needed us too much. We used all kinds of behaviors—from intimidation to whining—to control people, but we didn't realize how much they were controlling us.

All of our behavior, no matter how warped or painful, God can and will use for a purpose. Our reasoning may have been conscious and logical, or more likely, these reactions became instinctive and ingrained in our subconscious perceptions. We believed there was a significant payoff to these behaviors: the illusion of safety through avoidance or control, and the illusion of real connections with people through enmeshed, absorbing relationships. Throughout our lives, all of our actions made perfect sense to us—until now.

At this point in the journey, we recommend that you go back over the timeline you drafted of your life earlier in the book, including all the major events and relationships. What has been the most significant discovery for you? What is a pattern that developed in the way people treated you? Did you develop a pattern of relating to others based on your relationship with your parents or primary caregivers? Have these patterns affected your relationship with God and what you believe about him?

Before you recognized the patterns in your life, you may have felt locked in to reacting to the same people and situations in the same way, time after time. But no more; now you can make new, healthy choices. When Alicia completed her timeline and reflected with her counselor, she remarked, "This is the hardest thing I've ever done, but it's the most liberating. Now I feel that all my feelings have been validated. I used to believe that there was something horribly wrong with me because I felt so angry and afraid, but I don't feel that way anymore. I finally understand why I felt that way."

Reframe the Meaning of the Story

As we take these steps and gain insight, many of us realize that we've seen ourselves as victims all our lives. Tragically, our wounds have become translated into our identity. As much as we hate to admit it, we believed we were helpless and hopeless, responding passively or defiantly to any perceived threat. Victims are inherently demanding and bitter. They demand that people pay for what they've done to them, they demand that someone fill the hole created by the wound, and they demand that no one ever hurt them again. These unrealistic demands only leave them vulnerable to more hurts, so they become victims all over again.

Reframing our story doesn't mean we deny the wounds that have occurred. Instead, we challenge our beliefs about God (if we've seen him as disinterested or cruel) and ourselves (as hopeless or defiant victims), and see everything that has happened to us through a new set of lenses. The truth is that we have been hurt and victimized, but these wounds no longer have to define our identity. The story of Joseph illustrates how even someone who was betrayed and abandoned can reframe his story.

Joseph was Jacob's favorite son, but his ten older brothers resented his father's affection for him. One day, Jacob asked Joseph to travel some distance to check on his brothers, but when they saw him, they decided to do away with him. They wanted to kill him, but his brother Reuben convinced them to throw him into a cistern. When a Midianite caravan came by on the way to Egypt, Judah suggested they sell Joseph for twenty shekels of silver—two pieces each.

In Egypt, Joseph was sold to an official named Potiphar. After serving him faithfully, the official's wife tried to seduce the handsome young Jew. When Joseph fled from her, she told her husband that he had tried to rape her. Potiphar must have known better because he didn't kill Joseph. Instead, he had him thrown into prison. There, the warden noticed such integrity and skill in the young man that he put him in charge of the prison.

Years later, the pharaoh had trouble with two of his servants, the baker and the cupbearer, so he sentenced them to prison. There, the two men had alarming dreams. Joseph interpreted them; and as he predicted, the cupbearer was restored to his role, but the baker was executed. The cupbearer promised to help Joseph get out of prison, but he forgot about him—until the pharaoh also had disturbing dreams.

The cupbearer told the pharaoh about Joseph, and suddenly, he found himself standing in front of the ruler of the most powerful nation on earth to interpret his dreams. Joseph correctly interpreted the pharaoh's troubled dreams, and it gave the pharaoh great peace and comfort. In response, he made Joseph prime minister and put him in charge of the entire kingdom. During seven years of plenty, Joseph gave orders to store grain for the upcoming famine.

Then, a year or two into the region-wide famine, Joseph's ten brothers traveled to Egypt, looking for food. They eventually came before Joseph, but he didn't let them know who he was. Instead, he tested them to see if they had changed, or if they were as selfish and hateful as they had been when they sold him to the caravan over twenty years before.

Finally, he was convinced that they had learned their lessons, and he told them who he really was. They were astonished, and they wondered if he would take revenge and kill them. "But Joseph said to them, 'Don't be afraid. Am I in the place of God? You intended to harm me, but God intended it for good to accomplish what is now being done, the saving of many lives. So then, don't be afraid. I will provide for you and your children.' And he reassured them and spoke kindly to them."[5]

Joseph could have identified himself only and always as a victim of his brothers' hate, but he chose to reframe his story. And the phrase "You intended to harm me, but God intended it for good" may be one of the most powerful reframes in the story of anyone's life. He saw the events of his life through God's lens, and he believed that God had used betrayal, abandonment, false accusation, delay, and harsh conditions in prison to strengthen him and give him an opportunity to serve God even more. Joseph realized that God's purpose for his life was much bigger than comfort and applause. God never promises those things, but he promises to use every event in our lives to produce good and to glorify God.

In a similar way, Jesus suffered unjustly, but he always had a bigger view of the Father's purposes than just getting revenge on those who hurt him, or having a legion of angels appear to rescue him. When we become painfully aware of the depths of our suffering, we can identify to a degree with Jesus. He knows exactly how we feel because he suffered shame, pain, and abandonment, too. Knowing he understands our pain and shame gives us tremendous comfort.

Reframing our story into one that glorifies God is a choice and a process. At some point, we make a decision to think differently about our past. We may make a firm commitment to put new lenses into our eyes, but it takes time to learn to see more clearly. Gradually, and with flashes of insight, we acknowledge that the lessons we've learned through suffering are treasures to our hearts, we appreciate God's love far more than before, and we realize we have developed compassion for others who are hurting. We would never have chosen this path, but we've gained so much by walking it that we'd never choose any other.

Many years ago a prisoner was released after many years in a Soviet gulag, a camp where convicts worked fourteen hours a day with very little food. Millions died under these conditions, and death was the prescribed end for these millions who had become nothing more than slave labor to the Soviet state. When the prisoner was released, however, he walked through the gates to freedom, then turned and walked to the gray concrete wall. He bent down and kissed it. He said, "Thank you, gulag. This is where I found God." Some of us have been in prison camps of abuse, heartache, loneliness, and shame. When we can reframe our story like Joseph and this Soviet prisoner, we too will thank God for the lessons we've learned through our suffering.

Restore Hope and Meaning

As we learn to write our timeline and reframe our stories, a flood of memories fills our minds. To restore hope and meaning (or find them for the first time), we need to grieve our losses, forgive those who have hurt us, and learn new relational skills. Many psychologists say it takes up to two years to grieve a major loss. Anxious, avoidant, and fearful people have suffered major losses; and many would also admit that their entire adult life has been consumed by grief.

The story we have already written has helped us put a face on the wound and a shape on our loss. In the past, we may have minimized the pain by saying, "Oh, it's not that bad." We may have excused those who hurt us by claiming, "He couldn't help it. It's not really his fault." Or we denied the reality of the wound altogether, shoving the memories down so deep that we later had a hard time even remembering the events. But the process of rediscovery has brought back all the pain, and now it's time to do the serious work of grieving.

People in our culture aren't very good at grieving. We think life should be fun, easy, and trouble-free, so we push away any thought of processing emotional pain—but it's necessary in order to find peace and joy. We can't, however, grieve alone. Remember one of the key principles in our meta-theory of relationship: *We were wounded in relationships, and we are healed in relationships.* We simply must have someone to walk this road with us, to give us perspective when we're confused, to laugh with us when we find something funny, and to cry when our hearts are broken.

When we start grieving, we may realize that we have to deal with multiple wounds from many different people, and it gets pretty complicated. The sheer weight of all that happened can feel overwhelming, and any single traumatic event may be devastating. The process occurs in layers. We grieve as much as we can, and a few months later, we realize we need to grieve a bit more. That doesn't mean we haven't grieved; it only means that we have more pain to process. By God's grace, he doesn't show us the full measure of our pain all at once, or we'd be shattered. He reminds us of as much as we can take whenever we're ready to handle it, and even then, it's hard enough. But grief doesn't last forever. We find moments of sunlight breaking through the gloom, and later, the sunlight takes over and joy becomes a more consistent reality in our hearts.

As we grieve, we choose to forgive—and forgiveness sets us free. When we see ourselves as victims, bitterness causes us to cling to our anger and hurt. Our whole identity is wrapped up in being "the one who was wronged," so we don't want to forgive and forfeit our identity. The healing process, though, helps us see that the payoff of bitterness isn't what we want out of life. To be whole and happy, we have to choose to forgive those who offended us. We choose to forgive because we've been forgiven. Paul wrote, "Get rid of all bitterness, rage and anger, brawling and slander, along with every form of malice. Be kind and compassionate to one another, forgiving each other, just as in Christ, God forgave you."[6]

Who are the ones we are "kind and compassionate" toward? The very ones who have been the object of our bitterness. How can this happen? Only by choosing to forgive—only by inviting and allowing God to remove the enmity. We don't forgive because the person is sorry, has changed, or promises to never do it again. That may happen, but it may not. We choose to forgive just as in Christ, God forgave us. Pastor Tim Keller asks, "If you had a trillion dollars in the bank, how hard would it be to forgive someone who owes you a hundred? But if you are broke and hungry, how hard is it to forgive that hundred-dollar debt?"[7] His point is that we need to realize how much we've been forgiven—our bank accounts are overflowing with God's grace—and out of that wealth of God's forgiveness for our sins, we choose to forgive others.

When we forgive, we leave justice in God's hands. Paul wrote, "If it is possible, as far as it depends on you, live at peace with everyone. Do not take revenge, my friends, but leave room for God's wrath, for it is written: 'It is mine to avenge; I will repay,' says the Lord."[8] It's not easy to forgive someone who has abused or abandoned us. The wound is deep, and the person may not be the least bit sorry, or even acknowledge the wrong at all. But forgiveness is also limited and unilateral. We forgive, but we don't necessarily trust. Forgiveness isn't the same thing as reconciliation. In fact, it's foolish to trust someone who hasn't proved to be trustworthy. That's not faith, it's stupidity—and it is not an essential part of forgiveness.

Choosing to forgive is an excruciating process. It certainly brings peace, but not at first. In the early stages, we are faced with the painful reality of our pain and the person's offense. To take steps on this journey, we have to go deeper into the heart of God, to experience his love, forgiveness, and power more than ever before. As we learn to deal with the pain and pathology of our past, we learn to trust him more.

During the process of grieving and forgiving, we also develop a range of new skills we can use in relationships. We learn to speak the truth, to let others make their own choices instead of demanding a particular response, to move toward people instead of hiding behind walls of self-protection, to assign appropriate responsibility, to confront those who hurt us, and to do it in a way that provides a step forward in the relationship, and to use our painful feelings (chiefly fear, hurt, and anger) as triggers to reflect, identify misconceptions, think rightly, and make healthy choices.

Rebuild Relationships with People and God

Landon traveled this path of healing to pursue God and healthy relationships in his life. When he learned about forgiveness, he was, like most of us, initially resistant. "I'm not going to forgive them," he defiantly told a friend, "because I'll have to trust them—and I'm not going to do that!" When he discovered that forgiveness and reconciliation are two different things, he made the courageous choice to forgive his parents for years of abuse.

As he healed and learned new skills about how to relate to difficult people, he offered both of them an open door to relate in a healthy way, based on truth and respect, with the hope of building trust they had never experienced. His father took him up on his offer. Together, they talked about the past, resolved past wounds, and found forgiveness and healing. Before his father died of cancer, Landon and his dad spent many long hours enjoying each other's company. "It was wonderful," Landon reported. "In those few months we had together, all the bitterness, resentment, and distrust melted away. Today, I have only happy memories of my father. Those last months overshadow three decades of distrust we suffered before."

His mom, though, refused to take his hand and walk toward reconciliation. When he talked to her about the past, she insisted that he had made up all the events that he said had hurt him. She angrily accused him of "ruining the family." For the rest of her life, Landon told her, "Whenever you want a relationship of trust and respect, let me know. My door is open." But she never walked through it. During those years, he continued to grieve and forgive his mother. The knife of hurt was extracted from his heart, but Landon and his mother had only a cordial relationship.

During all this time, Landon's relationship with God was transformed. The entire process of being honest about his pain, identifying the wounds, grieving, forgiving, and learning new skills revolutionized his relationship with God. He no longer saw God as cruel, aloof, and demanding. He began to relate to God as a loving Father, and he saw Christ's sacrifice as a clear message of the passionate love of God—for him!

He had grown up as an anxious person, and for much of his life, he had secretly hoped God would swoop in and magically make his life a dream come true. When God consistently failed at this demand, Landon had grown bitter and cold toward God. But in the years of walking the journey toward truth and hope, all of this changed. An angry, demanding victim was changed into a grateful child of God. "I still have a long way to go," Landon confided. "I'm not what I should be, but thank God, I'm not what I was!"

We live in an instantaneous culture, and billions are spent every month by advertisers who scream at us 24/7 that we can "have it all, and have it all now." Is it any wonder that we expect to have exactly what we want immediately? We can get all the information on the Internet in a heartbeat, and we can buy coffee from all over the world at a drive-through window. Nothing, it seems, should take more than a few seconds of our time.

Spiritual life, however, doesn't operate at warp speed. Things that really matter require reflection and meditation. Relationships that happen on the fly may be fun, but they may not have much depth. We can't afford to have that kind of relationship with God. Throughout church history, people who really wanted to attach to God have practiced a few habits that are stepping-stones to connect with him more deeply. They aren't magic, and they don't guarantee anything. They simply provide time, space, and content for us to think about who God is and how he wants to relate to us. Some people call them "disciplines," but it's probably more appropriate to call them "coffee breaks with God." These healthy spiritual habits include Bible study, prayer, silence and solitude, and service.

Before we look at these, we want to say that we're not suggesting a single recipe or structure for spiritual growth. We are complex creatures, with different personalities, different aspirations, different habits, and different histories. What may be wonderfully stimulating for one person may be a bore for someone else. Though some books or speakers may promote their way to know God more intimately, we want to avoid a "one size fits all" approach. Try these, use varieties of them at different times, and find your own way to feed your spiritual hunger.

As you use these habits, be alert to your responses. Anxious people may hope these practices will work like magic and give them the connection they've always wanted. They'll be disappointed when they find that they are part of the long, sometimes grinding hike toward healing and hope. At first, ambivalent people don't see much need for any of these habits, unless they can excel in Bible study or service to prove themselves to others. Using them to deepen their relationship seems foreign, but as they heal, they can learn to value the relationship and use these practices to connect with God. Fearful people may, at the outset, feel very threatened by solitude because they associate it with painful isolation. They, too, can learn that these practices bring them to the heart of God, not away from him.

Many of us have countless varieties of each of these habits (and others we haven't mentioned) to help us connect with God. In his insightful book *The Life You've Always Wanted,* John Ortberg reminds us of the purpose of these habits: "Spiritual disciplines are not about trying to be good enough to merit God's forgiveness and goodwill. They are not ways to get extra credit, or to demonstrate to God how deeply we are committed to him. . . . But spiritual disciplines are simply a means of appropriating or growing toward the life that God graciously offers. This is why they are sometimes called 'a means of grace.'"[9]

The motivation to develop these habits is important. We begin, not with pride or fear, but with appropriate disappointment and longing. Ortberg observes, "Where does this disappointment come from? A common answer in our day is that it is a lack of self-esteem, a failure to accept oneself. . . . The older and wiser answer is that the feeling of disappointment is not the problem, but a reflection of a deeper problem— my failure to *be* the person God had in mind when he created me. It is the 'pearly ache' in my heart to be at home with the Father."[10]

We want to share just an idea or two about each one, but we encourage you to explore others you'd like to try. All of them are designed to help us connect with the Father's heart, to rebuild the most vital relationship in our lives so he becomes the source of truth, love, forgiveness, kindness, thankfulness, and joyful care for others in need. Practicing these disciplines helps us live and breathe new life. It's like oxygen to our body.

Bible Study

Find some uninterrupted time to read the Scriptures. Pick a book, perhaps the Gospel of John or Ephesians, and read it through three or four times. It doesn't matter how many days it takes. By the time you read it the third time, you'll see things you didn't see the first time or two. Then slow down and read it paragraph by paragraph, with a pen and paper to jot down what you see. A good study template is in Paul's second letter to Timothy (3:16–17). You can ask:

- What does this passage teach me?
- How does my life fall short of this truth?
- What am I going to do about it?
- How can I get this into my daily schedule?

Talk with a friend about what you're learning. Your interaction will crystallize your thinking and stimulate your faith (and your friend's, too).

Prayer

God isn't looking for some fancy, impressive prayer. He's looking for you. His desire is for you to connect with him. I (Tim) know that early on in our marriage Julie and I had a hard time connecting in a meaningful way. Did we go through the rituals? Yes. Did we connect with God? No.

Prayer has taken on a new meaning for us now. We enjoy praying together and with our kids. It's a beautiful conversation about what's going on in our lives, about his presence and his goodness, his work in and through us individually and together.

Prayer with God is both talking and listening. Avoid just reciting a list of the things you want him to do for you. In addition to your requests, spend time reflecting on his beauty. Delight in him, and then talk to him about your concerns of the day. As you pray, take time to be silent. He may remind you of passages of Scripture that relate to your concerns. One of the most helpful practices believers have found is praying through passages of Scripture. This practice keeps you focused on the Lord, reminds you of his character, and directs your thoughts as you pray.

An important component of prayer is *confession*, which means "to agree with." Like David, we pray, "Search me, O God, and know my heart. Try me and know my anxious thoughts."[11] As we pray and wait quietly, the Holy Spirit will remind us of attitudes and actions that displease God. Then we agree that we've done them, we agree that Christ has already forgiven us, and we agree that the right path is to make different choices next time. Confession invites us to "assign appropriate responsibility." As we grow in our faith, we aren't as black-and-white in our perspectives, so we no longer see people and situations as all good or all bad. Secure people (and those who are becoming more secure) are able to look reality in the eye and admit the things they did that were wrong, but they see clearly the sins of others, too. Insecure people either take all the blame on themselves or put all the blame on others—but a few of them vacillate between the two, driving themselves crazy and remaining stuck in their insecurity and clouded perception. Confession, then, isn't morbid self-examination to scrape any conceivable sin from our hearts. It's a partnership with the Spirit of God, inviting him to examine us, and then responding in faith to whatever he shows us. Learning to confess and repent is an essential element in a life that longs for God and pursues his path.

Before we move on I want to mention an ancient practice known as *lectio divina* (LD), which literally means "divine reading" and is being revived in all parts of Christendom these days. LD is a high synthesis of Bible reading and prayer that is done in silence and solitude, the topic of our next section. *Lectio divina* has been likened to a "feasting on the Word." It was put forth in the twelfth century in four moments: first taking a bite (*lectio*); then chewing on it (*meditatio*); next savoring the essence of it (*oratio*); and finally, digesting the Word and making it a part of the body (*contemplatio*). It is a systematic practice of contemplative prayer that allows the seeker to pray through whole books of the Bible in a way that invites God to come alive.

Silence and Solitude

Some of us can't imagine being alone and unplugged for any length of time, but we urge you to try it. You may be surprised how clear your mind becomes. You may need a few minutes to clear out the noise and focus on the Lord, but even a few minutes of quiet can be wonderful for your mind, body, and soul. Find a place and a time when there are no distractions. Turn off your phone and all other devices that are nearby.

When we are quiet, we may hear his soft voice more clearly than any other time during the day—and it is his still, small voice that we want to learn to hear in our inner, spiritual ear. As we spend time alone, we realize how much we need God to give us wisdom for each decision, love for those who annoy us, and peace in difficult circumstances. As we practice this habit, we will probably find that we want to spend even more time alone because it's so refreshing.

Service

The closer we get to God, the more he gives us his heart for others. We may have begun as self-absorbed, wounded people who desperately needed God's healing, but as we connect with him and experience his goodness and grace, we take on his heart of compassion for others. It is the exact duplicate of the secure-base experience of the needy child who, after being cuddled and reassured by the parent, is reoriented to exploring the world "out there" with renewed vigor.

We want to help, and we're not too particular about how he uses us. We may be involved in a structured ministry at church or in a civic organization, or we may spontaneously help people God brings across our path. We need to be careful, though, that we don't give, and love, and serve to the point of exhaustion. God wants us to serve him and help others from a full, overflowing heart, not because we think we have to. As we are involved in touching others' lives, we reflect often on how God has transformed us. Helping others then becomes a feedback loop of grace that is amazing, and inherently therapeutic.

No wonder Jesus said it is more blessed to give than to receive.

He Really Does Love You, He Really Is There

As you practice each of the spiritual disciplines we just mentioned, keep in mind how your God attachment affects or infects each one. If you're predominantly anxious and feel guilty when you sense you're not doing something right, give yourself a break. Your self-punishment and poor view of yourself doesn't bring glory to God, because it's not how he sees you anyway. Ask God to help you through these feelings to truly connect with him in a secure way; he really *does* love you. If you're primarily avoidant or fearful, ask God to help you to trust that he *is* capable of being there for you and loving you. Seek him with all of your heart, even when he feels distant. He really is there for you.

The path of pursuing God takes us through valleys and up to mountaintops. For most of us, we first have to walk down into our pain and experience God's healing before we can come up on the other side. As we walk with him and see him at work, he changes our story, our identity, our motivation, and our ability to give and receive love. It's a difficult path, but there's nothing that fills our heart nearly as much.

CONSIDER THIS: Can you breathe? Are you getting oxygen into your life? Your heart? Your lungs? It's hard to breathe with no air.

And to truly live in a vibrant relationship with God, we all need spiritual oxygen. To learn how we breathe, visit www.godattachmentbook.com.

12

Spiritual Rehab

The first purgation or night is bitter and terrible to sense. . . . Since, then, the conduct of these beginners upon the way of God is ignoble, and has much to do with their love of self and their own inclinations. . . . God desires to lead them farther. He seeks to bring them out of that ignoble kind of love to a higher degree of love for him, to free them from the ignoble exercises of sense . . . and to lead them to a kind of spiritual exercise wherein they can commune with him more abundantly.
—St. John of the Cross[1]

AT A WEEKEND SEMINAR at their church, Marsha's friend promised her that God would work in her life. Marsha had been struggling all of her life to connect with God. Her father was domineering and harsh. Nothing she ever did was good enough to please him. Until she left home after college, he bitterly judged every choice she made.

She moved across the country to get away from him, but his words—and the look of disgust on his face—haunted her every day. All those years, Marsha's mom was just as traumatized. She sometimes tried to stand up for her daughter, but an icy blast of her husband's rage immediately caused her to back down. Now, Marsha was forty-two years old and had two children in high school, and she desperately wanted to change how she felt and acted. The seminar offered hope.

The speaker was nationally known. He shared some principles of emotional healing, and he told his own story of being "miraculously delivered" from years of fear, shame, and doubt. It sounded pretty good to Marsha and the 300 others at the event. In the last session, the speaker asked people to close their eyes and envision the worst abuse they'd ever experienced, and then he told them to imagine Jesus coming in and stopping the hurt from taking place. He told them, "From this moment, you'll never feel any more hurt, fear, or anger from the event. Jesus stopped it. You won't even remember the event after today." Marsha could hear sobs from all across the room, including her own. After the speaker closed the seminar in prayer, grateful people mobbed him. Marsha excitedly told her friend, "It's finally happened. I'm completely free from my past! I'll never have to feel those awful feelings again."

Four days later, the euphoria wore off, and the gnawing, painful shame returned. For a couple of days, Marsha told herself that her negative emotions were just the result of some bad pizza, but she couldn't deny that the awful feelings had come back. She felt devastated. When her friend called to talk, she didn't answer the phone. After Marsha avoided her for several days, her friend showed up at her house. Marsha acted very strangely, and they had an awkward conversation. Finally, her friend asked, "Marsha, what's wrong? I've tried to call you, but you haven't answered. What's happened in the past few days?"

Marsha choked back her tears. "It didn't work for me."

"What didn't work?"

"The promise of healing. Those awful feelings and memories are back. I'm sure it worked for everybody else, but not for me." Marsha burst into bitter tears.

Idealism and Broken Promises

When we're wounded we tend to look for quick fixes (if we look for any at all), and there seems to be no shortage of books and speakers that make bold promises of marvelous and instantaneous transformation. Some promote psychological techniques, and others communicate sweeping promises from the Bible. To see quick change, some of us gravitate toward New Age healing or the human potential "you can do it now" movement. Some Christian groups use catchy phrases like "Get into the jet stream of God's Spirit." They promise that if we believe the right things or follow the right techniques, we'll overcome any nagging pain or sinful habit. And they trot out dozens of testimonies to prove their point.

The goal of good Bible teaching isn't to make the biggest and most glowing promises; it is to teach God's truth accurately, so that we have a strong blend of hope and realistic expectations about the process of change. And for most of us "it doesn't come easy." Do we believe in miracles? Yes. And we pray for them often—expectantly. But again for most of us, miracles are the exception, not the rule in this life. When teachers promise more than God intends to deliver—such as complete and instantaneous healing for any relational wound—they mean well, but they are being cruel to their listeners.[2]

But, some might argue, aren't the promises of God's love, forgiveness, and healing true? Yes, certainly they are, but we live between the "already" and the "not yet." We experience a taste of the wonder of God's grace and peace now, but we'll enjoy far more when we see him face-to-face. In this life, we "groan," waiting for that day when all tears will be wiped away and justice will reign. The complete fulfillment of his promises, though, will come later.

Those of us with insecure attachments are particularly vulnerable to lofty promises. We have suffered under the burden of others' sins for years, and we want to feel better now! Our expectations—often embraced as a new and empowering faith—are so high that we are ready to believe anyone who promises the quick fix. Suffering the way we have suffered isn't fair, and we believe the speakers who promise that God will make it all right immediately—if we just believe the right truths or follow the right procedures.

Emotional and spiritual healing is certainly possible, but it happens far more like rehab than the miracle surgery, far more like the slow-turning rheostat bringing light incrementally than a light switch. Wrong answers to life's two crucial questions—Am I worthy of love? and Are others capable of loving me?—aren't resolved in an instant. We may begin the process of change at a moment in time, but healing emotional damage is far more like rehabilitation from a tragic car accident than instantaneously turning on a light.

When a person lies broken and bleeding in the street after a wreck, emergency medical personnel stabilize the person and rush him or her to the hospital. There, specialists set bones and operate on internal injuries, but the person doesn't get up from the table healthy and whole. After days of recovery, the patient leaves the hospital and begins a long regimen of physical rehabilitation. For months, he or she gives focused attention to healing the wound and strengthening the damaged bones and muscles.

Almost universally, patients report wanting to quit during the rehab process because of the time and agony of making slow and barely discernible gains. At some point, however, they begin to see signs of genuine gains, and they feel more hopeful. Throughout the process, some have needed professionals to help them take the necessary steps, the encouragement of a family member or trusted friend, and a large measure of tenacity to keep going, no matter what. We have talked frequently about walking with someone we can trust through this process, and that's because insecurity is most often overcome by living and relating in secure attachment relationships.

The metaphor of physical rehab as a description of emotional and psychological healing isn't as sexy or glamorous as the promise of instant healing, but it's a far more accurate description of the real process God takes us through as we address our relationships and learn to connect with him and others.

Recognizable Stages

For centuries, people have noticed stages of growth in human development and spirituality. Let's look at a few examples from the worlds of psychology and spiritual life.

Babies are born with some basic capabilities and distinct temperaments, but they go through dramatic changes on the way to adulthood and then to growing old. According to psychologist Erik H. Erikson, each individual passes through eight interrelated developmental stages (Erikson calls them "psychosocial stages"). Each stage is characterized by a different psychological crisis, which must be resolved by the individual before he or she can move on to the next stage. If the person copes with a particular crisis in a maladaptive manner, he or she will endure more struggles with that issue later in life. The first three stages are:

1. *Infancy*, in which the crisis is learning to trust.
2. *Toddler*, when the child begins to gain confidence toward autonomy or lapses into self-doubt.
3. *Early childhood*, as the child learns to balance eagerness for adventure with responsibilities in social interaction.

During these three critical stages, children develop their sense of security and confidence to take risks of exploration, with the promise of finding a safe haven if things don't go well.

To describe spiritual growth, Philip Yancey uses the simple but profound model of *child, adult,* and *parent*. In the first phase, we're like children who focus on rules to shape our behavior, and we often have unrealistic expectations of God, the church, and spiritual life. In the adult stage, motivations and the Seeking System change profoundly. We learn to practice spiritual disciplines in order to know God more intimately, not to follow some strict set of rules to prove ourselves or control our behavior. We understand that some of our questions won't be answered in this life, and we are at peace with that fact. Parents live to give themselves to their children. In this stage of spiritual maturity, we feel safe and secure in God's love, and we delight in helping others take steps of progress.[3]

In his first letter to the churches, the apostle John makes a distinction as he gives instructions to three groups of people (1 John 2:12–14). Similar to Yancey's model but writing to a patriarchal society, John identifies them as "dear children," "young men," and "fathers." The "dear children" includes all of his readers. He encourages them to reflect on the foundational truths of God's love and our genuine connection to him as our Father. He sees the "young men" as the lions of the faith, fighting against the powers of darkness. "Fathers" are the wise, trusted leaders of the community, who have their position by virtue of their long experience of knowing, trusting, and following God through good times and bad.

St. John of the Cross was a Spanish Christian mystic in the sixteenth century. In his book *Ascent of Mount Carmel,* he describes three stages of a devout person's relationship with God. First, we seek God entirely for pleasure's sake. We delight in his love for us, and we enjoy the blessings of his forgiveness. Later, as we grow closer to God and he illumines our hearts, we have a clearer grasp of our inherent sinfulness. In this phase of growth, we understand his unconditional love more deeply, and we bask in his grace. None of us is immune to the difficulties of life, and sometimes we enter "the dark night of the soul" (or "spirit"). In these troubling times, we are faced with what we truly believe about God.[4] Like Job, we suffer terribly, but we cry out, "Though he slay me, yet will I trust in him."[5]

Then, we don't delight in pleasures or blessings; we delight in being united with God. To John of the Cross, every event, no matter how pleasant or painful, was a stepping-stone to enter more deeply into the heart of God. He observed, "If an experience fails to engender humility, charity, mortification, holy simplicity, and silence, etc., of what value is it? In this faith God supernaturally and secretly teaches the soul and, in a way unknown to it, raises it up in virtues and gifts. When together with the words and concepts the soul is loving God and simultaneously experiencing this love with humility and reverence, there is indication that the Holy Spirit is at work within it. Whenever he bestows favors, he clothes them with this love."[6]

When we begin our spiritual journey, our minds and hearts are focused on what God will give us, but on the way our motivations change, becoming more God-centered than self-centered. As we are filled with the wonder of God's love, wisdom, and strength, former obsessions and cares become secondary. Only one thing really matters: knowing, loving, and delighting in God.

As we apply the principles of rehabilitation and growth to our need to seek and attach to God, we will use three stages: *security, exploration,* and *compassionate action.* Even if we didn't have a safe haven growing up, we can find God to be a safe haven now. Even if we didn't feel confident enough to take risks and explore our worlds when we were kids, we can begin to take bold steps as we heal. And as we find the answer is yes to the two crucial questions in our lives, we will enjoy helping others find safety and security in their relationship with God, too.

As we look at these stages, we need to remember that God doesn't promise to protect his children from struggles, heartache, or failure. The experience of difficulties need not threaten our faith if we understand God's purposes for them. J. I. Packer noted:

> God . . . is very gentle with young Christians, just as mothers are with very young babies. Often the start of their Christian career is marked by great emotional joy, striking providences, remarkable answers to prayer, and immediate fruitfulness in their first acts of witnessing; thus God encourages them, and establishes them in "the life." But as they grow stronger, and are able to bear more, he exercises them in a tougher school. He exposes them to as much testing by the pressure of opposed and discouraging influences as they are able to bear—not more (see the promise, 1 Corinthians 10:13), but equally not less (see the admonition, Acts 14:22). Thus he builds our character, strengthens our faith, and prepares us to help others.[7]

The experience of difficulties, then, may challenge our perceptions of God's goodness and purpose, but times of suffering give us the opportunity to see him more accurately, trust him more deeply, and gain compassion for others who endure suffering, too.

As we begin to examine these stages, remember that a person doesn't make it from being broken and bleeding on the street after an accident to restored health without help. A team of skilled and caring people help each step of the way. Finding the right people to help us on this journey is essential, but we also need to realize our inherent resistance. Some of us distrust all people we meet, no matter how much we need them or how they've proven to be trustworthy. We are isolated, and we prefer to stay that way. Emotional and spiritual rehab, though, doesn't just happen by reading books and participating in self-improvement exercises. These can help, but only if we're engaged with someone who walks securely with us through the long, difficult process of healing.

Others have the opposite problem: we long so desperately to be connected to someone, we cling to anyone who shows us some interest. People like this need to take steps toward independence and healthy emotional connections with people and God. Virtually all of us suffer from the common human problem of self-deception. We've seen the world through a particular set of glasses for so long that we're absolutely convinced that our perceptions are accurate—but they're not. We need someone to speak the truth to us, and to speak it with grace so that we can hear it. We don't need a dozen trusted friends or counselors—just one or two. With them, we can learn the most important lessons we've ever learned, and we can experience God's healing love in the core of our hearts. Without them, we may learn a few principles, but we won't have the insight we need to apply those truths to our deepest wounds and highest hopes. We need someone to help us learn to attach.

Stages and Styles

Some of the principles of rehab apply to all four attachment styles, but many of them apply in unique ways for different people. Let's look at how each style goes through the stages of security, exploration, and compassionate action.

Secure

Those of us who grew up in a safe, supportive, affirming family environment have a distinct advantage as we take steps of spiritual growth. The good models of our parents (and other adults) give us a picture of what a healthy person looks like. We have developed a clearer image of someone who delights in loving relationships, enjoys giving and receiving love, and responds thoughtfully to life's difficulties. In this environment, we internalized the powerfully positive messages of unconditional love and affirmation, even when we took risks and failed. With this confidence, those of us who are secure were willing to ask hard questions about life and God, and have learned to live in the tension between the ideal and the real. This environment certainly doesn't guarantee that we will grow up to trust God and love him with all our hearts, but it at least invites us to make a connection between our parents' strong love and the description of God in the Bible.

When we're secure, we are willing to take risks and explore our world, and when we grow up, our sense of adventure remains intact. As believers, we discover our spiritual gifts, and we see God use them to touch people's lives. We get involved in church or other organizations because we want to make a difference. In relationships, we're open but not naive. In our family environment, we learned that trust is the most important ingredient in any relationship, and we treasure relationships of trust wherever we go. We realize, though, that not everyone is trustworthy. Trust must be earned, and it must be nurtured and protected. When trust is strained or broken, it takes attention, forgiveness, and hard work to rebuild it. We are willing to take risks as we explore the possibilities God has put in front of us, but we realize there are no guarantees. We don't get bent out of shape when things don't work out. Instead, we dust ourselves off, learn from the situation, and try something else.

Living in a secure relationship provides the foundation for being confident in our skills and abilities to touch people's lives. Our experiences and the lessons we learned from exploring the world around us and engaging others gives us confidence that God can use us. We also realize we will always have mixed motives, so we aren't surprised when our default mode shifts to selfishness. We practice repentance as a lifestyle, and we delight in helping people. We are effective, but not cocky. We realize that every talent and every opportunity is a gift from God.[8] We realize also our limitations in helping people. The needs of some are simply beyond the scope of our compassion and ability to meet them, so we find other resources to help. Secure attachment doesn't mean we're perfect, but that we grow spiritually with clear perception, good role models, and confidence that failure doesn't mean the end of the world.

From Anxious to Secure

Coming to see others as capable of loving us, yet not feeling worthy of love, can lead us to seek relationships rather than material possessions to calm us when we're anxious. Though we sometimes feel isolated, we compulsively pursue relationships in our longing to feel connected to someone. We are full of self-doubt, and we feel oppressed by shame. To begin to experience security, we have to stop expecting good results from redoubling our efforts to please people to win their approval. Instead, we have to face our fears and false beliefs. We won't be able to accept God's love until we can acknowledge, "I don't believe God really loves me," or "I believe his love is conditional—I have to meet him halfway." Though we may not think we believe this, we live as if we do.

Honesty is the first step toward healing, and it is easy to be overwhelmed by doubt and shame when we honestly face our doubts and limits about faith in God. That is why a trusted, secure friend who won't abandon or fail us is so critical. It's in a secure relationship that we can contrast our previous, painful experiences with the genuine, openhanded love of a true friend and the wonderful truth of God's amazing grace. In a thousand important moments of insight, we can say, "That's what I used to believe, but now I know the truth about God."

In the stage of security, we can gather new information about God and draw important contrasts with our family experiences, but we have to internalize those truths in our exploration of the world around us. Here is where we take risks to disengage from the controlling person in our lives and create new boundaries of safety and independence.

Dominating people, though, have sometimes knowingly or unknowingly used their promises of intimacy and acceptance to manipulate those of us who are anxious and longing to connect. Once we courageously set boundaries and learn to function differently in these unhealthy relationships, we come to discover that it's okay to speak the truth about our feelings and new choices. Like acquiring any new skill, learning to be in healthy relationships includes a lot of wins and losses. In this challenging phase of exploration, there's a good chance we're going to feel torn between the known and the unknown, perceived safety with those we learned we can't trust, and the fear of being unconnected to anybody. Be prepared to vacillate: wanting to set boundaries, and yet feeling completely disconnected when you do. If we can muster the courage to be strong and keep gaining more perception about the love of God for us, that we truly are worthy of his love, we'll find a new world opens up to us, as we gain a healthy sense of independence, the ability to relate to people without fear or control, and the wisdom to see through the deceptive message that we're somehow not worthy of love.

Anxious about approval and love, many of us tend to gravitate to needy people, because we feel valid, needed, and loved by them. Once we realize our motives for helping the needy were really about us trying to feel loved, we can move toward emotional stability and begin caring for others with openhanded love—not demanding appreciation or a particular response from those we help. The journey of gaining wisdom and strength gives us wonderful insights to share with people who are struggling with anxiety in relationships, but we can say no when the burdens of responsibility are too great. Some of the most compassionate, wise, and effective caregivers in the family of God are men and women who grew up in a cloud of anxiety, but experienced emotional and spiritual rehab in God's family.

From Avoidant to Secure

Some of us were raised in families where we didn't receive much support when we cried out for help. Instead, we experienced condemnation or isolation. In this environment, we grew up thinking, "I'm okay, but you're not." We concluded that people in general, and authority figures in particular, aren't trustworthy. In times of stress, we believed, "I can't trust anybody to be there for me, and if God isn't going to be there for me either, then I can do it myself."

To find security in our relationship with God, those of us who are avoidant need to face the reality of our defiant isolation, our over-inflated view of our self, and our propensity to rely on our abilities to give us a semblance of stability and purpose. Moments of failure threaten us more than most. Instead of redoubling our efforts to win at all costs, we need to listen to a secure friend we can trust who speaks the truth to us in love. Though we have a tendency to push away anyone who tries to lovingly correct us, many different kinds of losses, disappointments, or "rock-bottom" experiences can trigger our sense of desperation to listen. Turning to God requires the realization that there are no other options and that he really is capable of loving us and is accessible when we need him most.

To explore the world around us means continually moving toward relationships and away from rigid self-reliance. Though feeling vulnerable has seemed like a fate worse than death, gradually opening our heart to someone (yes, maybe just one) and sharing our true feelings could be the best thing in our journey toward intimacy with God. This is a real challenge for many of us, though, because we haven't even been aware of any emotions—except anger—for many years. Opening up in a secure relationship, however, could lead us to an awareness of the full range of our emotions—hope and fear, love and anger, calm and anxiety. As we take risks to be connected to people, we're sometimes going to be disappointed and tempted to think, "I knew it would be like that. There's no use to even try." But a secure friend will keep speaking truth with grace, inviting us to stay connected and to keep taking risks to have an authentic relationship.

Since our avoidance has led us to rely on ourselves, taking action is usually natural for us. But now we have to learn to be motivated in a completely different way. Where we used to be aggressive, perhaps dominating people and situations to prove ourselves or help others, now we learn to help people out of our genuine love for them.

As we continue to grow spiritually and heal emotionally, our friends may begin to use words to describe us that would have been awkward to hear years before: *kindness*, *gentleness*, and *compassion*.

From Fearful to Secure

Those of us who endured abuse and abandonment as children have many hurdles to overcome as we pursue God's rehab assignment; but as we experience his healing love, we often may become the most appreciative and secure of all. Some of the most courageous people in the world are those who have looked at the face of hell in their own hearts and have trusted God to heal them, cleanse them, and give them something to live for. In their families, they answered a loud and heartrending no to both crucial questions. They didn't believe they were worthy of love, and they were sure no one really loved them. They internalized all the twisted, evil messages, and they may have concluded, "When I'm abused, it makes perfect sense—because I deserve it."

The Scriptures tell us wonderful truths about the love of God. He heals the brokenhearted and binds their wounds. He is, after all, the Great Physician. The psalmist reminds us:

Blessed is he whose help is the God of Jacob,
>   whose hope is in the LORD his God,
the Maker of heaven and earth,
>   the sea, and everything in them—
>   the LORD, who remains faithful forever.
He upholds the cause of the oppressed
>   and gives food to the hungry.
>   The LORD sets prisoners free,
the LORD gives sight to the blind,
>   the LORD lifts up those who are bowed down,
>   the LORD loves the righteous.
The LORD watches over the alien
>   and sustains the fatherless and the widow,
>   but he frustrates the ways of the wicked.
The LORD reigns forever,
>   your God, O Zion, for all generations.
>   Praise the LORD.[9]

Who are the people God cares for? The oppressed, the hungry, prisoners, the blind, those who are bowed down, the aliens, the fatherless, and the widows—anyone who feels unloved, unwanted, rejected, and disconnected. None of us is beyond the reach of God's kindness. For those of us who are fearful to find security in our relationship with God, we need someone who will be Christ's secure arms to show the warmth of his affection and his mouth to articulate his grace. Everything in the fearful person says, "I want to be in relationship with you, come close to me; but I don't trust you! Stay away from me." Admitting this fear and distrust is an important step. Slowly and painfully, years of isolation begin to dissolve. The hard shell of self-protection begins to show signs of cracks, and we begin to wonder, "Maybe, just maybe, somebody cares about me."

We do this because—remember—the source of our comfort has also been the source of our pain.

As in the other relational styles, the exploration stage is where we take risks to connect, and it's where we face our deepest fears. As we begin, we doubt anyone will be there if we need them, but we trust the voice of a secure friend who encourages us to keep reaching out. Every little bump in relationships seems like a catastrophe, and we often want to quit at the slightest provocation.

In this important stage of rehab, we have to do the hard work of facing our deepest wounds, grieving, forgiving, and learning how to connect to people in healthy adult–adult relationships. One of the most important skills we learn in this stage is to be aware of our feelings. Painful, powerful emotions have been one of our most significant threats, but now we learn to identify them and use them to manage our impulses and compulsive behaviors. Through this process we learn that our feelings aren't necessarily our enemy, but a valuable ally in our struggle to become whole and strong.

Though we may still have a few quirks in our perceptions and personalities, our journey from fearful to secure in our relationships with God and others added a wealth of wisdom to share. No one has to tell us how hard it is to make progress; we know. No one has to convince us that healing is a process and not a light-switch event; we've been there. And no one needs to help us understand the transforming power of love; we've experienced it; it has changed our lives, and we're more than happy to share it with others.

The Need for Community

Sometimes preachers' messages and the songs we sing give the wrong impression of spiritual life. We sing that we only need God, and "it's all for you." In the sense that Christ is the "author and perfecter" of life, that's true, but God has put each believer in the body of Christ. To be whole and healthy, and to function properly as we seek to bring God's kingdom to earth, we need each other. In fact, God has made us not only for himself but also for each other. Truly, no man is an island. We simply can't thrive on our own. We need each other more than we know.

As we've seen, when we're wounded we have difficulties in relationships. We either demand too much of others or we expect too little; we become enmeshed as we lose ourselves in our thirst to be connected to someone, or we are so emotionally defended that we can't form meaningful relationships at all. Like all human endeavors, the body of Christ is flawed because it is made up of flawed individuals. We have to be wise about whom to trust, but we simply won't make progress if we don't find someone who is secure and trustworthy. When we find a friend, a counselor, a pastor, or a group that is committed to authentic relationships, we find something beautiful.

What does it look like? How does it operate? There are many descriptions in the Bible, but Paul wrote, "Love must be sincere. Hate what is evil; cling to what is good. Be devoted to one another in brotherly love. Honor one another above yourselves. Never be lacking in zeal, but keep your spiritual fervor, serving the Lord. Be joyful in hope, patient in affliction, faithful in prayer. Share with God's people who are in need. Practice hospitality."[10]

Throughout the New Testament, we see relationships in God's family described by the phrase "one another." Three of these uses are instructive. In John's first letter, he tells us to love each other the way Christ loves us.[11] In his letter to the Romans, Paul tells us to accept each other "just as Christ accepted you."[12] And to the Ephesians, Paul said to forgive each other "just as in Christ, God has forgiven you."[13]

Do you see the pattern? We don't have to grit our teeth and try to come up with love, acceptance, and forgiveness of others. We experience these things in our relationship with God, and then we express them to others as they overflow from our hearts. There is a massive and deeply connected flow—a triangle that includes God, yourself, and your family and other believers. If we have trouble loving, accepting, and forgiving difficult people in our lives, we need to go back to the source to drink more deeply.

When we enter spiritual rehab, we come as needy people who long to soak up God's love from his people. In the process of building security, God brings along someone to speak truth and love, and to demonstrate God's kindness to us. When we feel secure in him, we can take risks and realize we are still safe in our relationships with those we trust. This is a turning point. From then on, each risk to connect is based on a past experience of safety.

The healing process brings life, hope, and joy to troubled hearts; and soon, those of us who had been anxious, avoidant, or fearful begin to give love, strength, and security to other hurting people. In a healthy church, this cycle becomes a normal process, whereby members are always reaching out to those who feel disconnected and hope-less. As these hurting people experience God's love, empowered by God's Spirit and shared by God's people, their hearts are full to over-flowing, and they then reach out to others. And the cycle of love and secure attachment continues.

CONSIDER THIS: It takes grace, patience, and mercy to live in secure relationships. Pray continually for these virtues.

To learn more about how to live out a secure relationship with God practically, visit the Web site for the chapter 12 video.

13

The Power of Wonder

*My profession is to be always on alert
to find God in nature . . .*
—Henry David Thoreau[1]

I (Tim) recently took a trip out west with my daughter, Megan, for our annual father-daughter trip. As we were driving up the mountain to go skiing, she began telling me about the biology and anatomy classes she's currently taking. "Dad," she said, "I don't see how anybody could study the human body, the intricacies of the way our bodies are built, down to the very smallest of cells, and not see the intelligent design and order of how we were created. It seems harder to not believe in God than to believe in him once you see how perfectly all of the systems function."

As we talked about her class and the amazement of God's created order, Megan said, "Dad, look at those mountains. I've never seen anything so beautiful and enormous. It just confirms to me what I am learning in anatomy."

The Psalmist wrote that "The heavens declare the glory of God; the skies proclaim the work of his hands."[2] And Paul wrote that it was through the created order of the world that we can clearly see who God is, so that they are without excuse.[3] A sense of wonder—of exploring a great unknown mystery—is essential to an authentic relationship with God. In fact, the deeper our faith in him, the better able we are to grasp his greatness and goodness.

But again, our relationship with our parents or significant others has a strong influence on our concept of God. People whose parents provided plenty of protection and support are more easily able to understand and grasp God's transcendence and beauty, but those whose parents were absent or abusive instinctively see God as distant, disengaged, or disgusted with them. Our style of attachment with God— whether secure or insecure—can influence our orientation to the adventure and mystery of knowing him. And though it is a tougher challenge for some, all of us can learn new truths about God's nature and experience a sense of wonder that greatly enhances our relationship with him.

Take a moment now and consider your own experience with God. Go back to the ways you said you viewed God earlier in the book. Now think about how you view his majesty, awe, and wonder. Have you ever looked at the stars? The mountains? Creation? And just sat in awe? If not, consider why.

Amazed

In his book *Recapture the Wonder,* Ravi Zacharias teaches powerfully about the progression of boredom in today's culture, to the point that adults are seldom amazed by anything—especially in the Western world, where nearly everything has been domesticated and made safe.[4]

Today's generations are caught up in the cult of the next thing. And it's no wonder. With technological advances such as iPods, iPhones, and text messaging, we very rarely understand the concept of spending too much time or giving too much attention to one place or with one person.

When Isaac Newton set out to discover the laws of nature, including gravity and the law of entropy, he wanted to demonstrate the way God orchestrated the universe. His discoveries honored the God who created the laws of nature, as well as the scientist who uncovered them. More recently, Stephen Hawking wrote, in *A Brief History of Time,* "We want to make sense of what we see around us and to ask: What is the nature of the universe? What is our place in it and where did it come from? Why is it the way it is?"[5] Newton and Hawking both looked at the universe and wondered at its immensity and intricacy.

Our amazement at creation gives us a glimpse of the greatness of God, but it leaves us asking some hard questions. We marvel at the natural world and the inventions of humans, but something seems to be missing. In our hearts, we know something just isn't right. French physicist and philosopher Blaise Pascal tells us where our longing originates. He wrote:

> What else does this craving, and this helplessness, proclaim but that there was once in man a true happiness, of which all that now remains is the empty print and trace? This he tries in vain to fill with everything around him, seeking in things that are not there the help he cannot find in those that are, though none can help, since this infinite abyss can be filled only with an infinite and immutable object; in other words by God himself.[6]

There is, in Pascal's famous phrase, "a God-shaped vacuum" in the heart of every person, a longing for meaning and intimacy that calls us to pursue everything that is beautiful and wonderful. Too often, we try to fill that hole with things or people or gadgets—with money, sex, and power, as Richard Foster's classic book tells us.[7] These may thrill us for a while, but soon we feel even more frustrated and empty. Only a sense of wonder that leads to a deeper knowledge of God truly satisfies.

Creation Declares His Glory

As a couple of Pennsylvania natives, we grew up understanding the nature of hard work and a love for the outdoors. In fact, we recently took an elk-hunting trip together to Colorado to get away and experience the power of the Rocky Mountains and the smell of fresh country air. I'll (Josh) never forget the first night we were there and headed out into the woods. Seeing the color of the Colorado fall and smelling the freshness of the clean, crisp air kept me (at least for a little while) from getting cold. But before long the tingling sensation of the freezing Colorado air at dusk began to sting the little bit of my exposed face. Until I heard one of the most beautiful sounds I have ever heard in my life: the call of a bugling elk in the wild.

A century ago, many people worked on farms and interacted with nature every day. Their work was backbreaking, but they were in touch with the cycles of the seasons, the birth of animals, and the mystery of growing things. They fought droughts, thunderstorms, and wildfires, but these spoke of the awesome nature of God's creation. Today, most of us are sheltered from the inconveniences of nature. We buy our food prepackaged, and while we might grow some tomatoes in the backyard, we aren't really connected with the soil, the beauty of nature, or the dangers of the physical world. A brief glance at the vastness and intricacies of creation reminds us that the God who created it all must be incredibly powerful and creative—and certainly, he must have a sense of humor—but taking that glance requires some deliberate action on the part of a city-dweller who has been cut off from the sources of food, energy, and reasons for this safe environment.

Having grown up in a family of eight in central Pennsylvania, I (Tim) learned to appreciate what it meant to work for food, and being in the woods is always a great reminder for me. On the second day of our elk trip to Colorado, I remember coming through the woods as a herd of elk was barreling across the road in front of us. As my older brother Jim, Josh, and I lined up along the road, I stood in the middle, my brother Jim was to my left, and Josh was to my right—the elk running from left to right directly in front of us.

Then we heard the sound Josh just mentioned: a bugle so loud you knew there was a bull about to step into our crosshairs. And sure enough: a beautiful trophy 6x6 down on simultaneous shots. One by Josh. The other by me. A successful hunt all the way around.

What does bagging that elk have to do with this chapter? Nothing more than understanding that the trip itself was a wondrous reminder of our need for a transcendent God who reveals himself in the middle of nowhere, just as much as he shows up in meeting our everyday need for food, shelter, and love. That he is not only the God who walks beside us on our trip as we venture through the woods but also the God who is in the stars and the universe, as we sit and stare at the dark sky on the 8-degree frozen tundra of Colorado. A friend. And a transcendent, powerful creator.

God of the Heavens

In 1923, an unknown astronomer looked through a telescope one night and realized that a clump of light was actually another galaxy. Edwin Hubble's name is now attached to the most powerful telescope in the world—or actually, out of this world. As an orbiting observatory, it has given us a picture of wonders deep into the universe, as far back as only a few years after creation. The sheer size of the universe is staggering, but the Bible tells us that God simply spoke and the stars were flung into space. He didn't even sweat!

The first astronomer, Ptolemy, counted 1,056 stars in the sky. After Galileo invented the telescope, far more came into view. With only a 1-inch version, we can see 225,000 stars, but a 100-inch telescope enables us to see 1.5 billion stars. The largest telescopes available on land show us 1 billion galaxies, each containing about 100 billion stars, but the Hubble has allowed astronomers to see 200 billion galaxies, each containing about 200 billion stars.

Astronomer Hugh Ross concluded:

> So the total number of stars in these galaxies adds up to about forty billion trillion—and that's without the estimated ten billion trillion stars contained in the unobserved dwarf galaxies. Somewhere around fifty billion trillion stars make their home in the observable universe. That's a mind-boggling number—written numerically it is the number fifty followed by twenty-four zeroes: 50,000,000,000,000,000, 000,000,000. A comparison may make it more comprehensible: if that same number of dimes were packed together as densely as possible and piled into 1,500 feet high stacks (as high as some of the world's tallest skyscrapers), they would cover the entire North American continent.[8]

Distances in space are so large that scientists calculate them in *light-years*. That's the time it takes light to travel in a year at 186,000 miles per second, or about 6 trillion miles. The nearest star to us in our own Milky Way galaxy is Alpha Centauri, about 4.3 light-years away, and astronomers have looked back into space to see star formation 13.7 billion years ago! That's an incredibly long way and a long time. In his textbook *Astronomy,* Dr. Arthur Harding wrote, "Who can study the science of astronomy and contemplate the star-lit heavens with a knowledge of the celestial bodies, their movements and their enormous distances, without bowing his head in reverence to the power that brought this universe into being and safely guides its individual members?"[9]

On the other end of the spectrum of size is God's creation of the human body. In his book *More Than Meets the Eye,* physician Richard Swenson observes that the strands of DNA are wound so tightly that if the DNA from a single cell were stretched, it would be over 5 feet long. But that strand is incredibly narrow—only 50 trillionths of an inch wide. All of the DNA from a human body could be compressed into an ice cube, but if each cell's DNA were stretched end to end, it would reach at least ten billion miles![10]

Another fascinating calculation is the odds that life as we know it in the universe could develop to the incredible complexity of human life by evolutionary processes. One of the first serious attempts at calculating these mind-numbing odds was done by Frank Salisbury. In a now-out-of-date article entitled "Natural Selection and the Complexity of the Gene," and published in the prestigious journal *Nature,* he was the first researcher to identify a scientific problem with these odds and suggest possible avenues of research toward a solution.[11]

First, Salisbury calculated that the odds against life beginning in the known expanse and age of the universe are 1 in 10^{415}—that is, 1 followed by 415 zeroes. In another article by Salisbury in 1971, "Doubts about the Modern Synthetic Theory of Evolution" in *American Biology Teacher,* Salisbury calculated the number of possible arrangements of nucleotides in a "medium protein" 300 amino acids long, arriving at 10^{600}, or ten to the 600th power—600 zeroes.[12]

The dedicated evolutionist Carl Sagan, at a 1973 conference on the Search for Extraterrestrial Intelligence (SETI), calculated the odds against a *specific* human genome being assembled by chance as 1 in $10^{2,000,000,000}$ (in other words, the genome of a specific person, and not just any human).[13] Even so, any number with *2 billion* zeroes behind it is truly beyond comprehension. It also strongly suggests that many evolutionists will not change their beliefs against God, even when the evidence indicates an overwhelming likelihood that it took an intelligent designer to put it all together so intricately rather than the operation of chance by random selection operating over billions of years.

Probably the most well-known book on the battle between evolution and creation is *Scientific Creationism* by Henry Morris. He assumes that a fixed twenty amino acid types are necessary for human life, and that 1,500 sequential steps are needed to achieve a "protein molecule." From this, Morris calculates the odds against this ever happening as 1 in 10^{450}. Contemplating the further development of an intelligible human from there, Morris comes up with the final figure of 1 chance in $10^{299,843}$. Again, that is one with nearly 300,000 zeroes following it, against the evolution of life.[14] And you thought your chances of winning the lottery were bad.

What does this glimpse at the vastness of space and the intricate construction of the human body tell us? It teaches us that God is so great that we can trust him with our biggest problems, and he is involved in even the smallest details of our lives. David reflected on God's creation of the human body, and it inspired him to worship:

> My frame was not hidden from you
> > when I was made in the secret place.
> > When I was woven together in the depths of the earth,
> > your eyes saw my unformed body.
> > All the days ordained for me
> > were written in your book
> > before one of them came to be.
> How precious to me are your thoughts, O God!
> > How vast is the sum of them!
> Were I to count them,
> > they would outnumber the grains of sand. (Ps. 139:15–18)

The Wonder of the Cross

Violent death, it seems, is the only appropriate way to deal with the depth of our selfishness. Many years before Jesus set foot on earth,

God instructed the people of Israel to sacrifice animals as a symbol of the cost of forgiveness. The sight of so much blood may have become familiar to the Jews, but it seems odd and abhorrent to modern sensibilities.

When Jesus spent time with his followers, he told them over and over that he would be killed. For centuries, the prophets predicted that the Messiah would come to earth and die as the ultimate lamb of God to "take away the sins of the world." No matter, Jesus' men couldn't fathom that this would really happen. Even on the last night before his arrest, they failed to grasp the significance of his intention to give his life in their place and ours.

Today, we wear gold crosses around our necks and put big ones on the steeples of our churches. Familiarity may not breed contempt, but it can cause serious misunderstanding. We need to remember that the cross was the most horrific form of execution ever devised by man, meant to inflict excruciating pain and expose the person to ridicule. People have often asked, "Who killed Jesus?" Was it the Jewish leaders, the crowd who yelled, "Crucify him, but give us Barabbas," or was it the Roman governor Pilate?

The answer is that the death of Christ was always God's plan, and Jesus went to the cross willingly. To be sure, he cringed as he anticipated the full fury of pain he would endure, but he was willing to face the agony for helpless sinners like us. Still, Jesus was well aware that it was his choice to die. When the soldiers came to arrest him, Peter grabbed a sword and cut off the ear of the high priest's servant. (He was a fisherman, not a warrior, so he missed what he was aiming to cut!) At that moment, Jesus told him, "Put your sword back in its place . . . for all who draw the sword will die by the sword. Do you think I cannot call on my Father, and he will at once put at my disposal more than twelve legions of angels? But how then would the Scriptures be fulfilled that say it must happen in this way?" (Matt. 26:52–54).

Angels aren't the little creatures we see on Valentine cards. They are awesome beings, so powerful that whenever they appeared to people, their first words had to be, "Don't be afraid!" A legion was a thousand soldiers, so Jesus was saying that he could have called an entire army of angels, enough to wipe out the human race. That was his choice: to wipe us out or rescue us, to save his life or save us, to avoid suffering or endure the greatest physical and spiritual suffering ever imagined. He chose you.

I'll (Josh) never forget the day I was driving down the road and actually saw a sign outside of a church that wasn't corny. It was around Easter time, and as I drove by I can still remember the overwhelming feeling of awe that sunk in as I read the words, "Why did Jesus die for you?" It's as if God were speaking directly at me.

Ask yourself that question now. What helps you grasp the meaning of Jesus' sacrifice for you? What makes it real to you? People have tried to put their wonder and gratitude into songs for a long time. Charles Wesley was one of the most gifted songwriters in the history of the faith. In a beautiful song about the wonder of grace, he described the moment he grasped God's love:

> Long my imprisoned spirit lay,
> fast bound in sin and nature's night;
> thine eye diffused a quickening ray;
> I woke, the dungeon flamed with light;
> my chains fell off, my heart was free,
> I rose, went forth, and followed thee.[15]

The biography of Jesus isn't just a nice story about a good man who was misunderstood and mistakenly killed by evil people. His death was no accident. It had been planned since the beginning of time. We didn't deserve his sacrifice because we are good people, and we didn't do anything to twist God's arm. He gave himself willingly, giving up his comfort, his reputation, and his life for people who didn't even care—and even for those who hated him. It's hard for us to understand the depth of his love that drove him to do this for us, but it's good to try.

Near and Far

The Scriptures tell us about two starkly different aspects of the nature of God. He is, at the same time, "as near as our breath" and "far above all" creation. He delights in "holding our hand," but he "dwells in unapproachable light." He calls us his "friends," but he is the "king over all." The terms to describe this paradox are *transcendence* and *immanence*—and both are true about God. If we focus only on the nearness of God, his immanence, we may find him to be a very nice God, but we won't worship him as the awesome, all-powerful God of the universe. We'll take him for granted, and we'll see him as our helper, but we won't be in awe of him. To get a more accurate picture, let's look at the transcendent nature of God.

For three millennia, people focused primarily on the greatness of God. For 1,500 years before Christ, at the time of Moses, until about 1,500 years after Christ, believers' worship centered on God's awe-inspiring transcendence. By the time Martin Luther began the Protestant Reformation 500 years ago, the Catholic Church's Mass had been spoken in Latin for generations of illiterate farmers and their families (who spoke not a word of Latin). The priests chanted, lit candles, waved censers of smoke, and led worship behind screens that separated them from the people. To the men and women in those churches, God seemed distant, majestic, and aloof.

During the Reformation, bands of Protestants smashed the statues of saints and the screens that separated priests from the people, and symbolically separated them from God. Salvation, the Reformers taught, was based on God's grace, not our efforts to earn his approval. Their message was that God is approachable, not unreachable—turning fifteen centuries of church practice upside down. Those decades of the early sixteenth century saw a powerful movement toward balance between the transcendence of God—that he is far above anything we can imagine—and immanence—that he is near and accessible.

In recent years, however, we have swung strongly toward immanence, toward knowing God intimately, as a friend. In an effort to make Jesus seem more approachable, the church has lost a sense of his greatness.

We need to be careful not to embrace God's grace at the expense of his greatness. Has this been the case with you? Have you related to God purely as a friend? As if he isn't the all-powerful Creator of the universe? Or have you been treating him as a waiter—somebody who is just here to serve you and give you what you want or need?

Take time right now to sit and consider the awe and majesty of the Creator God. Schedule time tonight to lie outside on your back, gazing at the stars. Go for a hike this weekend, and instead of focusing on getting to the top, just enjoy the journey, taking notice of the trees and beauty around you. Fit into your life time to go and experience the created order of God, experiencing and worshipping his beauty and vastness.

Pastor and author A. W. Tozer wrote about the essence of true worship:

> The purpose of God in sending his Son to die and rise and live and be at the right hand of God the Father was that he might restore to us the missing jewel, the jewel of worship; that we might come back and learn to do again that which we were created to do in the first place—worship the Lord in the beauty of holiness, to spend our time in awesome wonder and adoration of God, feeling and expressing it, and letting it get into our labors and doing nothing except as an act of worship to Almighty God through his Son, Jesus Christ.[16]

One of the most striking images of Jesus is described in John's Revelation. John was one of Jesus' closest friends. When John referred to himself in his Gospel, he identified himself as "the disciple Jesus loved." Does that mean he was the only one Jesus loved? No, it means that the love of Christ was so overwhelming to John that it defined his identity. They were very close. In Revelation, the risen Christ appears to John, but the scene isn't what you'd expect when old friends meet to talk. John described the encounter:

> I turned around to see the voice that was speaking to me. And when I turned I saw seven golden lampstands, and among the lampstands was someone "like a son of man," dressed in a robe reaching down to his feet and with a golden sash around his chest. His head and hair were white like wool, as white as snow, and his eyes were like blazing fire. His feet were like bronze glowing in a furnace, and his voice was like the sound of rushing waters. In his right hand he held seven stars, and out of his mouth came a sharp double-edged sword. His face was like the sun shining in all its brilliance.[17]

The Jesus John had known so well now looked unlike anything he had ever seen! He had gotten a glimpse of Christ's glory at the transfiguration, but this was categorically different. John described his reaction: "When I saw him, I fell at his feet as though dead. Then he placed his right hand on me and said: 'Do not be afraid. I am the First and the Last. I am the Living One; I was dead, and behold I am alive for ever and ever! And I hold the keys of death and Hades.'"[18]

An accurate picture of his friend overwhelmed John. When he saw Jesus, he fainted, and he had to be revived by hearing Jesus' familiar, loving voice and feeling the warmth of his hand. At that moment, John had a pretty good understanding of both the transcendence and the immanence of Christ!

When we were in Colorado, I (Josh) realized how often I think of God as a good buddy more than an awesome king. But wonder is seldom inspired by a buddy. Have you experienced this? A time when you were awakened to the majesty and wonder of the king of the universe who created every little bone in your body, knows the number of hairs on your head, and yet is the God who created the vast mountains and entire universe?

In his matchless grace, God has made himself approachable, but the writer to the Hebrews tells us we "approach the throne of grace" (Hebrews 4:16). It's the throne of the Ruler of All, the King of the awesome expanse of the universe. But God is not one or the other, either unapproachable and "far above all" or close friend. He is both, and that is a source of true wonder.

Author Philip Yancey quotes British philosopher and theologian G. K. Chesterton and comments on Chesterton's insight: "In a memorable phrase that became the virtual cornerstone of his theology, G. K. Chesterton said, 'Christianity got over the difficulty of combining furious opposites, by keeping them both, and keeping them both furious.' Most heresies come from espousing one opposite at the expense of the other."[19]

Our faith weakens when we focus on one at the expense of the other. Certainly, God "dwells in unapproachable light" and we can't imagine the full scope of his greatness, but he loves us enough to make himself known to flawed, weak people on a speck of dust in the cosmic landscape. Those truths are "furious opposites" that inspire us and instill a sense of wonder.

Wonder Shapes Our Hearts

Delighting in beauty, love, and strength changes us from the inside out. As we dig deeper into God's greatness and goodness, our hearts are filled with wonder, and our desires are changed. Our fears gradually melt as we realize how much our Heavenly Father loves us. And we are energized, wanting to honor him in everything we do. The combination of his transcendence and immanence convinces us that he is a safe haven, a source of security for even anxious, avoidant, and disorganized hearts.

The process of learning to trust God, though, is a struggle for most of us. It would be nice if our lives would suddenly change just by reading some encouraging verses, hearing a nice message, or studying an inspiring book, but trust in any relationship is a product of courage, risk taking that results in security, and time. Some of us refuse to take even the smallest step of trust until we have all the answers, but in our relationship with God, we sometimes have to realize that he has all the answers even when we don't.

In most cases, building trust involves first recognizing our lack of trust and the patterns of self-protection. Many people love the encouraging verse at the end of Isaiah 40. The prophet reports:

> . . . but those who hope in the LORD
> will renew their strength.
> They will soar on wings like eagles;
> they will run and not grow weary,
> they will walk and not be faint. (Isa. 40:31)

This encouragement, though, comes at the end of a process that gave insight and prompted a change in perspective. It began with an honest expression of disappointment about God:

> Why do you say, O Jacob,
> and complain, O Israel,
> "My way is hidden from the LORD;
> my cause is disregarded by my God"? (Isa. 40:27)

They thought God had abandoned them, and they weren't happy about it. They blamed God for not coming through like they thought he should. Isaiah then reminded them of God's character and explained that God delights in touching the lives of people who need him and trust him. He begins by asking them a couple of questions, and then he answers the questions himself—in a way designed to increase trust and security:

> Do you not know?
>> Have you not heard?
>> The LORD is the everlasting God,
>> the Creator of the ends of the earth.
>> He will not grow tired or weary,
>> and his understanding no one can fathom.
> He gives strength to the weary
>> and increases the power of the weak.
> Even youths grow tired and weary,
>> and young men stumble and fall;
> but those who hope in the LORD
>> will renew their strength.
>> They will soar on wings like eagles;
>> they will run and not grow weary,
>> they will walk and not be faint. (Isa. 40:28–31)

What does this mean to those of us who struggle in our relationship with God? It means that we're not alone and that God wants to connect with us to reassure us. People have always found it difficult to grasp the nature of a God who is both tender and mighty. A good beginning point is to simply be honest, to express our doubts and disappointments. From there, we search the Bible and talk to friends to find out the truth. Quite often, the truth is right in front of us, but it's hard to grasp—just like Jesus lived with the disciples every day but they often failed to understand who he really was.

A Deeper Faith

Spiritual maturity and enlightenment, however, don't come only from happy moments and pleasant reading. Far more often, we learn about God and about our relationship with him in the crucible of great difficulties. When we face deep disappointments, we have to wrestle with what we believe. We can't skate along any longer or dodge the hard questions about life. When our lives are shaken or shattered, we have to find something or someone to trust. Those of us who couldn't trust parents for safety may find it hard to trust God, but he promises that if we seek, we'll find him, and if we knock, he'll open the door. The process may take time, and we may have to remove boulders of doubt before we can replace them with strong homes of faith. But the struggle is incredibly valuable.

As we connect with the pursuer God, we'll find that our preconceptions of him have been deficient, and in some cases, terribly wrong. We may have assumed that all authority figures don't care about us, use us for their own purposes, or only want to hurt us. Gradually, we learn that God is different. The story of Jesus slowly convinces us that God truly loves us—in fact, he's crazy about us! Good crazy. The one who tenderly cares for us is the one who spoke creation into existence. Slowly, preconceived and fallacious ideas melt away, and new and truer perceptions of God take root in our hearts. Instead of resisting him, we are thrilled by his affection, and we want to know more about him. We may always carry scars from our past wounds, but we realize that scars are signs of healing.

Sometimes, our hearts will soar like an eagle, and we delight in God—thanksgiving and worship flow out of us like strong rivers. At other times, we run alongside him to do what he wants us to do, and we enjoy each step of the way. But there are times in all of our lives that we face deep, dark valleys. All we can do then is to cling to his hand as we take one step at a time. We may feel like quitting, but we find the courage to take one more step with him. As finite beings, we realize we'll never have the full picture of our circumstances in the way an all-knowing God understands them, but we learn to trust him even when we don't understand.

Elisabeth Elliot and her husband, Jim, served as missionaries in Ecuador, but Jim and several other men were killed by a tribe of Indians they had hoped to lead to Christ. Elisabeth grieved, but she decided to stay and translate the New Testament into the tribe's language. In a wonderful twist of grace, some of the men who had killed her husband later came to Christ and became her friends. After long months of labor to translate the Scriptures, she flew back to

America. On the way, all her work was lost. With bold faith, she didn't blame God or give up on his plan for her life. She commented on the mystery of God's will and her commitment to trust him even when she didn't understand his ways:

> There are many things that God does not fix precisely because he loves us. Instead of extracting us from the problem, he calls us. In our sorrow or loneliness or pain he calls— "This is a necessary part of the journey. Even if it is the roughest part, it is only a part, and it will not last the whole long way. Remember where I am leading you. Remember what you will find at the end—a home and a haven and a heaven."[20]

Not everyone is tested by the loss of those they love most, however. Remember that God never allows those things that would overwhelm us—that would shipwreck our faith and love for him. By God's grace, he will use even our disappointments to deepen our faith and give us more understanding of his character. He never promised that we'd understand all he's doing, but he assures us that no matter what happens, we can trust him. That kind of faith depends on a strong sense of wonder at God's greatness and goodness.

That's why we can't ever get over the wonder of it all.

CONSIDER THIS: Instead of asking God for anything this week or treating him like a buddy, just sit in solitude and meditate on his majesty. Treat him like a King. (And to see how to do this, visit us at www.godattachmentbook.com.)

14

Your Life Counts

I know your deeds, that you are neither cold nor hot.
I wish you were either one or the other!
So, because you are lukewarm—neither hot nor cold—
I am about to spit you out of my mouth.
—Jesus[1]

A FEW YEARS AGO Josh and I (Tim) led a men's spiritual retreat at Wintergreen Ski Resort here in Virginia. Before each session we showed videos clips from movies that emphasized a key point we were trying to make and that also connected with the hearts of the men there. Scenes from movies like *Kingdom of Heaven, Braveheart, Gladiator, Cinderella Man,* and *Walk the Line.* Scenes about passion, courage, purpose, tenacity, wisdom, meaning, freedom . . . and fighting to the bitter end for it.

End products in the life of someone who has learned to be attached to God.

But more than that, they were also necessary equipment for the journey. When we begin this journey, we may not know where to find them (let alone know how to use them), but soon we realize that we have to if we're going to make any progress at all.

• • •

Few people who know Bethany today would have recognized her as the same person if they had met her a few years before. When she was a child, her father was a crack addict. To stay one step ahead of the law, he moved the family every few months to towns nearby. Bethany and her two little brothers changed schools so often that they never had any sense of stability. But her father was the least of her worries. Bethany's mother was a sadistic monster, sexually abusing her and beating her unmercifully if she cried out in pain. Her mom threatened to kill her if she told anyone, and Bethany knew it wasn't an empty threat. To outsiders, though, her mother was the most respected member of the family. Each day, she put on her uniform and went to work as a physician's assistant at the local hospital. Everyone thought she was a model citizen, especially if they knew what a bum her husband was.

When Bethany was nine years old, she couldn't take the abuse any longer, so she told her aunt what was happening at home. She hoped her aunt would be outraged, stop the abuse, and ask her to live in her home. Instead, her aunt didn't believe her and insisted that she was making up the stories of abuse. After Bethany walked out of her house, the aunt called her mother and reported all she had said. When Bethany walked in the door of her house, she met a firestorm of fists and blows from a frying pan. When her mother picked up a butcher knife and lunged at her, Bethany jumped back. The blade cut her arm, but she escaped out the back door. She didn't dare go to a doctor to stitch up the wound. She kept it bandaged very tightly to keep the skin together until it healed.

During many of the ordeals of sexual abuse and beatings, Bethany dissociated. She later remarked, "To protect myself the best way I could, I left my body. I floated near the ceiling, watching all that was going on. It helped me escape the pain."

When her friend Stephanie heard her story, she asked, "Where was your dad?"

"High or in jail."

"Did you try to talk to him about your mom?" Stephanie asked as her anger rose. "Wasn't he willing to stop her?"

"Yes," Bethany said softly. "I talked to him a couple of times, and he knew exactly what was going on. But he was as terrified of my mother as I was."

"And where were your brothers during all these horrible times?"

Stephanie said through clenched teeth. "Didn't they hear what was happening? Why didn't they stop it?"

Bethany sighed. "Of course, they knew, but Mother threatened them that she'd kill me first and then them if they ever told anybody. They kept quiet. They were so afraid that they never lifted a finger to help me."

In this kind of environment, Bethany's attachment style wasn't just fearful—it was shattered. Today, however, she has the look in her eye of a combat veteran who has fought and survived a war's most difficult battles. There isn't a trace of self-pity or bitterness, only a deep sense of gratitude to God and for some wonderful friends who have walked with her on her path of healing. A friend told her, "Bethany, you are one of the bravest people I've ever known!"

She laughed. "Well, thank you, but to survive, I didn't have any choice but to face my pain and take steps forward."

When she was in her thirties, Bethany's life was a disaster. She was abusing prescription drugs to numb the pain in her heart, and she was in her fifth or sixth bad relationship with demanding, abusive men. "Finally," she recalled, "I told a friend at work what had happened to me and that I couldn't stop finding men who used me and then dumped me. She was alarmed, and she told me life didn't have to be that way. I know it may sound strange, but I didn't know any other way to live. I assumed my relationships would always be abusive. It seemed completely normal."

In months of therapy and support groups, God walked with Bethany toward truth, love, and peace. "It was the hardest thing I've ever done," she remembered. "But my life is so different today. I have real friends, I can laugh, I don't die when I make a mistake, and I really believe that God loves me." People are drawn to her because they appreciate her rich wisdom, her quick smile, and her genuine love for people, but many of them have no idea where she's come from. "I don't tell my story very often," she relates. "I tell people when I think it will help them, but there's a whole life to live now. I don't want to live in the past, but I'll go there if I think God might want to use my story to help somebody." Bethany is a wonderful example of someone who has courageously walked through the stages of security, exploration, and compassionate action. She is living proof that even the most damaged among us can experience God's love and strength in supportive relationships. All it takes is a backpack full of tenacity, courage, kindness, and wisdom.

Finding Him

When our attachment to God is weak, strained, or nonexistent, we try to fill the hole in our hearts with other things. It's human nature. We are driven to please people to win a loving connection with them, but we always fear that we'll say or do something that will cause them to reject us. We compare our stuff with others', and we think that if we have just a little bit bigger house, nicer car, better vacations, or faster boat, we'll finally be happy. But no matter how much stuff we have, it never seems to be enough to fill the void in our souls. We long for comfort, pleasure, and excitement, so we spend more than we can afford on the latest gadgets, fun-filled trips, and sports, but when the thrill wears off, we feel empty again. Trying to fill our lives with people, things, and fun satisfies for a moment, but ultimately, they are treads on a perpetual rat race that leads to nowhere.

Saint Augustine knew very well what it felt like to pursue things to fill his heart. In his spiritual autobiography, *Confessions,* he details his quest for "disordered loves." He explains that there's nothing wrong with appreciating beautiful bodies, great sex, delicious food, great friends, a wonderful family, and other good things in life, but only if they remain in second or third place in our affections. When they occupy the central spot, the place reserved for God alone, then our loves become disordered.

Then, like throwing a wrench into a machine, our lives quickly self-destruct. Too often, our solution to the gnawing emptiness is to pursue those loves even more fiercely. Sooner or later, like the younger brother in Jesus' story of the prodigal son, we "come to our senses." We realize that all of our pursuits have led us deeper into compulsive behavior, strained relationships, and existential despair. We've been attached to the wrong things, or unattached to anything, and we need to make some changes before it's too late.

Muse on this: Saint Augustine defined moral evil as choosing the good things God created over God himself. Sin, then, is pursuing lasting happiness where it can't be found, drinking water from a well that only makes us thirstier. In the opening lines of his book, he proclaims the ultimate value statement: "You have made us for yourself, O God, and our hearts are restless until they find their rest in you."[2]

Jesus' words "Follow me" are both a summons from a king and an invitation from a friend. Either way, we refuse to respond to this heavenly invitation at our peril. He calls us to follow him because he is the ultimate authority as Creator and Savior, so we respond in obedience to his summons. But at the same time, he reaches out to us as friends to invite us to join him in the greatest adventure people have ever known.

In his book *The Call,* author Os Guinness observes that many believers in our culture compartmentalize their lives into two buckets: the sacred and the secular. Most Christians go to church two or three times each month. Some attend a Bible study or small group, and a few carve out time for personal devotions several times a week. Far too often, they leave God behind when they walk out the doors or close the book. For the rest of the day (the vast majority of time), they live as if God doesn't exist. This dualism of compartmentalized hypocrisy surfaces in two different ways. One way is that which values only those things that are considered strictly religious, and the other elevates the mundane above the spiritual. Guinness observes:

> The truth of calling means that for followers of Christ, "everyone, everywhere, and in everything" lives the whole of life as a response to God's call. Yet, this holistic character of calling has often been distorted to become a form of dualism that elevates the spiritual at the expense of the secular. This distortion may be called the "Catholic distortion" because it rose in the Catholic era and is the majority position in the Catholic tradition. Protestants, however, cannot afford to be smug. For one thing, countless Protestants have succumbed to the Catholic distortion as Wilberforce nearly did. Ponder, for example, the fallacy of the contemporary Protestant term "full-time Christian service"—as if those not working for churches or Christian organizations are only part-time in the service of Christ. For another thing, Protestant confusion about calling has led to a "Protestant distortion" that is even worse. This is a form of dualism in a secular direction that

not only elevates the secular at the expense of the spiritual, but also cuts it off from the spiritual altogether.[3]

As we understand the nature of Christ, that he is both transcendent and immanent, and our relationship to him is as God's beloved children, we'll learn that we belong to him all day every day (in Guinness's term, "everyone, everywhere, and in everything"). Our bodies may be in church, at work, in the car with kids, on the courts, or between the sheets, but we are his 24/7. No matter where we go or what we are doing, we are vitally connected to the God of the universe.

This fact, though, is double-edged. His love never fails, and we can depend on him for wisdom and strength at all times, but he expects obedience out of love at all times from his children. When we are in the middle of the healing process, we might resent any suggestion that God wants us to obey, but as we continue to attach to him, we gain insight into his heart, and we learn to obey out of profound gratitude. In fact, obedience motivated by thankfulness is a sure sign of progress, and is the proper motivation for everything that moves the Seeking System forward.

If only for this life we have hope in Christ,
we are to be pitied more than all men.
But Christ has indeed been raised from the dead.
—Paul[4]

Life's Most Difficult Tests

It was the spring of 1993. Though only thirteen years old at the time, I (Josh) remember it like it was yesterday.

I woke up earlier than I needed to for school, as I did most mornings, to say good-bye to my dad before he left for work. As he was leaning over next to the kitchen table to tie his shoes, I noticed him sit back up in his chair, then quickly fall back and slouch into it, throwing his arms at his sides as he surrendered to the task, groaning in anguish. He was visibly exhausted and frustrated. I knew he had not been feeling well, but this was bad. Later that morning, after I left for school, my stepmother took him to the family doctor. He was admitted into the local hospital later that afternoon for an irregular heartbeat and fatigue. I was scared.

That week, as his condition worsened, they decided to transfer him to Hershey Medical Center in Hershey, Pennsylvania, one of the top cardiology hospitals in the nation. After his transfer my mom thought it best for me to get away from the situation. My dad agreed.

That weekend my mom and her fiancé (who later became my stepfather) took me with them to the camping lot we had along the Susquehanna River to swim and fish. They meant it as a chance for me to get my mind off of my dad's condition.

Good intentions. Bad idea.

The only thing I remember about that weekend is that I lay prostrate on the floor of the boat late one night, and bawled uncontrollably over my dad, who, at just thirty-four years old, had developed congestive heart failure. I didn't want to fish that weekend. I feared deeply my dad would die.

Though he survived, I grieved the loss of my dad in other ways. When he got out of the hospital I was no longer able to wrestle with him as I used to or run or play football in the backyard anymore. It was a sad time for me. My dad and I had played together often.

The beauty in all of it was that, though I grieved the loss of the dad I knew, I rediscovered a whole new dad I hadn't met before. His bad heart forced us to connect in new ways. And it opened up my heart to be appreciative of every single moment I now share with him and take every memory, silly quirk, joke, or serious moment together as a gift. Now we go to a Phillies game every year for Father's Day. We play cards. We laugh. And just do stupid stuff to make the most of every opportunity.

Sometimes I just like to sit with him and reminisce, and enjoy the wonder of the father-son relationship we share.

As I was forced to change the way I related to my dad I came to see aspects of who he was that I had never seen before. This is exactly what will happen to you as you become more secure in your relationship with God. You will learn to relate to him in new, even fun ways. You will see aspects of who he is you never imagined. And you will learn to trust that he loves you more than you ever thought possible.

When you were mired in anxiety and confusion, it was hard to trust God's goodness and greatness. Many of us demanded that God protect us from all hurt, and some of us even expected him to guarantee an easy life—or we avoided him altogether. We interpreted every difficulty in our lives as one more sign that God didn't care. As our hearts heal, though, we realize that testing, pruning, and suffering are simply parts of life. There are no guarantees that God will protect us from difficulties, but we have his solemn promise to use every event, no matter how painful, to draw us closer to himself—if we'll let him. Before, we wanted God's blessings, but we really didn't want him; we found him useful, but we didn't really love him. Now our hearts, our perceptions, and our motivations are changing. We're learning to reframe our life's story—from childishness to adulthood, from victimization to maturity.

We hope you now realize that every event in your life comes from, or comes through, the hand of God, and the ultimate statement of your identity is that you are his. Jesus told us, "Never will I leave you; never will I forsake you" (Heb. 13:5). In response to his gracious promise, we can tell him, "Lord, I belong to you." We carry that insight into every circumstance we encounter. When God gives us wonderful encouragement, we can rejoice and say, "Lord, I belong to you, and I realize you are the one who gave me this gift. Thank you so much!"

When we are lonely, we can pour our hearts out to God and say, "Lord, I belong to you, and I know you are with me right now."

When we are filled with self-pity, envy, or jealousy because life doesn't seem fair, we can pray, "Lord, I belong to you, and you have the right to determine my circumstances."

And when we face difficulties and excruciating decisions, we can tell him, "Lord, I belong to you, and I know you will lead me and use this situation to make me more dependent on you, no matter how it turns out."[5]

When we feel out of control, we don't have to give up in despair. God will use every struggle, heartache, and moment of confusion to teach us life's most important lessons. In his letter to the Christians in Rome, Paul explained this point. Paul concluded that suffering is God's classroom. He wrote: "We also rejoice in our sufferings, because we know that suffering produces perseverance; perseverance, character; and character, hope. And hope does not disappoint us, because God has poured out his love into our hearts by the Holy Spirit, whom he has given us" (Rom. 5:3–5).

Another translation says that we "exult" in our tribulations. *Exult* means "to take delight in." We don't take delight in the suffering itself. Instead, we delight that suffering causes us to draw closer to God, and it produces godly character in us. We can learn a lot from Paul's perspective about suffering.

Holding God's hand through difficult times requires a tenacious mind and a tender heart. When everything in us wants to run away from God and our pain, we need to cling to him, just like Julie and I want our kids to come to us when they're hurting. We also need to remember Christ's sacrifice as a model for our courage to follow God in hard times and stay strong in our faith.

During the dark days of World War II, Dietrich Bonhoeffer faced suffering and death at the hands of his Nazi captors, but he remained cheerfully obedient to God until the day he was executed. What did it take for him to remain spiritually and emotionally strong in such an ordeal? He wrote, "Who stands fast? Only the man whose final standard is not his reason, his principles, his conscience, his freedom, or his virtue, but who is ready to sacrifice all this when he is called to obedient and responsible action in faith and in exclusive allegiance to God—the responsible man, who tries to make his whole life an answer to the question and call of God. Where are these responsible people?"[6]

Those who are attached to the wrong things or who remain unattached aren't the people Bonhoeffer was looking for, but countless men and women have answered his call. These are the brave ones who have looked inside their own hearts; found pain, emptiness, and deceit; and turned to God for forgiveness and healing. In a rich, vibrant, growing relationship with Christ, they have found genuine love in him and in his people. Jesus' summons to follow him is incredibly demanding.

Over and over again, he called men and women to put him first in their lives, and he calls us to make the same choice. As the old hymn accurately states, "Love so amazing, so divine, demands my soul, my life, my all."[7] In one account, "Then Jesus said to his disciples, 'If anyone would come after me, he must deny himself and take up his cross and follow me. For whoever wants to save his life will lose it, but whoever loses his life for me will find it. What good will it be for a man if he gains the whole world, yet forfeits his soul? Or what can a man give in exchange for his soul?'"[8] To Jesus, and to those who have followed him and found him faithful, complete devotion to him makes perfect sense. Gaining all the wealth and popularity in the world, he explained, is worthless compared to knowing him.

The apostle Paul understood very well that suffering is part of the Christian life. As he followed Jesus, he experienced ridicule, natural disasters, and heartache. In the middle of his most articulate letter, Paul asks and answers several questions he thought the Christians in Rome might be asking. He knew that it was their natural tendency to interpret trouble as a sign that God had left them high and dry, so he wrote:

> Who shall separate us from the love of Christ? Shall trouble or hardship or persecution or famine or nakedness or danger or sword? As it is written:
> "For your sake we face death all day long; we are considered as sheep to be slaughtered."
> No, in all these things we are more than conquerors through him who loved us. For I am convinced that neither death nor life, neither angels nor demons, neither the present nor the future, nor any powers, neither height nor depth, nor anything else in all creation, will be able to separate us from the love of God that is in Christ Jesus our Lord.[9]

Who needs to hear this assurance? All of us do: those who are beginning the journey out of anxiety, avoidance, and disorganization; those who feel threatened and need reassurance when they take steps to explore a new world of relationships; and those who have made significant strides in attaching to God but feel knocked down by unforeseen heartaches. We cling to God's mercy and kindness no matter what happens.

Your Life Counts

Under the warmth of God's love, our shell of self-protection cracks, our hard heart melts, and our loves become reordered. In his creativity (and his humor), God has made us with very different personalities and talents, but knowing God produces a common passion in all of us: a deep desire for our lives to count. As our hearts are filled with the love of God, his grace overflows and we want others to experience his love, too. One lady expressed her heart by defining her purpose. She wrote:

> I want to live my life very *purposely*, regularly reviewing and praying over my purpose in life, loving God intensely, cherishing and inspiring my husband, praying for and keeping connected spiritually with my children, loving women and seeking to lay spiritual foundations in their lives.
>
> I want to live *faithfully*, believing God for what I cannot see. I want to believe that God can do in my children's lives what I cannot do.
>
> I want to live *creatively*, creating beauty and warmth in my home, around my table, and in my Bible study. Creativity adds sparkle to a focused, purposeful life.
>
> I want to live *paradoxically*. I want to go against my selfish nature, against our culture, giving a little bit more than I feel like giving, going the second mile, being like Jesus.[10]

As we heal and grow, we long for our God to use us to touch people's lives. We may naturally gravitate to people in whose faces we see reflections of ourselves in our painful past, those who are wounded and see no way forward. We've been there. We know how it feels, and we know how to take a step at a time toward honesty and strength. As the circle of our lives expands far beyond the dot of self-absorption, we reach out to help family members, friends, neighbors, and people we've never met before.

As we mature, that healing spirit that has been so inwardly focused for so long begins to turn inexorably outward, shining its light on the needs of others. We hang around people who are taking compassionate action, our passion fuels each other, and we join hands in doing things we couldn't have dreamed of before. We find we truly care about other people, and we boldly pray along with World Vision founder Bob Pierce: "Let my heart be broken by the things that break the heart of God."

We used to find convenient excuses for not helping other people, but no longer. Everyone, we now know, is our neighbor. That was Jesus' message when he told the story of "the good Samaritan." Luke records Jesus' story. The Samaritans were ethnic and spiritual outcasts. The Jews hated them, and the Samaritans returned the favor. In the story, a man traveling from Jerusalem to Jericho was robbed and beaten by thieves. As he lay beside the road, a priest came by, but he didn't try to help. Then a Levite came by, but he didn't help the man, either.

Finally, a Samaritan walked by, saw the man's plight, and cared for him. He bandaged his wounds and took him to an inn to recuperate. He paid the innkeeper two silver coins—enough to cover room and board for two months. Jesus asked, "Which of these three do you think was a neighbor to the man who fell into the hands of robbers?"[11] The answer was obvious: "the one who had mercy" on the wounded man.

What or whose predicament breaks your heart? Today, in a world of Internet communications and convenient worldwide air travel, we know about and can actually touch the lives of virtually every person on the planet. The opportunities are almost endless. Hundreds of thousands of people invest a small amount each month to care for hungry children and share Christ's love through Compassion International. Many different organizations travel to Africa to build hospitals and provide food for people ravaged by HIV/AIDS.

People are outraged by the plight of human sex trafficking, and they are taking steps in American cities and around the world to help women come out of sex slavery into freedom. More locally, we can make a difference by volunteering at crisis pregnancy centers and donating food and clothing to homeless shelters. It's not enough for many of us, though, to just write a check. We want to be involved, to roll up our sleeves and pitch in, to see the look of despair change to hope, and to see lives changed.

Some people may protest to any one of us, "What you're doing isn't making much of a dent." But we respond, "No, it's not much, but it's something, and we believe it matters to God." In fact, when we reach out to touch a life, Jesus said we are doing it for him, too. Every time we put an arm around a discouraged friend, invite a stranger in to have a bite to eat, give a coat to someone who is cold, or visit someone who is sick or in prison, in a mystical way Christ is the recipient of our efforts. Jesus said, "I tell you the truth, whatever you did for one of the least of these brothers of mine, you did for me."[12]

N. T. Wright, the Bishop of Durham, in England, is a champion of social justice in the church. He notes that we don't have to have grand and glorious schemes to make a difference. Even the smallest act of compassion can change a person's life, and someday in the New Heaven and New Earth, we'll understand each act's significance. In his book *Following Jesus,* he wrote:

> Every act of justice, every word of truth, every creation of genuine beauty, every act of sacrificial love, will be reaffirmed on the last day, in the new world. The poem that glimpses truth in a new way; the mug of tea given with gentleness to the down-and-out at the drop-in center; the setting aside of my own longings in order to support and cherish someone who depends on me; the piece of work done honestly and thoroughly; the prayer that comes from heart and mind together; all of these and many more are building blocks for the kingdom. We may not yet see how they will fit into God's eventual structure, but the fact of the resurrection, of God's glad reaffirmation of true humanness, assures us that they will.[13]

Questions and Answers

In our quest to find God, we began by exploring the question of whether God even exists. The evidence, we found, points to him as the Creator, and the historical record of the resurrection of Jesus assures us that we can trust him. But most of us don't begin our journey as an intellectual pursuit. We had some presuppositions about God based on our life experiences. Those, we've found, are much more powerful in shaping our faith (or lack of it) than we imagined.

We've had to take a long, hard look at the damage, and we've had to do some heavy lifting to trust God to repair our hearts. In this book, we've used metaphors like a hike in the Grand Canyon and physical rehabilitation to describe how we make progress in healing and faith, and we've seen that we simply can't make it on our own. The people who walk beside us are dearer than a brother or sister. They are the hands of God to care for us.

As we've walked with God and our friends, we've come face-to-face with our answers to the two crucial questions every person instinctively asks. Many of us have had to admit that the answer to at least one of those questions was a painful no. We've wrestled with our demanding victim mentality, our self-protective measures that kept people and God away from us, and our compulsion to fill our lives with things instead of letting God fill our hearts. Through all of this, we've slowly discovered that God is much different from how we presumed. Slowly, the scales have fallen from our eyes, and we see him much more clearly. We realize that we can't make him into a God of our own construction; we take him as he is, and we worship him for his love, kindness, and awesome power. We remember that Mrs. Beaver told Lucy, "Oh no, dearie, he's not safe, but he's good." And she's right. We can't control God, but we can trust him. Along the journey, we find that his love, wisdom, and presence genuinely satisfies.

Jonathan Edwards was one of the greatest theologians in American history, but his scholarship wasn't dry and boring. His study of God led him to adore him. In his book *The Christian Pilgrim*, he observed, "The enjoyment of God is the only happiness with which our souls can be satisfied. To go to heaven, fully to enjoy God, is infinitely better than the most pleasant accommodations here. Fathers and mothers, husbands, wives or children, or the company of earthly friends, are but shadows; but God is the substance. These are but scattered beams, but God is the sun. These are but streams. But God is the ocean."[14] To know God now is a taste of heaven on earth.

Now, at the end of the book, you have a choice to make. Actually, if you've read this far, you've probably already made it. You long for something more. You picked up this book because you hoped it would offer some insights about the path to know him; and as you've read, you've realized that your doubts and resistance are rooted in your distorted childhood attachments and your human selfishness and sin. We can know a lot about someone by studying a biography, but we can't say we truly know the person unless we begin a relationship. That's what God offers. Throughout the Scriptures, God proclaims to anyone who will listen, "I will be your God, and you will be my people." It's an offer to have him as Savior, Father, and friend.

Perhaps you've heard his gracious invitation and you've reached out to take his hand, but maybe you're still waiting for "the right moment" or "a special feeling" or something else. God is incredibly patient, and he's willing to wait until we reach for him. But he is the dividing point of each life as well as that of history. In the face of Christ's humility and sacrifice, we simply can't remain distant and passive. To one of the early churches, Christ said, "I know your deeds, that you are neither cold nor hot. I wish you were either one or the other!" (Revelation 3:15).

Our encouragement to you at the end of this book is to look at the beautiful face of Christ, and then embrace him with all your heart. Don't keep him at arm's length forever. To the same church, he offers his invitation, "Here I am! I stand at the door and knock. If anyone hears my voice and opens the door, I will come in and eat with him, and he with me."[15] Jesus isn't stuck in the pages of a dusty old book, and he's not floating out there in the cosmos somewhere. He's as close as your breath, and he's patiently, persistently knocking on your heart's door.

When we let him in, we begin a relationship of love, adventure, mystery, laughter, and purpose. We know him, and he knows us—everything about us, even those things we don't know about ourselves—and he delights in us still.

Perhaps you've had a relationship with God for many years, but you've had secret doubts about where you stand with him. In reading this book, we hope you've been able to identify the source of some of those doubts so they can be dissolved in God's strong love. No matter how much we know about God, there's still much more to learn. And no matter how much we cherish him, he is still far more wonderful. For the rest of our lives, and all of eternity, our challenge and joy will be to know him more deeply—and in that pursuit, we'll find our greatest joy.

I (Tim) want to go back to one of my last conversations with my earthly father about my Heavenly Father. He said, "If you seek him you will find him, and you'll be blessed in him." God changes everything. Follow him . . . and you'll never be the same. And it's because of him that I'll see you again.

The choice has been and will always be simply ours to make. God will do his part if we will do ours.

CONSIDER THIS: You matter to God. So much that he gave his only Son for you. He is alive. He does matter. And a relationship with him changes everything.

Our prayer is that you will truly connect with God in ways you never imagined you could. Visit www.godattachmentbook .com for your next steps.

Epilogue
Knowing God

THE CHOICE IS YOURS.

God loves you and invites you to be in a relationship with him through Jesus Christ. The Bible says:

"All have sinned and fall short of the glory of God." (Romans 3:23)

"Therefore, just as sin entered the world through one man, and death through sin, and in this way death came to all men, because all sinned." (Romans 5:12)

But the good news is:

"God so loved the world that he gave his only son that whosoever believes in him will not perish but have eternal life." (John 3:16)

"For everyone who calls on the name of the Lord will be saved." (Romans 10:13)

It should be really obvious by now that *God loves and longs for a relationship with YOU! He wants you in heaven with him* (John 17:24) *and to live an abundant life full of His love* (John 10:10).

However, because he loves you, he refuses to control you. He allows you to make the decision for yourself. The choice is yours.

The following prayer from your heart to God's heart changes everything:

> *Almighty God, Everlasting Father, I believe that you love me*
> *so much that you gave up your one and only Son to die for my*
> *sins. I believe he died, was buried, and rose from the dead on*
> *the third day. I therefore confess my sins and turn my life over*
> *to you today. Come into my heart and save me as you promised.*
> *I daily surrender my life into your hands. In Jesus' name. Amen.*

Congratulations! If you have prayed that prayer you now know you'll be in heaven with God forever. But it's just the beginning. Ephesians 1:3 says that you now have been blessed with every spiritual blessing in the heavenly *places* in Christ (NKJV). According to that entire passage, God has granted us his spiritual power for our everyday life.

The Next Step (for all of us):

Find a godly mentor of the same sex to help guide you and walk with you on your spiritual journey as your relationship with God deepens. The biggest obstacle you will face from here on out will be your tendency to turn away from God to the things you used to turn to for safety, comfort, and relief. And when you turn to something or someone other than God, this is called sin. When you turn from God for relief, you act as though you do not trust him to be there for you. And it ultimately puts a barrier between you and your relationship with God. God wants you to connect to him . . . to believe him in the now.

Throughout the book we have mentioned the distorted views about God that you may have developed based on your relationships with your parents, primary caregivers, or others in your life. Though these circumstances and events have probably affected or infected your relationship with God, and may prevent you from trusting him, it does not excuse you from sinful, selfish behaviors—because your behaviors are your responsibility. Remember, problems are never the issue in life; it's what you do with the problems.

God calls us to more—to understand and know him more intimately than you ever thought possible. If you believe Jesus Christ is who he says he is—then come to him with a spirit of expectation. And live what you believe.

The choice is yours.

Notes

Chapter 1: Does God Matter?

1. Friedrich Wilhelm Nietzsche, *The Gay Science* (New York: Vintage, 1974), 119.

2. 1 Sam. 17:26.

3. Paraphrase of 1 Sam. 17:32–37.

4. 1 Sam. 17:43–44.

5. 1 Sam. 17:45–46.

6. See "Wisconsin Parents Get Probation Plus Jail in Daughter's Prayer Death," Associated Press, http://origin.foxnews.com/story/0,2933,560941,00 .html (retrieved October 13, 2009).

7. Joe Kovacs, "Maher: Bush is 'Gilligan who cannot find his a—.'" *World Net Daily*, February 21, 2007, http://70.85.195.205/news/printer-friendly .asp?ARTICLE_ID=54367.

8. See story: D. Edwards, "F.C. Little League Father Starts Petition for 'Religious Freedom,'" July 15, 2009, http://fcnp.com/news/4745-fc-little-league-father-starts-petition-for-religious-freedom.html.

9. Retrieved from a keynote address delivered by Major General Bob Dees at a Wildfire Men's Conference, October 9, 2009; verified statement was e-mailed word for word from Maj. Gen. Dees to Joshua Straub on Monday, October 26, 2009.

10. "Jihad and Terrorism-Palestinians," Middle East Media Research Institute, February 7, 2006, http://www.memri.org/report/en/0/0/0/0/0/0/1601 .htm.

11. This story and telephone conversation are based on my (Tim) best recollections as a teenager. It may or may not reflect actual events as they happened.

12. J. Jeffries McWhirter, "Religion and the Practice of Counseling Psychology," *Counseling Psychologist,* 17, no. 4 (1989): 613–616.

13. Charles Gilbert Wrenn, *The World of the Contemporary Counselor* (Boston: Houghton Mifflin, 1973), 109.

14. Ibid.

15. Sigmund Freud, *New Introductory Lectures on Psychoanalysis, A Philosophy of Life, Lecture 35,* 1933 (New York: Vintage New Ed edition, 2001).

16. Carl Rogers, *On Becoming a Person* (Boston: Houghton Mifflin, 1961), 8.

17. Stevan Lars Nielsen and Albert Ellis, "A Discussion with Albert Ellis: Reason, Emotion and Religion," *Journal of Psychology and Christianity,* vol. 13, issue 4 (2003): 327–341. Also found at http://myauz.com/janr/articles/lect13rebt .pdf (accessed March 10, 2010).

18. Os Guinness, *Long Journey Home: A Guide to Your Search for the Meaning of Life* (Colorado Springs: Waterbrook Press, 2003), 26.

19. See Justin Barrett, *Why Would Anyone Believe in God?* (Walnut Creek, CA: Altamira Press, 2004); and Justin Barrett, "Is the Spell Really Broken? Bio-Psychological Explanations of Religion and Theistic Belief," *Theology and Science* 5 (2007): 57–72.

20. Albert Einstein, as quoted by Alan Lightman, *A Sense of the Mysterious: Science and the Human Spirit* (New York: Vintage, 2006), 42.

21. Guinness, *Long Journey Home,* 26.

22. Walt Kelly, *Pogo: We Have Met the Enemy, and He Is Us* (New York: Simon & Schuster, 1972).

Chapter 2: God Obsession

1. Søren Kierkegaard, *Repetition and Philosophical Crumbs* (New York: Oxford University Press, 2009), 60.

2. B. A. Robinson, "Religions of the World: Number of Adherents; Growth Rates," Ontario Consultants on Religious Tolerance, http://www.religioustolerance .org/worldrel.htm (accessed October 10, 2009).

3. Ibid.

4. Ibid.

5. Ibid.

6. *Time* Archive, "Search Results for 'Jesus,'" *Time,* http://search.time.com/ results.html?N=46&Nty=1&Ns=p_date_range%7C1&Ntt=jesus&x=53&y=9 (accessed October 16, 2009).

7. Newsweek Web Exclusive. "The God Debate," *Newsweek,* April 9, 2007, http://www.newsweek.com/id/35784.

8. Frank Newport, "Who Believes in God and Who Doesn't?" Gallup, June 23, 2006, http://www.gallup.com/poll/23470/Who-Believes-God-Who-Doesnt.aspx.

9. Russell Ash, *The Top 10 of Everything, 1997* (New York: DK Publishers, 1996), 112.

10. Religion BookLine, "Three Reviews from Publishers Weekly's Web-Exclusive Reviews Annex," *Publishers Weekly*, July 12, 2006, http://www.publishersweekly.com/article/CA6351852.html?nid=2287#review2.

11. Religion BookLine, "Web-Exclusive Interviews: Week of 6/26/06," *Publishers Weekly*, June 26, 2006, http://www.publishersweekly.com/article/CA6346265.html?q=70+million+left+behind+series.

12. "Best Sellers," *New York Times*, October 13, 2009, http://www.nytimes.com/pages/books/bestseller/.

13. Internet Movie Database, "All-Time Box Office: USA," http://www.imdb.com/boxoffice/alltimegross.

14. Box Office Mojo, "Movies: Fireproof (2008)," http://www.boxofficemojo.com/movies/?id=fireproof.htm. These numbers were retrieved October 18, 2009.

15. Steve Crabtree and Brett Pelham, "What Alabamians and Iranians Have in Common," Gallup, February 9, 2009, http://www.gallup.com/poll/114211/alabamians-iranians-common.aspx.

16. Ibid.

17. John Meacham, "The End of Christian America," *Newsweek*, April 13, 2009, http://www.newsweek.com/id/192583.

18. "Religion," Gallup, http://www.gallup.com/poll/1690/religion.aspx? (accessed October 13, 2009).

19. Allen E. Bergin and Jay P. Jensen, "Religiosity of Psychotherapists: A National Survey," *Psychotherapy*, 27, no. 1 (Spring 1990): 3–7.

20. David Kinnaman and Gabe Lyons, *Unchristian: What a Generation Really Thinks About Christianity . . . and Why It Matters* (Grand Rapids: Baker Books, 2007), 15.

21. Ibid.

22. "A New Generation Expresses Its Skepticism and Frustration with Christianity." *Barna Group*, September 24, 2007, http://www.barna.org/barna-update/article/16-teensnext-gen/94-a-new-generation-expresses-its-skepticism-and-frustration-with-christianity.

23. Bergin and Jensen, "Religiosity of Psychotherapists," 3–7.

24. "For Easter Worship, Obama Picks Episcopal Church," Associated Press, April 13, 2009, http://www.google.com/hostednews/ap/article/ALeqM5jn4ZlxW24L322-0sC7NftpnM_YZQD97H3V0O0.

25. Hugh Ross, *Why the Universe Is the Way It Is* (Grand Rapids: Baker Books, 2008), 117.

26. Dwight Goddard, *A Buddhist Bible* (Boston: Beacon Press, 1994), 409.

27. Mohandas K. Ghandi, *An Autobiography: The Story of My Experiments with Truth* (Boston: Beacon Press, 1993; originally published 1929), page xxviii.

28. C. S. Lewis, *The Problem of Pain* (New York: HarperOne, 2001), 70.

29. Arthur Bennett, ed., *The Valley of Vision* (Edinburgh: Banner of Truth Trust, 1975), 388.

30. Os Guinness, *Long Journey Home: A Guide to Your Search for the Meaning of Life* (Colorado Springs: Waterbrook Press, 2003), 24.

31. Heb. 11:6 (NKJV).

Chapter 3: Crisis of Belief

1. Philip Yancey, *Reaching for the Invisible God* (Grand Rapids: Zondervan, 2002), 38.

2. As quoted by Os Guinness, *Long Journey Home: A Guide to Your Search for the Meaning of Life* (Colorado Springs: Waterbrook Press, 2003), 314–315.

3. C. S. Lewis, *The Problem of Pain* (New York: HarperOne, 2001), 91.

4. Tim Keller, *The Reason for God: Belief in an Age of Skepticism* (New York: Dutton, 2008), xviii.

5. Brenda Branson and Paula Silva, "Domestic Violence Among Believers: Confronting the Destructive Secret," *Christian Counseling Today,* 13, no. 3 (2005): 18–22.

6. "Costs of Intimate Partner Violence Against Women in the United States," Centers for Disease Control and Prevention, National Centers for Injury Prevention and Control, 2003, http://www.ncadv.org (accessed October 19, 2009).

7. Paul Strand, "Exposing Porn: Science, Religion, and the New Addiction," *CBN*, August 14, 2003, http://www.freerepublic.com/focus/f-news/964363/posts.

8. Jerry Ropelato, "Internet Pornography Statistics," Internet Filter Review, http://internet-filter-review.toptenreviews.com/internet-pornography-statistics .html (accessed October 19, 2009).

9. Ibid.

10. Mark O'Keefe, "Internet Porn a Guy Thing? Not Really, Online Rating Service Says," *Charlotte Observer,* http://www.nationalcoalition.org/ statisticspornography.asp (accessed October 19, 2009).

11. Gary Langer, "ABC News Poll: Sex Lives of American Teens," *ABC News,* May 19, 2006, http://abcnews.go.com/Primetime/PollVault/ story?id=1981945&page=1.

12. Statistics from National Coalition Survey of Pastors, Mike Genung, "How Many Porn Addicts Are in Your Church?" *Crosswalk,* http://www .crosswalk.com/1336107/ (accessed October 19, 2009).

13. "Statistics: Eating Disorders and their Precursors," *National Eating Disorders Association*, 2006, http://www.nationaleatingdisorders.org/p.asp?Web Page_ID=286&Profile_ID=41138 (accessed October 19, 2009).

14. Susan Ice, "Statistics," *Eating Disorders Coalition for Research, Policy, and Action*, http://www.eatingdisorderscoalition.org/reports/statistics.html (accessed October 19, 2009).

15. "Poll: Have you ever wished you could surgically change something about your body?" *Seventeen Magazine*, October 1, 2007, http://www.seventeen .com/health-sex-fitness/special/plastic-surgery-poll-0807.

16. Kathleen Berger, *The Developing Person: Through the Life Span* (New York: Worth Publishers, 2006), 354.

17. U.S. Census Bureau statistics, "The Father Factor: Facts on Fatherhood," *National Fatherhood Initiative*, http://www.fatherhood.org/father_factor.asp (accessed October 20, 2009).

18. M. Scott Peck, *The Road Less Traveled* (New York: Simon & Schuster, 2003), 15.

19. John 16:33.

20. Henry David Thoreau, *Early Spring in Massachusetts: From the Journals of Henry David Thoreau* (New York: BiblioBazaar, 2008), 224.

21. Tim Keller, *The Reason for God: Belief in an Age of Skepticism* (New York: Dutton, 2008), xviii.

22. Judg. 6:36–37.

23. H. B. Noble, "Dr. Viktor E. Frankl of Vienna, Psychiatrist of *The Search for Meaning*, Dies at 92," *New York Times*, September 4, 1997, http://www.nytimes .com/1997/09/04/world/dr-viktor-e-frankl-of-vienna-psychiatrist-of-the-search-for-meaning-dies-at-92.html.

24. Victor E. Frankl, *Man's Search for Meaning* (Boston: Beacon Press, 1992), 84.

25. Ibid.

26. Ibid., 7.

27. Ibid., 72.

28. John Calvin, *Calvin's Institutes* (Louisville, KY: Westminster John Knox Press, 2001), 7.

29. Frankl, *Man's Search for Meaning*, 7.

30. Dallas Willard, *The Divine Conspiracy: Rediscovering Our Hidden Life in God* (San Francisco: HarperCollins, 1988), 386.

31. Paraphrase of Blaise Pascal, *Pensées* (New York: Penguin Classics, 1997), 45.

32. C. Fayard, M. J. Pereau, and A. Ciovica, " 'Love the Lord with All Your Mind': Explorations on a Possible Neurobiology of the Experience of God and Some Implications for the Practice of Psychotherapy," *Journal of Psychology and Christianity*, 28, no. 2 (2009): 171.

33. D. Keltner and J. Haidt, "Approaching Awe, a Moral, Spiritual, and Aesthetic Emotion," *Cognition and Emotion,* 17 (2003): 306.

34. For more information into this research, see Fayard, Pereau, and Ciovica, " 'Love the Lord with All Your Mind,'" 167–181; D. Hay and P. Socha, "Spirituality as a Natural Phenomenon: Bringing Biological and Psychological Perspectives Together," *Zygon,* 40 (2003): 589–612; Keltner and Haidt, "Approaching Awe," 297–314; J. Haidt, "The New Synthesis in Moral Psychology," *Science,* 316 (2007): 998–1002.

There are a number of interesting studies currently taking place to discover how innate longing for God is, and how the brain functions when we're in a relationship with God. It's important to note that these researchers vary in their beliefs about God. Despite what they believe, their approach is based on a value system and motive for studying this particular topic. Therefore, even the most notable researchers and theories in the understanding of how the brain functions in relation to God and our ability to seek the transcendent are speculative and contingent on further research. First and arguably the most notable is Andrew Newberg, a neuroscientist at the University of Pennsylvania. Newberg uses different types of techniques including single photon emission computed tomography, or SPECT, and functional magnetic resonance imaging (fMRI) to scan the brains of individuals from different religious backgrounds and degrees of commitment to their faith. Though his studies have shown variable results, generally speaking he has found that regardless of faith background, spiritual exercises practiced by individuals activate the same neural pathways and parts of the brain. For further understanding of Newberg's research, see Andrew Newberg and Mark Robert Waldman, *How God Changes Your Brain: Breakthrough Findings from a Leading Neuroscientist* (New York: Ballantine Books, 2009), and Andrew Newberg and Mark Robert Waldman, *Why We Believe What We Believe: Uncovering Our Biological Need for Meaning, Spirituality, and Truth* (New York: Free Press, 2006).

35. Hay and Socha, "Spirituality as a Natural Phenomenon," 596.

36. Fayard, Pereau, and Ciovica, " 'Love the Lord with All Your Mind,'" 171.

37. See Justin Barrett, *Why Would Anyone Believe in God?* (Walnut Creek, CA: Altamira Press, 2004); and Justin Barrett, "Is the Spell Really Broken? Bio-Psychological Explanations of Religion and Theistic Belief," *Theology and Science,* 5 (2007): 57–72.

38. P. Granqvist and L. A. Kirkpatrick, "Religious Conversion and Perceived Childhood Attachment: A Meta-Analysis," *International Journal for the Psychology of Religion,* 14, no. 4 (2004): 226.

39. Ibid., 226; P. Granqvist, "Religiousness and Perceived Childhood Attachment: On the Question of Compensation or Correspondence," *Journal for the Scientific Study of Religion,* 37, no. 2 (1998): 350–367; L. A. Kirkpatrick

and P. R. Shaver, "Attachment Theory and Religion: Childhood Attachments, Religious Beliefs, and Conversion," *Journal for the Scientific Study of Religion,* 29 (1990): 315–334; G. G. Loveland, "The Effects of Bereavement on Certain Religious Attitudes," *Sociological Symposium,* 1 (1968): 17–27; C. M. Parkes, *Bereavement: Studies of Grief in Later Life* (New York: International Universities Press, 1972); and C. Ullman, "Cognitive and Emotional Antecedents of Religious Conversion," *Journal of Personality and Social Psychology,* 43 (1982): 183–192.

40. Fayard, Pereau, and Ciovica, " 'Love the Lord with All Your Mind,'" 167–181.

41. Os Guinness, *Long Journey Home: A Guide to Your Search for the Meaning of Life* (Colorado Springs: Waterbrook Press, 2003), 28.

42. Fayard, Pereau, and Ciovica, " 'Love the Lord with All Your Mind,'" 168.

43. Rev. 3:20.

Chapter 4: Human Hardware and Software: Made for Relationships

1. For a more complete review of how early caregiving relationships affect the brain function of an infant, see Allan N. Schore, "Effects of a Secure Attachment Relationship on Right Brain Development, Affect Regulation, and Infant Mental Health," *Infant Mental Health Journal,* 22, no. 1/2 (Jan.–April 2001): 7–66.

2. For a thorough understanding into the nature of this study and its findings, see "Hardwired to Connect: The New Scientific Case for Authoritative Communities, Executive Summary," *Institute for American Values,* September 9, 2003, http://www.americanvalues.org/html/hardwired_-_ex_summary.html.

3. Ibid.

4. Ibid., 1.

5. Ibid., 2.

6. Ibid., 3.

7. C. B. Thomas and K. R. Duszynski, "Closeness to Parents and the Family Constellation in a Prospective Study of Five Disease States: Suicide, Mental Illness, Malignant Tumor, Hypertension, and Coronary Heart Disease," *Johns Hopkins Medical Journal,* vol. 134, no. 5 (May 1974): 251–270.

8. For further empirical reading on how core relational beliefs (or internal working models) are developed, see M. D. S. Ainsworth, "The Development of Infant-Mother Attachment," in *Review of Child Development Research,* eds. B. M. Caldwell and H. N. Ricciuti (Chicago: University of Chicago Press, 1973), 1–94; M. D. S. Ainsworth, M. Blehar, E. Waters, and S. Wall, *Patterns of Attachment: A Psychological Study of the Strange Situation* (Hillsdale, NJ: Erlbaum, 1978); J. P. Allen, C. Moore, G. Kuperminc, and K. Bell, "Attachment and Adolescent Psycho-Social Functioning," *Child Development,* 69 (1998): 1406–1419; J. Bowlby,

Attachment and Loss: Vol. 1, Attachment (New York: Basic Books, 1969); J. Bowlby, *Attachment and Loss: Vol. 2, Separation: Anxiety and Anger* (New York: Basic Books, 1973); J. Bowlby, *Attachment and Loss: Vol. 3, Loss: Sadness and Depression* (New York: Basic Books, 1980); N. Kaplan and M. Main, "Internal Representations of Attachment at Six Years as Indicated by Family Drawings and Verbal Responses to Imagined Separations," in *Attachment: A Move to the Level of Representation,* April 1985 symposium conducted at the meeting of the Society for Research in Child Development, Toronto, Ontario, Canada; M. Main, N. Kaplan, and J. Cassidy, "Security in Infancy, Childhood and Adulthood: A Move to the Level of Representation," in *Growing Points in Attachment Theory and Research,* eds. I. Bretherton and E. Waters, *Monographs of the Society for Research in Child Development,* 50 (1985): 66–104.

9. M. Main, N. Kaplan, and J. Cassidy, "Security in Infancy, Childhood and Adulthood: A Move to the Level of Representation," in *Growing Points in Attachment Theory and Research,*" eds. I. Bretherton and E. Waters, *Monographs of the Society for Research in Child Development,* 50 (1985): 66–104.

10. Bowlby, *Attachment and Loss: Vol. 2.*

11. Daniel Siegel, *The Neurobiology of We,* 2008 Audio Workshop, Mindsight Institute.

12. This section is supported by the following seminal research: Ainsworth, "Development of Infant-Mother Attachment," 1–94; Ainsworth, Blehar, Waters, and Wall, *Patterns of Attachment;* Bowlby, *Attachment and Loss: Vol. 1;* Bowlby, *Attachment and Loss: Vol. 2;* Bowlby, *Attachment and Loss, Vol. 3;* Main, Kaplan, and Cassidy, "Security in Infancy, Childhood and Adulthood," 66–104. The information was included in an article by Gary Sibcy and Tim Clinton, "New Directions: Core Relational Beliefs," *Christian Counseling Today,* 16, no. 3 (2008): 29–32.

13. "Your Views of God Say a Lot About You, Study Shows," *Jet,* October 2, 2006, http://findarticles.com/p/articles/mi_m1355/is_13_110/ai_n16807277/.

14. L. A. Kirkpatrick and P. R. Shaver, "Attachment Theory and Religion: Childhood Attachments, Religious Beliefs, and Conversion," *Journal for the Scientific Study of Religion,* 29 (1990): 315–334.

15. Ibid.

Chapter 5: Your Attachment Style

1. Arthur Bennett, ed. *The Valley of Vision* (Edinburgh: Banner of Truth Trust, 1975), 268.

2. D. W. Griffin and K. Bartholomew, "Models of Self and Other: Fundamental Dimensions Underlying Measures of Adult Attachment," *Journal of Personality and Social Psychology,* 67 (1994): 430–445.

3. K. Bartholomew, "Avoidance of Intimacy: An Attachment Perspective," *Journal of Social and Personal Relationships*, 7 (1990): 147–178; K. Bartholomew and L. Horowitz, "Attachment Styles Among Young Adults: A Test of a Four-Category Model," *Journal of Personality and Social Psychology*, 61 (1991): 226–244.

For a deeper understanding of attachment styles, see the following resources: M. D. S. Ainsworth, "Patterns of Attachment," *Clinical Psychologist*, 38: 27–29; M. D. S. Ainsworth, "The Development of Infant-Mother Attachment," in *Review of Child Development Research*, eds. B. M. Caldwell and H. N. Ricciuti (Chicago: University of Chicago Press, 1973), 1–94; M. D. S. Ainsworth, "Attachments Across the Life Span," *Bulletin of the New York Academy of Medicine*, 61 (1985): 792–812: M. D. S. Ainsworth, "Attachment and Other Affectional Bonds Across the Life Cycle." in *Attachment Across the Life Cycle*, eds. C. M. Parkes, J. Stevenson-Hinde, and P. Marris (New York: Routledge, 1991), 33–51; M. D. S. Ainsworth, M. Blehar, E. Waters, and S. Wall, *Patterns of Attachment: A Psychological Study of the Strange Situation* (Hillsdale, NJ: Erlbaum, 1978); J. P. Allen, C. Moore, G. Kuperminc, and K. Bell, "Attachment and Adolescent Psycho-Social Functioning," *Child Development*, 69 (1998): 1406–1419; Bartholomew, "Avoidance of Intimacy," 147–178; Bartholomew and Horowitz, "Attachment Styles Among Young Adults," 226–244; K. A. Brennan, C. L. Clark, and P. R. Shaver, "Self-Report Measurement of Adult Romantic Attachment: An Integrative Overview," in *Attachment Theory and Close Relationships*, eds. J. A. Simpson and W. S. Rholes (New York: Guilford Press, 1998), 46–76; Tim Clinton and Gary Sibcy, *Why You Do the Things You Do: The Secret to Healthy Relationships* (Nashville: Integrity, 2006); Hazan and Shaver, "Romantic Love Conceptualized as an Attachment Process," *Journal of Personality and Social Psychology*, vol. 52, no. 3 (1987): 511–524.

4. Ps. 107:35.

5. 2 Cor. 4:6.

6. Eccles. 4:9.

7. Ps. 27:10.

8. Dan Allender, *The Healing Path: How the Hurts in Your Past Can Lead You to a More Abundant Life* (Colorado Springs: Waterbrook Press, 2000), 96.

9. Taken from Tim Clinton and Gary Sibcy, *Why You Do the Things You Do: The Secret to Healthy Relationships* (Nashville: Thomas Nelson, 2006), 46–48. Do Not Reproduce, Copy, Duplicate or Disseminate without permission of author.

Chapter 6: Meeting God One-on-One

1. "Lee Strobel Quotes," *The Case for Christ*, http://www.quotesea.com/Quotes.aspx?by=Lee+Strobel.

2. R. F. Baumeister, "Religion and Psychology: Introduction to the Special Issue," *Psychological Inquiry,* 13 (2002): 165–167; L. A. Kirkpatrick, "An Attachment-Theoretical Approach to the Psychology of Religion," *International Journal for the Psychology of Religion,* 2, no. 1 (1992): 3–28.

3. Harold Koenig, Michael McCullough, and David Larson, *Handbook of Religion and Health* (New York: Oxford University Press, 2001).

4. Linda K. George, David B. Larson, Harold G. Koenig, and Michael E. McCullough, "Spirituality and Health: What We Know, What We Need to Know," *Journal of Clinical and Social Psychology,* 19, no. 1 (2000): 108.

5. Ibid., 109.

6. Ibid.

7. Ibid.

8. For a more in-depth study on the nature of child deaths in families that neglected medical care for faith healing, see S. M. Asser and R. Swan, "Child Fatalities from Religion-Motivated Medical Neglect," *Pediatrics,* 101 (1998): 625–629.

9. Kenneth Pargament, Harold Koenig, Nalini Tarakeshwar, and June Hahn, "Religious Coping Methods as Predictors of Psychological, Physical, and Spiritual Outcomes Among Medically Ill Elderly Patients: A Two Year Longitudinal Study," *Journal of Health Psychology,* 9, no. 6 (2004): 713–730.

10. George et al., "Spirituality and Health," 109.

11. Tim and Josh have been working with Dr. Gary Sibcy on God-attachment research for the past decade. For more information on this research you can refer to Josh's doctoral dissertation, for which Dr. Sibcy was chair, Joshua Straub, *God Attachment, Romantic Attachment, and Relationship Satisfaction in a Sample of Evangelical College Students,* doctoral dissertation, Liberty University, 2009. In addition, see Tim Clinton and Gary Sibcy, *Why You Do the Things You Do: The Secret to Healthy Relationships* (Nashville: Integrity, 2006); and Tim Clinton and Gary Sibcy, *Loving Your Child Too Much: How to Keep a Close Relationship with Your Child Without Overindulging, Overprotecting, or Overcontrolling* (Nashville: Integrity, 2006).

12. Paul Granqvist, "Building a Bridge Between Attachment and Religious Coping: Tests of Moderators and Mediators," *Mental Health, Religion & Culture,* 8, no. 1 (2005): 35–47.

13. J. Bowlby, *Attachment and Loss: Vol. 2, Separation: Anxiety and Anger* (New York: Basic Books, 1973), 23.

14. L. A. Kirkpatrick and P. R. Shaver, "Attachment Theory and Religion: Childhood Attachments, Religious Beliefs, and Conversion," *Journal for the Scientific Study of Religion,* 29 (1990): 315–334.

15. Ibid.

16. Ibid.

17. M. Pollner, "Divine Relations, Social Relations, and Well-Being," *Journal of Health and Social Behavior,* 30 (1989): 92–104.

18. B. L. Fredrickson, "How Does Religion Benefit Health and Well-Being?: Are Positive Emotions Active Ingredients?" *Psychological Inquiry,* 13 (2002): 209–213.

19. T. N. Sim and B. S. M. Loh, "Attachment to God: Measurement and Dynamics," *Journal of Social and Personal Relationships*, 20 (2003): 373–389.

20. L. A. Kirkpatrick, *Attachment, Evolution, and the Psychology of Religion* (New York: Guilford Press, 2005).

21. B. Hunsberger, B. McKenzie, M. Pratt, and S. M. Pancer, "Religious Doubt: A Social Psychological Analysis," *Research in the Social Scientific Study of Religion,* 5 (1993): 27–51.

22. K. I. Pargament, *The Psychology of Religion and Coping: Theory, Research, Practice* (New York: The Guilford Press, 1997).

23. G. D. Kaufman, *The Theological Imagination: Constructing the Concept of God* (Philadelphia: Westminster, 1981), 67.

24. Larry Crabb, *Finding God* (Grand Rapids: Zondervan, 2003), 18.

25. J. I. Packer, *Knowing God* (Downers Grove, IL: InterVarsity Press, 1973), 227.

Chapter 7: When It's Hard to Connect

1. Blaise Pascal, *Pensées* (New York: Penguin Classics, 1997), 45.

2. J. R. Dickie, A. K. Eshleman, D. M. Merasco, A. Shepard, M. Vander Wilt, and M. Johnson, "Parent-Child Relationships and Children's Images of God," *Journal for the Scientific Study of Religion*, 36, no. 1 (1997): 25–43; B. E. Blaine, P. Trivedi, and A. Eshleman, "Religious Belief and the Self-Concept: Evaluating the Implications for Psychological Adjustment," *Personality and Social Psychology Bulletin*, 24 (1998): 1040–1052.

3. C. Gilligan and J. Attanuaci, "Two Moral Orientations," in *Mapping the Moral Domain*, eds. C. Gilligan, J. V. Ward, and J. M. Taylor (Cambridge, MA: Harvard University Press, 1988); C. Gilligan and G. Wiggins, "The Origins of Morality in Early Childhood Relationships," in *Mapping the Moral Domain*, eds. C. Gilligan, J. V. Ward, and J. M. Taylor (Cambridge, MA: Harvard University Press, 1988); L. Kohlberg and R. Kramer, "Continuities and Discontinuities in Childhood and Adult Moral Development," *Human Development*, 12 (1969): 93–120.

4. Dickie et al., "Parent-Child Relationships," 25–43; Blaine, Trivedi, and Eshleman, "Religious Belief and the Self-Concept," 1040–1052.

5. Ibid.

6. Ibid.

7. Ibid.

8. Dickie et al., "Parent-Child Relationships," 42; L. A. Kirkpatrick and P. R. Shaver, "Attachment Theory and Religion: Childhood Attachments, Religious Beliefs, and Conversion," *Journal for the Scientific Study of Religion*, 29 (1990): 315–334.

9. Philip Yancey, *Reaching for the Invisible God* (Grand Rapids: Zondervan, 2000), 117.

10. John 20:28.

11. John 20:29.

12. John 11:16.

13. 1 John 3:4 (AMP)

14. Jer. 17:9.

15. Eccles. 7:20.

16. Rom. 3:23.

17. 1 John 1:8.

18. Rom. 6:23.

19. 1 John 1:9.

20. Luke 15:7.

21. Tim Keller, *The Prodigal God* (New York: Dutton, 2008).

22. 2 Cor. 5:21.

23. Oswald Chambers, *My Utmost for His Highest*, January 20 (Grand Rapids: Discovery House Publishers, 1935), 2008.

24. 1 John 2:2.

25. Eph. 1:7.

26. John 1:12–13.

27. St. Augustine, *Confessions* (New York: Penguin, 1961), 120.

28. Dallas Willard, *The Spirit of Disciplines: Understanding How God Changes Lives* (San Francisco: Harper and Row, 1988), viii.

29. Phil. 2:6–11.

30. St. Augustine, *Sermons for Christians and Epiphany*, trans. Thomas Comerford Lawler, *Ancient Christian Writers*, no. 15 (Westminster, MD: Newman Press, 1952), 107.

31. James 1:13–16.

32. Martin Luther, *A Commentary on St. Paul's Epistle to the Galatians* (New York: James Clarke, 1953), 101.

33. Ps. 34:8.

Chapter 8: Exploring Your Seeking System and What Happens When It Goes Awry

1. Ernest Becker, *The Denial of Death* (New York: Free Press, 1976), 284.

2. Thomas Merton, *No Man Is an Island* (New York: Mariner Books, 2002), 3.

3. Simon and Garfunkel, "I Am a Rock," *Sounds of Silence* (Nashville: Sony, 2001).

4. Gerald May, *Addiction and Grace* (New York: Harper and Row, 1988), 3.

5. Eccles. 6:7.

6. Helen Fisher, *Why We Love: The Nature and Chemistry of Romantic Love* (New York: Henry Holt, 2004), 3. For more information into the understanding of dopamine and the chemicals core to the process of romantic love and attachment, see H. Fisher, A. Aron, and L. Brown, "Romantic Love: An fMRI Study of a Neural Mechanism for Mate Choice," *Journal of Comparative Neurology*, 493 (2005): 58–62; L. Slater, "This Thing Called Love," *National Geographic*, 209, no. 2 (2006): 32–49.

7. Jaak Panksepp, *Affective Neuroscience: The Foundation of Human and Animal Emotions* (New York: Oxford University Press, 1998), 144. Also see C. Fayard, M. J. Pereau, and A. Ciovica, " 'Love the Lord with All Your Mind': Explorations on a Possible Neurobiology of the Experience of God and Some Implications for the Practice of Psychotheraphy," *Journal of Psychology and Christianity*, 28, no. 2 (2009): 171.

8. For a more in-depth look at the studies linking the experience of God to dopamine neurotransmission, see Paul Granqvist, "Religion as a By-Product of Evolved Psychology: The Case of Attachment and Implications for Brain and Religion Research," in *Where God and Science Meet: How Brain and Evolutionary Studies Alter Our Understanding of Religion: Vol. 2, The Neurology of Religious Experience*, ed. P. McNamara (Westport, CT: Praeger, 2006), 105–150; P. McNamara, R. Durso, A. Brown, and E. Harris, "The Chemistry of Religiosity: Evidence from Patients with Parkinson's Disease," *Where God and Science Meet: How Brain and Evolutionary Studies Alter Our Understanding of Religion: Vol. 2, The Neurology of Religious Experience*, ed. P. McNamara (Westport, CT: Praeger, 2006), 105–150; M. Ostow, *Spirit, Mind, and Brain: A Psychoanalytic Examination of Spirituality and Religion* (New York: Columbia University Press, 2007); Jaak Panksepp, *Affective Neuroscience: The Foundation of Human and Animal Emotions* (New York: Oxford University Press, 1998); M. Persinger, "Experiential Stimulation of the God Experience," in *NeuroTheology: Brain, Science, Spirituality, Religious Experience*, ed. R. Joseph (San Jose, CA: University Press, 2003), 279–292.

9. U. Schjodt, H. Stodkilde-Jorgensen, A. Geertz, and A. Roepstorff, "Rewarding Prayers," *Neuroscience Letters*, 443 (2008): 165–168.

10. "Discover Presents the Brain: An Owner's Manual," *Discover*, Spring 2007, http://www.discovermagazine.com.

11. Panksepp, *Affective Neuroscience*, 144.

12. L. Slater, "This Thing Called Love," *National Geographic*, 209, no. 2 (2006), 32–39.

13. 2 Cor. 4:16–18.

14. Tim Keller, "Hell: Isn't the God of Christianity an Angry Judge?" From the sermon series titled *The Trouble with Christianity: Why It's So Hard to Believe It*, October 22, 2006, http://sermons2.redeemer.com/sermons/hell-isnt-god-christianity-angry-judge.

15. Tim Keller, *The Reason for God: Belief in an Age of Skepticism* (New York: Dutton, 2008), 78. For a better understanding on how good things become idols and addictions in our lives, see Keller's *The Reason for God* as well as his *Counterfeit Gods: The Empty Promises of Money, Sex, Power and the Only Hope That Matters* (New York: Dutton, 2009).

Chapter 9: The Grand Delusion

1. Matt. 5:20.
2. Prov. 12:15.
3. Ps. 28:3.
4. John 8:1–5 (MSG).
5. John 8:5–9 (MSG).
6. Matt. 23.
7. Matt. 23:29–32 (MSG).
8. See Deut. 17:7 (MSG).
9. John 8:9–11 (MSG).
10. Matt. 9:10–13 (MSG).

11. J. P. Moreland (2007), *How Evangelicals Became Over-Committed to the Bible and What Can Be Done About It*, a presentation to the 2007 Evangelical Theological Society meeting in San Diego, http://blog.christianitytoday.com/ctliveblog/archives/2007/11/postcard_from_s.html.

12. E. Allison Peers, trans., *The Dark Night of the Soul: A Masterpiece in the Literature of Mysticism by St. John of the Cross* (New York: Image Books, Doubleday, 1990), 38 (original work published in 1584). For more on St. John of the Cross and his developmental spirituality, see John H. Coe, "Musings on the Dark Night of the Soul: Insights from St. John of the Cross on a Developmental Spirituality," *Journal of Psychology and Theology*, 28, no. 4 (2000): 293–307.

13. Eph. 5:22–33 (MSG).
14. Eph. 1:3.

15. Ps. 42:1–2.

16. Exod. 33:13–18.

17. Dennis Prager, *Happiness Is a Serious Problem* (New York: Regan Books, 1998), 4.

18. Matt. 7:13–14.

19. Ibid.

20. Isa. 29:13.

21. A. W. Tozer, *Man: The Dwelling Place of God* (New York: Meadow Books, 2008), 102.

22. Paul Vitz, *Faith of the Fatherless: The Psychology of Atheism* (Dallas: Spence Publishing, 1999), 12.

23. Tozer, *Man: The Dwelling Place of God*, 19.

24. Christopher Hitchens, *God Is Not Great: How Religion Poisons Everything* (New York: Hachette, 2007), 16.

25. Philip Yancey, *Rumors of Another World: What on Earth Are We Missing?* (Grand Rapids: Zondervan, 2003), 19. Also see Paul Vitz's explanation of the innate desire to seek God found throughout all cultures in history; Vitz, *Faith of the Fatherless*.

26. Vitz, *Faith of the Fatherless*.

27. Ibid., 16. Also see Paul Vitz, "Truth Journal: The Psychology of Atheism," *LeaderU*, July 14, 2002, http://www.leaderu.com/truth/1truth12.html; and Paul Vitz, "Support from Psychology for the Fatherhood of God," *Homiletic and Pastoral Review*, vol. xcvii, no. 5 (February 1997): 7–19.

28. Vitz, *Faith of the Fatherless*, 16.

29. Ibid., 141.

30. Eugene Kamenka, *The Philosophy of Ludwig Feuerbach* (New York: Praegar, 1970), 151.

31. Vitz, *Faith of the Fatherless*, 141.

32. Ibid., 142; also see R. Monk, *Bertrand Russell: The Spirit of Solitude, 1872–1921* (New York: Free Press, 1996).

33. Vitz, *Faith of the Fatherless*, 144.

34. Interview with Peter Kreeft, in Lee Strobel, *The Case for Faith: A Journalist Investigates the Toughest Objections to Christianity* (Grand Rapids: Zondervan, 2000), 9.

35. Luke 7:41–42.

36. Luke 7:43.

37. Luke 7:44–47.

38. Vitz, *Faith of the Fatherless*, 147.

Chapter 10: The Risk of Grace

1. See Gal. 5:1.
2. See John 10:10.
3. See Matt. 16:24.
4. Retrieved from www.dictionary.com.
5. Timothy F. Lull, *Martin Luther's Basic Theological Writings*, 2nd ed. (Minneapolis: Augsburg Fortress, 2005), 101.
6. Larry Crabb, *Inside Out* (Colorado Springs: NavPress, 2007), 8.
7. See Col. 2:14 (NASB).
8. See 1 Cor. 6:20 (NASB).
9. Philip Yancey, *Rumors of Another World* (Grand Rapids: Zondervan, 2003), 145.
10. Mark Twain, "Pudd'nhead Wilson's New Calendar," *Following the Equator* (New York: Collier, 1897), 238.
11. Yancey, *Rumors of Another World*, 145.
12. 2 Cor. 7:8–10.
13. John 13:38.
14. See John 21:1–22.

Chapter 11: Spiritual Oxygen

1. Hosea 6:3 (NASB).
2. John 17:3.
3. Eph. 3:16–19.
4. Philip Yancey, *Reaching for the Invisible God* (Grand Rapids: Zondervan, 2000), 101–102.
5. Gen. 50:19–21.
6. Eph. 4:31–32.
7. Tim Keller, "The Prodigal God." Audio series, http://www.theprodigalgod .com.
8. Rom. 12:18–19.
9. John Ortberg, *The Life You've Always Wanted* (Grand Rapids: Zondervan, 2002), 46–47.
10. Ibid., 13.
11. Ps. 139:23 (NIV).

Chapter 12: Spiritual Rehab

1. E. Allison Peers, trans., *The Dark Night of the Soul: A Masterpiece in the Literature of Mysticism by St. John of the Cross* (New York: Image Books, Doubleday, 1990), 61–62 (original work published in 1584).

2. For more on this, see "These Inward Trials," in *Knowing God*, by J. I. Packer (Downers Grove, IL: InterVarsity Press, 1973).

3. Philip Yancey, *Reaching for the Invisible God* (Grand Rapids: Zondervan, 2000), 211–246.

4. St. John of the Cross, *Ascent of Mount Carmel* (Chicago: Wilder Publications, 2008), Book 2, Chapter 29, Numbers 5, 7, and 11.

5. Job 13:15 (KJV).

6. St. John of the Cross, *Ascent of Mount Carmel*.

7. J. I. Packer, *Knowing God* (Grand Rapids, MI: InterVarsity Press, 1979), 246.

8. See 1 Cor. 4:7 and Rom. 12:3.

9. Ps. 146:5–10.

10. Rom. 12:9–13.

11. See 1 John 4:10–11.

12. Rom. 15:7.

13. Eph. 4:32.

Chapter 13: The Power of Wonder

1. *The Journal of Henry David Thoreau*, vol. 2 (Salt Lake City: Peregrine Smith Books, 1984), 472.

2. Ps. 19:1.

3. Rom. 1:20.

4. Ravi Zacharias, *Recapture the Wonder* (New York: Integrity, 2005).

5. Stephen Hawking, *A Brief History of Time* (New York: Bantam, 1988), 171.

6. Blaise Pascal, *Pensées* (New York: Penguin Classics, 1997), 425.

7. Richard Foster, *The Challenge of the Disciplined Life: Christian Reflections on Money, Sex, and Power* (New York: Harper One, 1989).

8. Hugh Ross, *Why the Universe Is the Way It Is* (Dartmouth: Baker Books, 2008), 31.

9. Arthur Harding, *Astronomy* (Garden City, NY: Doubleday, 1940), 19.

10. Richard Swenson, *More Than Meets the Eye* (Colorado Springs: NavPress, 2000), 65.

11. Frank Salisbury, "Natural Selection and the Complexity of the Gene," *Nature*, 224 (Oct. 25, 1969): 332–333.

12. H. Frank Salisbury, "Doubts About the Modern Synthetic Theory of Evolution," *American Biology Teacher,* vol. 33, no. 6 (1971): 335–338.

13. Carl Sagan, ed., *Communication with Extraterrestrial Intelligence* (Cambridge, MA: The MIT Press, 1974), 175.

14. Henry Morris, *Scientific Creationism* (Houston: Master Books, 1974).

15. Charles Wesley, "And Can It Be That I Should Gain," *Psalms and Hymns* (1738), http://www.cyberhymnal.org/htm/a/c/acanitbe.htm.

16. A. W. Tozer, *Worship: The Missing Jewel* (Chicago: Christian Publications, 1996), 7–8.

17. Rev. 1:12–16.

18. Rev. 1:17–18.

19. Philip Yancey, *Reaching for the Invisible God* (Grand Rapids: Zondervan, 2000), 92.

20. Elisabeth Elliot, *The Path of Loneliness* (Grand Rapids: Servant Publications, 2001), 107.

Chapter 14: Your Life Counts

1. Rev. 3:15–17.

2. St. Augustine, *Confessions* (New York: Penguin, 1961), 3.

3. Os Guinness, *The Call* (Nashville: Word Publishing, 1998), 32.

4. 1 Cor. 15:19–20.

5. Adapted from a newsletter by Iris Lowder, 1998.

6. Dietrich Bonhoeffer, *Letters from Prison* (New York: Touchstone, 1997), 5.

7. Isaac Watts, "When I Survey the Wondrous Cross," *Hymns and Spiritual Songs* (1707).

8. Matt. 16:24–26.

9. Rom. 8:35–39.

10. Phyllis Stanley, quoted by Linda Dillow in *Calm My Anxious Heart* (Colorado Springs: NavPress, 1998), 105.

11. Luke 10:36.

12. Matt. 25:40.

13. N. T. Wright, *Following Jesus* (Grand Rapids: Eerdman's, 1994), 113.

14. Jonathan Edwards, *The Christian Pilgrim,* cited by Dr. Bob Pyne in *Bibliotheca Sacra,* April–June 2006.

15. Rev. 3:20.

Printed in the United States
By Bookmasters